THE STOCK OPTIONS MANUAL

THE STOCK OPTIONS MANUAL

GARY L. GASTINEAU

Kidder, Peabody & Co., Incorporated

SECOND EDITION

McGRAW-HILL BOOK COMPANY

*New York   St. Louis   San Francisco   Auckland   Bogotá
Düsseldorf   Johannesburg   London   Madrid
Mexico   Montreal   New Delhi   Panama
Paris   São Paulo   Singapore
Sydney   Tokyo   Toronto*

Library of Congress Cataloging in Publication Data

Gastineau, Gary L
  The stock options manual.

  Bibliography: p.
  Includes index.
  1. Put and call transactions. I. Title.
HG6041.G38 1979   332.6'45   78-12505
ISBN 0-07-022970-8

  6 7 8 9 10 11   BKP BKP   8 9 8 7 6 5

*The author is not engaged in rendering legal, tax, accounting, or
similar professional services. While legal, tax, and accounting
issues covered in this book have been checked with sources
believed to be reliable, some questions—particularly in the area of
taxes—have not been resolved by the Internal Revenue Service or
the courts, and the accuracy and completeness of such information
and the opinions based thereon are not guaranteed. If legal,
accounting, tax, investment, or other expert advice is required,
the services of a competent practitioner should be obtained.*

  *The investment strategies outlined in this book are not suitable
for every investor, and no specific investment recommendations are
intended. Readers should satisfy themselves by a careful reading
of The Options Clearing Corporation prospectus and by seeking
competent investment advice that they thoroughly understand the
risks as well as the potential rewards of trading in options.*

The editors for this book were W. Hodson Mogan and Ruth L. Weine,
the designer was Elliot Epstein, and the production
supervisor was Teresa F. Leaden. It was set in VIP Palatino
by Monotype Composition Company, Inc.

Printed and bound by The Book Press, Inc.

To my wife and family for their help and encouragement

Contents

FOREWORD

The success of the Chicago Board Options Exchange has both modified and strengthened the fundamental tenets of capital market theory. For 30 years most economists and students of portfolio theory have agreed that the buyer of common stocks faces two kinds of risk. One type of risk is a function of the fortunes of a particular corporation and that firm's relative valuation in the securities markets. If an investor diversifies his portfolio, he can eliminate most of the risk associated with his particular choice of corporation for investment.

A second kind of risk cannot be diversified away by purchasing the securities of a number of companies. It is the systematic or market risk that stems from the tendency of stocks to move up or down together. Some hedge funds and sophisticated individual investors have tried to reduce their exposure to this market risk by offsetting long positions in one security with short positions in another. The average investor has never really had the wherewithal to participate in these hedging activities. As a result, the theorist's argument that the buyer of common stocks cannot avoid market risk has been borne out in practice.

The Chicago Board Options Exchange not only provides a way to hedge the market risk of a large stock portfolio; it also enables the small investor to hedge his positions. With other securities exchanges now joining the CBOE in trading listed stock options, every investor can adjust the market risk of his portfolio to suit his personal preferences. The recognition of the functional relation between risk and rate of return is a cornerstone of modern portfolio theory. Stock options increase an investor's range of risk-return choices.

Popular investment publications usually portray stock options as instruments of speculation. Only recently have writers for some leading periodicals begun to explore the implications of stock options for the conservative investor. This new emphasis on the conservative uses of stock options is not without hazards. Reading many articles on options, one is left with the impression that an option buyer is a speculator and an option writer is a conservative investor. The real world is not so simple, as the reader of this book will soon learn.

The controversial aspects of options have been of limited interest and concern to most investors because option trading has been a small, obscure sector of the securities business. The recent bear market and the surprising success of the CBOE have expanded public interest in options and awakened renewed criticism of option trading. Neither the widespread interest nor the criticism has been based on a full understanding of what options can and cannot do. This book should prove helpful to the investor or portfolio manager who wants to expand his understanding of options. It should also focus any criticism of option trading on the few real regulatory problems rather than on some widespread but false impressions of the nature and place of options in the securities markets.

Albert Madansky
University of Chicago
April 1975

These comments seem even more pertinent as an introduction to the second edition.

A. M.
March 1978

PREFACE

Three major developments in the options markets led to the decision to publish this second edition of *The Stock Options Manual*. First, the Tax Reform Act of 1976 changed the tax status of option writing and extended the holding period required for long-term capital gains tax treatment on all securities holdings. As a consequence of these and other significant tax developments, the discussion of taxation in the first edition has been completely revised.

Second, options have become increasingly important in the management of institutional portfolios and in the development of portfolio theory at leading universities. New material covering these topics has been added.

Finally, the introduction of listed put options has markedly expanded the range of choices available to the investor. Appropriately, the discussion of puts has been expanded substantially.

In addition to making the almost obligatory changes and additions already listed, I have taken the opportunity afforded by the revision to expand the discussion of option evaluation and to examine the effect of options on investment performance. These important topics continue to be the subject of a considerable amount of uninformed commentary and speculation in the investment community. As the reader will discover, most of the controversy stems from a failure to ask appropriate questions or from a too ready acceptance of "conventional wisdom."

A number of people made important contributions to my understanding of key points discussed in the text and to the preparation of the manuscript itself. While it is impossible to remember the source of each suggestion, a number of individuals were conspicuously helpful. I am particularly indebted to Dr. Albert Madansky, not only for his useful comments, but for his crucial role in the development of the option evaluation model discussed in Chapter 7. Meyer Berman played the vital role of *shadchan* in bringing us together.

Other individuals who provided significant information or made important comments on the manuscript include Martin Askowitz, Jayusia P. Bernstein, Harriet Burnett, Hugh R. Covington, Samuel M. Feder, Katherine Finn, Beverly Gordon, Robert Kunzelman, Martin L. Leibowitz, Andrew A. Levy, Harry Markowitz, Edwin L. Solot, Seymour Suskin, and Paul A. Turitzin. Finally, I wish to acknowledge the assistance of Katherine Bender, Chana Birch, Darline Leslie, Mary Beth Minton, Catherine A. Swartz, and my wife, Nancy, for their help in preparing the manuscript. Many other contributions from my wife and other members of my family, while perhaps less tangible, were no less important.

Gary L. Gastineau

THE STOCK OPTIONS MANUAL

1 INTRODUCTION

The decision to write this book evolved from the personal conviction that there is a major deficiency in the literature on put and call options. A large number of books on options and related topics have been published or reprinted since the Chicago Board Options Exchange (CBOE) began listed trading of call options in April 1973; so the deficiency is certainly not quantitative. The problem with most of these books is that they are either too elementary or too technical for the intelligent investor who is looking for a comprehensive discussion of the investment characteristics of stock options but who lacks the mathematical background to tackle the specialized literature on capital market and portfolio theory. The advisory services are not much more helpful to the serious investor who wants to *understand* options.

In fairness, most of the basic option books and services do an excellent job of explaining the mechanics of the option market and the procedures for option trading to the beginning investor. On the other hand, the material available to the average investor rarely provides any really helpful insights into the evaluation of an option contract or into the impact of options on the risk-return characteristics of a portfolio. When specific option recommendations are provided, they are usually based on a discussion of the leverage features of the option contract and on a technical forecast of the direction of stock price movement. Occasionally a recommendation will be based on the relationship between present and historic option premiums.

In the author's judgment, the popular literature on options spends too much time translating a specific stock price forecast into the most leveraged way to play the expected move, and far too little time evaluating the risk-reward relationship of an option contract to its underlying stock. Leverage calculations and stock price forecasts have their place. Unless the forecast is unprecedentedly accurate, however, the option buyer who consistently pays more than a fair price for the options bought and the option writer who accepts inadequate premiums are virtually certain to experience substandard performance.

In contrast to the popular literature on options, a wealth of excellent material has been written by some of the finest minds in the academic community. Among the well-known economists who have done important work on options are Nobel laureate Paul Samuelson of M.I.T. and Burton Malkiel of Princeton, author of the best seller *A Random Walk Down Wall Street*. Other authors who have written key articles on options but who are not so well known outside the academic community are Fischer Black and Robert Merton of M.I.T.; Albert Madansky, Jonathan Ingersoll, and Myron Scholes of the University of Chicago; and Michael Parkinson of the University of Florida. Unfortunately, most of this academic literature is available only in specialized publications rarely found in neighborhood libraries. Furthermore, these articles are difficult to understand if the reader is not well versed in mathematics.

One of the principal purposes of this book is to make the significant findings of the academic community understandable and, it is hoped, useful to the intelligent investor. No attempt is made to explain the fine points of puts and calls to the investor who barely comprehends the difference between a common stock and a bond. On the other hand, most investors intelligent enough to use options can understand the investment characteristics and tax treatment of options and the principles behind the rational evaluation of an option contract. Investors who have a few years of experience with stocks and bonds should be able to use options rationally and effectively in investment programs.

The key concept which the investor must understand to make intelligent use of options is the *fair value* of an option contract. Option evaluation is the focus of most academic option literature but is rarely discussed in depth in books and articles prepared for broad distribution. Probably option evaluation is neglected by authors of most basic books on options for one or more of the following reasons:

1. The author does not understand option evaluation.

2. The fair value of an option is not the easiest concept to explain to the average reader.

3. It is easier to base option recommendations on stock price predictions than to worry about whether the option itself might be overpriced or underpriced.

4. Actually calculating the fair value of an option is even more difficult than explaining the concept.

Because of the importance of determining the fair value of an option contract before taking an option investment position, the significance of fair value will be briefly explained in this Introduction. If the reader finds this explanation difficult to understand, it is expanded in Chapter 7, Section A. If the reader has no difficulty with the explanation of fair value, everything else in the book should be readily understandable.
Fair value Assuming a call is not exercised or sold prior to its expiration date, its ultimate value will depend on the price of the underlying stock on the expiration date. Any price at which the call might be bought or sold during its life will reflect the buyer's and seller's respective estimates of the option's probable terminal value.

If the price of the stock is below the striking price of the call on the expiration date, the option is worthless to the buyer.

The option writer, under these circumstances, will get to keep the entire call premium. If the price of the stock rises above the striking price as the expiration date approaches, the value of the buyer's position will climb point-for-point with the stock price while the writer's position will deteriorate point-for-point.

Figure 1-1 depicts the gain and loss positions of a call buyer and an uncovered writer in a hypothetical call option transaction. In this example, which for illustrative purposes neglects the effect of commissions, the buyer has purchased and the writer has sold a call option with a striking price of $100 for an option premium of $10. Starting at the left-hand side of the graph, the top line illustrates the uncovered writer's profit and loss position. As long as the price of the stock does not exceed $100 on the day the option expires, the writer keeps the entire $10 option premium. If the price of the stock rises to $120, the writer loses the premium plus another $10 per share. The call buyer's profit and loss position, represented by the line that starts on the lower left-hand side of the graph, exactly mirrors that of the writer. If the stock stays below $100, the buyer loses the entire investment. If the stock rises to $120, the buyer

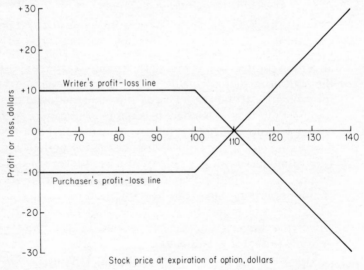

Figure 1-1. Profit-loss positions of the buyer and writer of a call.

gets back not only the premium but another $10 as well. If the stock sells at $110 at the end of the option period, neither buyer nor writer is better or worse off than before, except by the amount of commissions.

An important lesson to be learned from this graph is that the buyer's line and the writer's line move toward or away from the zero profit line together. If the option premium paid by the buyer increases by $1, the writer will receive $1 more. At every possible price of the stock on the expiration date, the value of the buyer's position will be reduced by the extra dollar paid for the option. Likewise, the writer's line will move up by $1 at every price because, at each possible price, the writer's position will be improved by the additional dollar received.

In their evaluation of a particular option, both buyer and writer consider, at least implicitly, a probability distribution of expected prices on the underlying stock at the date of expiration. The probability distributions envisioned by buyer and writer, respectively, may have different shapes. Neither of these hypothetical distributions need be objective or have any direct relationship to past or future distributions of price changes.

It is possible to derive a relatively neutral probability distribution of future prices for any stock. This distribution is based primarily on the present stock price, the past volatility pattern of the stock, and a careful appraisal of factors likely to affect volatility over the life of the option. The curve in Figure 1-2 shows what this probability distribution might look like. This distribution is not strictly objective in that certain of its parameters are based on human judgment. It is, however, approximately neutral with respect to the probable direction of stock price changes. Using this probability distribution, it is possible to estimate the *expected* profit from an option for the buyer or the writer. We need only multiply the profit or loss at each possible stock price by the probability that the stock will sell at that price on the expiration date. The sum of these probability-weighted values will give us the expected profit or loss for the investor who takes that position.

If we neglect the effect of commissions, present value

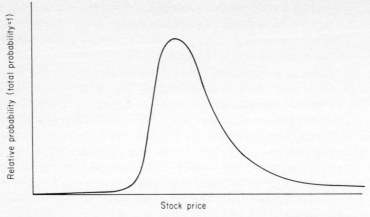

Figure 1-2. Estimated probability distribution of stock prices when option expires.

adjustments, and other considerations too complex for this brief explanation, it is possible to make the following statement: *For every option there is an option price or premium at which, given the probable distribution of stock prices on the expiration date and after an adjustment for risk, the expected profit to both the buyer and the writer is equal to zero. This option price is the fair value of the option.* To phrase this point differently, the fair value of the option is simply the option price at which both the buyer and the writer can expect to break even, excluding commissions and after adjusting for risk. They will not break even on each individual transaction. However, over a long period and after a large number of such transactions, they should expect no net risk-adjusted profit or loss on transactions made at fair value.

Though supply and demand determine option *prices*, the *value* of an option is determined largely by the volatility of the underlying stock. Of course, *price* and *value* will ordinarily be related. If large swings in the stock's price are common, the option buyer will be willing to pay a larger premium for a call because chances of profit from a large upswing are better. Likewise, the option writer will insist on a larger premium because chances of substantial loss are increased.

While more details of this explanation of option value will

be given in the sections on option evaluation, it is important that the reader understand at the outset that options are different from virtually any other asset in a very important respect. Because the option has a limited life and derives its value from the underlying common stock, the *price* of an option does not *necessarily* reflect the *value* of that option to a rational investor at every moment in time. Unless both the buyer and the writer use appropriate probability distributions of future stock prices in determining the price they are willing to pay or receive, the option price may differ significantly from fair value. A rational investor must consider whether an option is fairly priced *as well as* what he expects the stock price to do. Given the range of error inherent in any stock price prediction, consistently paying too much or receiving too little for an option contract will adversely affect investment results.

Superior investment results using options depend on the investor's ability (1) to buy options selling for less than fair value, (2) to write options selling for more than fair value, or (3) to predict accurately the *direction* in which the stock price will move. As difficult as it may be to determine the fair value of an option, it is probably easier to evaluate an option than to predict accurately and regularly whether a particular stock will rise or fall over the life of an option contract. Whether a technician, a fundamentalist, or an advocate of the random walk hypothesis, the reader can improve the odds by buying only undervalued options and writing only overvalued option contracts, consistent with other features of a personal investment strategy.

Other topics While our overall focus is on the effect of options on the risk characteristics of a portfolio and on option evaluation, an attempt has been made to include material that will be useful to any option investor, regardless of the technique used to make option decisions. In particular, the sections on taxes should be useful to investors interested in the implications of recent changes in the tax treatment of option contracts.

The sections on investment strategies should help either the beginner or the experienced portfolio manager to understand how one can use options to reduce or eliminate entirely the market risk of holding a diversified equity portfolio. While it is not possible to completely eliminate all types of investment risk with options, a carefully constructed, appropriately diversified portfolio of stock and option positions could give the investor a reasonably stable return on investment that is largely independent of the movement of broad market averages.

To avoid repeating or belaboring material familiar to nearly all option users, it will be assumed that the reader is familiar with The Options Clearing Corporation prospectus and has read one or more of the explanatory booklets published by the exchanges and distributed by brokerage firms. Several fairly complex equations have been reproduced in the section of the book which discusses option evaluation. However, these formulas are reproduced solely for the convenience of the mathematically inclined reader. No understanding of these equations is necessary to follow the argument of the text. While the reader may find high school algebra helpful, even this level of mathematical sophistication is not essential.

2 INVESTMENT CHARACTERISTICS OF BASIC OPTION CONTRACTS

Before we examine the investment characteristics of puts and calls, it will be helpful to define a few terms:

Option: A negotiable contract in which the writer, for a certain sum of money called the option premium, gives the buyer the right to demand, within a specified time, the purchase or sale by the writer of a specified number of shares of stock at a fixed price called the striking price. Unless otherwise stated, options are written for units of 100 shares. They are ordinarily issued for periods of less than 1 year.

Call option: An option to buy stock from the writer.

Put option: An option to sell stock to the writer.

Combination option: An option consisting of at least one put and one call. The individual option contracts which make up the combination are originally sold as a unit, but they may be exercised or resold separately.

Straddle: A combination option consisting of one put and one call with a common striking price and a common expiration date.

Striking price or exercise price: The price at which an option is exercisable, i.e., the price per share that the buyer of a call option must pay the writer for the stock or the price that the writer must pay the holder of a put option.

Option premium: The price of an option contract. In this book the convention of stating the option premium in terms of dollars per share under option is adopted. If the total premium for a 100-share option is $1,000, the option premium is given as $10.

Expiration date: The date after which an option is void.

Option buyer: The individual or, less frequently, the institutional investor who buys options.

Option writer: The individual or institutional investor who sells or writes options.

This list of definitions is basic and purposely short. Additional definitions of option terms appear in the Glossary. Readers should be certain that they are familiar with these basic terms before they continue reading.

No matter how intricate an option investment strategy the investor may adopt, *the principal result of any option purchase or sale is to modify the risk characteristics of an investor's position.* This feature of options can have an important impact on portfolio structure and on the investor's overall risk exposure. Most investors have found themselves at the mercy of trends in the stock and bond markets. Those who have been dissatisfied with a modest return on short-term debt instruments (the high short-term interest rates of the early 1970s are an exception to the historic pattern) have been forced to accept the market risks associated with investment in common stocks and bonds. Options can help reduce this market risk.

At times in the past an investor has been able to modify his risk exposure by splitting his portfolio between common stocks and bonds. Stock prices and bond prices have frequently been imperfectly correlated with one another. Whatever past patterns may have been, a variety of factors, such as more volatile interest rates and the broader impact of central banking activities in recent years, seem to have tied bond market and stock market fluctuations together.

As a result of the synchronization of recent bond and stock price movements, the investor who wishes to moderate his exposure to price fluctuations has been forced to reduce his exposure to both of these long-term security markets at the same time. While buying commercial paper and certificates of deposit damps fluctuations in the market value of a portfolio, few investors are willing to count on continuing high, short-term interest rates. Furthermore, the overall effect on a portfolio of swings in the value of the assets still invested in long-term securities may be greater than an investor finds acceptable, even after he switches part of his assets to short-term debt.

Stock options provide the investor with a unique way to modify his exposure to market risk. In particular, listed options traded on securities exchanges around the world are extremely versatile instruments for the modification of risk. This statement appears at odds with the popular view of call options as speculative tools which permit the small investor to obtain superior leverage on a small amount of capital. Options can fulfill much more important functions in an investment portfolio than this popular view suggests. Options can be of substantial aid to investors, large or small, who wish to modify the exposure of their portfolios to market fluctuations and improve their risk-adjusted return on investment.

Before undertaking a discussion of the diverse option investment strategies which may be required to achieve particular relationships of risk and reward, we must examine the risk-reward characteristics of the basic put and call contracts as they apply to the option buyer and writer. In contrast to most discussions of the risk-reward characteristics of options which focus on the position either of the buyer or the writer, this chapter stresses the interrelationships between the buying and writing positions. Also, rather than content ourselves with brief written descriptions of the investment characteristics of these option contracts, we will return to the graphic method of illustrating profits and losses used in the Introduction. (These graphs will be discussed in much greater detail in Chapter 4, Section A.)

The graph in Figure 2-1 illustrates the basic investment characteristics of a call option from the respective viewpoints of the buyer and the writer. As most investors who have any familiarity with options are aware, an option buyer can never

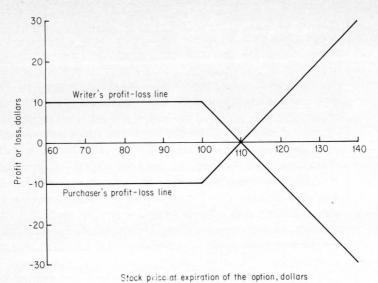

Figure 2-1. Profit-loss positions of the buyer and writer of a call.

lose more than the premium paid for the option contract. On the other hand, if the price of the stock rises substantially over the life of the call option, the buyer's potential reward is theoretically unlimited. This position is illustrated by the line which begins in the lower left-hand corner of Figure 2-1.

The uncovered or "naked" call writer's position is, in many respects, the exact opposite of the call buyer's position. As the line which begins in the upper left-hand corner of Figure 2-1 illustrates, the call writer keeps the entire premium unless the stock price rises above the exercise price at the time the option expires or is exercised. In return for the option premium received, the writer of the call agrees to sell the stock at the striking price, no matter how high the stock may go. If the writer does not own the shares covered by the option, the writer's position deteriorates by $1 per share for every point by which the price of the stock exceeds the exercise price.

The essence of the uncovered call writer's position is that he or she can earn no more than the amount of the option premium and can lose a large amount if the price of the underlying stock runs up. In contrast to the call buyer who is fixing the risk at the amount of the premium and accepting the possibility of a widely varying reward, the uncovered writer is fixing the reward at the amount of the premium and accepting a highly variable risk Figure 2-2 illustrates the profit and loss positions of the buyer and writer of an uncovered put. In return for a fixed premium, the buyer of a put obtains the right to receive a reward that increases as the price of the underlying stock declines. As in the case of the call, both the buyer and the writer of a put option fix one side of the risk-reward equation and permit the other side to vary.

The offsetting risk-reward features of the buying and writing positions are clarified by these graphs. Any profit to the option buyer is exactly offset by a loss to the writer, and vice versa. Neglecting transaction costs, *the net effect of an option transaction is simply a reallocation of risk and reward between buyer and writer.*

It is no accident that the word "premium" is used in both the insurance business and the option business. Option contracts, like insurance policies, are used to protect the investor, whether writer or buyer, from unacceptable risk. In

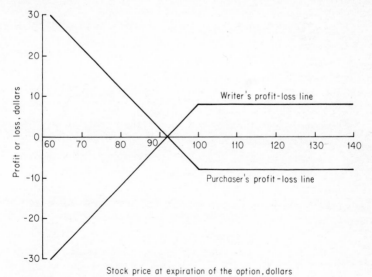

Figure 2-2. Profit-loss positions of the buyer and writer of a put.

these graphs, the option buyer appears to be in a position analogous to that of the owner of an insurance policy. The uncovered option writer is like the insurance underwriter who accepts risk in return for premium income. When options are incorporated in an overall portfolio plan, however, the risks and rewards can change remarkably. For example, the call writer who has a position in the underlying stock will actually be *reducing* the overall volatility or market risk of his portfolio by writing the option because the premium he receives protects his assets in the event of a price decline, while his writer's obligation limits his gain on the up side. Although options do not increase or decrease the total level of risk in the financial system, *both parties to a particular option transaction can reduce their portfolio risk simultaneously through a combination of stock, option, and short-term debt positions.* Chapter 4 will cover the ways in which this unusual and often desirable result can be accomplished. The purpose here has been to define and illustrate the risk-reward features of the simplest option positions to help the reader better understand the structure and functions of option markets. These markets will be the subject of the next chapter.

3 THE HISTORY AND STRUCTURE OF OPTION MARKETS

A. A SHORT HISTORY OF OPTIONS

Like any other financial instrument, options can serve either constructive or destructive purposes. The principal constructive feature of options is that they enable an investor to systematically increase or decrease the amount and kind of risk he accepts. Whether the option pertains to real estate or to securities, the seller or grantor of a call option typically forgoes the opportunity for further appreciation in the value of an asset he owns in return for the payment of an option premium which reduces his loss in the event the value of the asset drops. The buyer of a call option is able to control a larger quantity of assets through the payment of option premiums than he would be able to control if he purchased the assets outright. Though the option buyer benefits from any increase in the value of an asset, his potential loss is limited to the amount of the option premium.

Combinations of purchases and sales of options and related assets permit the astute investor to structure the risk-reward parameters of an investment position within the framework of permissible and available option contracts. The fact that an investor can structure risk and reward in a number of ways suggests that options should be a highly regarded financial tool, and that options should be widely used by investors with a variety of attitudes toward risk. In fact, options have not been highly regarded or widely used. Furthermore, the history of options is replete with occasions when unregulated option trading contributed to speculative boom and bust because options were used for questionable purposes.

Though the terms of option contracts have changed over the years, the concept of the option was in use by the ancients. Extensive research might uncover earlier examples, but the following quotation from Aristotle indicates that options were familiar to the ancient Greeks:

There is an anecdote of Thales the Milesian and his financial device, which involves a principle of universal application, but is attributed to him on account of his reputation for wisdom. He was reproached for his poverty, which was supposed to show that philosophy was of no use. According to the story, he knew by his skill in the stars while it was yet winter that there would be a great harvest of olives in the coming year; so, having a little money, he gave deposits for the use of all the olive presses in Chios and Miletus, which he hired at a low price because no one bid against him. When the harvest time came, and many wanted them all at once and of a sudden, he let them out at any rate which he pleased, and made a quantity of money. Thus he showed the world that philosophers can easily be rich if they like. . . .

Aristotle's *Politics*, Book One, Chapter Eleven, Jowett translation

The Greeks had no monopoly on the use of options. The Phoenicians and Romans reportedly granted options on cargos transported by their ships.

The use of options in these earlier civilizations appears to have been at worst harmless and probably constructive on balance. In contrast, the first extensive use of options after the Middle Ages occurred during the Dutch tulip bulb mania of the early seventeenth century. Options have never fully recovered from the tarnish they accumulated by association with this speculative episode.

Tulip bulb options were used in several ways. Dealers in

tulip bulbs would sell bulbs for future delivery based on call options granted them by growers. If they wished, growers could assure themselves of a minimum price on their bulbs by purchasing puts from dealers. All parties found they could adjust their risk exposure to what they considered appropriate levels. Options were particularly useful to growers in reducing their exposure to price fluctuations. Everything could have worked out reasonably well if there had been a regulatory mechanism to assure the option buyers that their contracts would be honored.

The tulip bulb option market was totally undisciplined. There were no financially sound option endorsers to guarantee that writers would fulfill their contracts. There were no margin requirements to keep speculators from ruining themselves and everyone who did business with them.

When the market in tulip bulbs broke in 1636, a number of writers of puts were wiped out. With the losers either unable or unwilling to pay and with no effective precedent to permit dealing with the situation quickly, the authorities called on the Provincial Council at The Hague to devise a solution which would restore credit to the nation. After exhaustive deliberations the Council advised that these contracts should be enforced. This sagacious decision accomplished nothing, it being as difficult to get blood out of a tulip bulb as out of a turnip. The courts refused to enforce the Council's impossible verdict, leaving holders of puts holding the bag. Writers were never required to perform on their contracts.

Neglect of other commerce during this period of tulipomania and delay in resolving the debts and dislocations caused by the collapse had an adverse effect on Holland's economy for many years after the tulip craze was over. The role of options in the excesses of the tulipomania and the fact that specific performance was not enforced on option contracts gave options a bad name throughout Europe. Ironically, the Dutch continued to use options in spite of their experience with tulip bulb contracts. Puts, calls, and straddles on the shares of the Dutch West India Company were traded in Amsterdam only a few years after the tulip bulb debacle.

Organized trading in puts and calls on securities began in

London late in the seventeenth century. In part because of the Dutch experience with tulip bulb options and in part because options were usually associated with speculative activity, considerable opposition soon developed to trading in stock options. Options were declared illegal by Barnard's Act of 1733. This legislation was not effective in stopping option trading, though it was not repealed until 1860. Option dealings continued throughout the period Barnard's Act was on the books. The scale of trading was modest, however, because many of the leading securities firms refused to have anything to do with options.

Puts and calls were traded in London until the financial crisis of 1931, when they were temporarily banned. Options were also banned for a period between World War II and the late 1950s. In 1958 option trading resumed on a small scale. Today the London option market has been eclipsed by the new European Option Exchange in Amsterdam.

Option trading in America began late in the eighteenth century. While options have never been banned in this country, as in London, options have been associated with some rather questionable practices over the years. For example, Russell Sage, widely credited with development of the modern put and call system, apparently devised the procedure for converting puts into calls to get around the usury laws.

Although the conversion process is described at length in Chapter 4, Section D, Sage's use of the technique to avoid usury restrictions is worth special mention as an example of the abuses possible with unregulated options. Sage bought the securities which were to serve as loan collateral from the investor who wanted to borrow money at a usurious rate and received a put option permitting him to sell the securities back to the investor at the purchase price. He then sold this investor a call. The premium on the call was calculated to permit Sage to earn the maximum interest rate the traffic would bear. The legal interest rate ceiling for a margin loan did not apply to the implicit interest rate charged for the option conversion. Unlike the typical owner of a call, Sage's customer participated fully in any rise *or fall* in the stock because the put he issued to Sage would be exercised if the stock dropped. If this technique had been widely used to circumvent margin and usury rules, it could have led to violent stock price fluctuations and, ultimately, to the deterioration of the market structure.

The so-called "bucket shops" (in which Jesse Livermore and many other speculators of the early twentieth century got their start) charged a small premium, typically $1 per share, to carry a speculator's position for a short period of time. If the stock declined, the speculator was, in effect, sold out. The bucket shops had devised an early form of the down-and-out call. Though the association with options is usually forgotten when the expression is used today, the term *bucket shop* retains its unfavorable connotations.

Many of the manipulative schemes of the 1920s were made possible by the practice of granting brokers options on certain stocks in return for an agreement to recommend those stocks to their customers. Stock pool operators and unethical promoters made extensive use of this kind of option. Many small investors were the victims of stock salesmen whose natural enthusiasm was augmented by ownership of these options.

Most large-scale abuses of stock options disappeared with the passage of the securities legislation of the 1930s. The lawmakers directed their attention to specific abuses involving options and established a constructive regulatory framework which dealt effectively with the misuse of options without destroying these useful tools. Occasionally, even today, a manipulative scheme uncovered by the Securities and Exchange Commission (SEC), the National Association of Securities Dealers (NASD), or one of the exchanges will feature grants of stock options to brokers or investment advisers who are expected to promote the stock to their clients. The use of inside information in the purchase of stock options has also surfaced, notably in the Texas Gulf case. On balance, however, abuses involving options have been relatively minor for the past 40 years. When major problems have cropped up, such as recent cases involving commodity options, the regulators have managed to deal with the situation.

The regulatory authorities have learned that the existence of a securities option market can even serve an important regulatory function. Large-scale option transactions that coincide with major events in a corporation's history can provide an important clue to the improper use of inside information.

The present regulatory environment effectively prevents the speculative abuses which led to the collapse of the Dutch economy in the seventeenth century and to the loss of faith in the securities markets during the depression of the 1930s. Option writers are now required to post adequate margin to ensure they will honor their contracts. Granting options to induce a broker or investment adviser to recommend a stock and buying options to take advantage of inside information are prohibited. In short, with rare exceptions, current regulations deal adequately with the historic abuses of the option contract. These regulations may have made it impossible to duplicate the shoestring leverage that was possible in earlier years, but they also ensure the viability of the securities option market under virtually all conditions.

B. STRUCTURE OF THE CONVENTIONAL OR OVER-THE-COUNTER OPTION MARKET

In spite of Wall Street's recent frenetic interest in options, trading volume in the conventional option market is much lower today than it was prior to the inauguration of the Chicago Board Options Exchange. As a result of the CBOE's success and the relative decline in conventional option volume, major structural changes in the conventional option market are likely during the next few years. Because of its declining relative importance and the high probability of structural changes, the conventional option market will not be discussed in great detail. Most books on options stress conventional options, and so the reader can easily find further information on topics mentioned only briefly here. The discussion of this market will focus on the role of the specialized put and call broker who is the heart of the over-the-counter option trading system and whose survival is threatened by listed option trading.

A glance at the figures in Table 3-1 suggests that prior to 1973 option trading volume was in a modest upward trend relative to volume on the New York Stock Exchange (NYSE).

Table 3-1. Comparison of Option Trading Volume and New York Stock Exchange Volume (All figures in thousands of shares of underlying stock)

Year	Conventional Option Volume	As a Percent of NYSE Volume	Listed Option Volume	As a Percent of NYSE Volume
1940	1,205	0.58		
1945	2,108	0.56		
1950	2,631	0.50		
1955	6,012	0.93		
1960	8,561	1.12		
1965	15,256	0.98		
1970	19,681	0.67		
1971	29,516	0.76		
1972	32,851	0.79		
1973	18,920	0.47	109,800	2.7
1974	N.A.	N.A.	564,458	16.1
1975	N.A.	N.A.	1,805,117	38.5
1976	N.A.	N.A.	3,214,089	60.0
1977	N.A.	N.A.	3,939,515	74.7

Conventional option volume figures are based on reports from members of the Put and Call Brokers and Dealers Association. These data include only sales of original options by writers and do not include sales by one dealer to another. Certain specialized options not processed by members of the Association such as down-and-out calls, up-and-out puts, and puts converted from listed calls are also excluded. Data for 1974 and subsequent years have not been compiled.

For 1973, listed option volume figures cover only the period during which the CBOE was open.

The decline in conventional option activity in 1973 was directly related to the opening of the CBOE.

Until 1973, the membership of the Put and Call Brokers and Dealers Association appeared relatively immune to the revenue shrinkage which has debilitated the rest of the securities business since the end of 1968. The revenues of option firms had risen and declined cyclically with changes in the popularity of options, but there was no reason prior to the CBOE "revolution" to doubt the economic viability of the approximately 30 firms that belonged to the Association. In contrast to the rest of Wall Street, these firms had operated for years with competitively negotiated "commission" rates. Even these competitive rates, however, were much higher than the CBOE commission rates on listed options because the conventional option market is a custom market with inherently higher transaction costs than the streamlined, standardized listed option market.

Lower transaction costs are not the only reason behind the overnight success of listed options. The sponsors and management of the CBOE did an outstanding job of educating registered representatives and the investing public to the virtues of options. Brokerage firms in search of new sources of revenue emphasized options for the first time. Any reluctance investors have shown in the past, based on the unknown size of the put and call dealer's spread (the difference between the premium paid by the buyer and the premium received by the writer), has disappeared with the introduction of the auction market and its published prices.

As a result of the outstanding success of listed option trading, several members of the Put and Call Brokers and Dealers Association were absorbed by NYSE member firms to provide the acquiring firm with in-house option expertise. Other members simply went out of business or resigned from the Association for other reasons. The remaining Association members found their revenues greatly reduced as investors abandoned the conventional option market for listed options. To understand why the long-term viability of independent conventional option houses is in doubt, it is necessary to understand the role of the put and call broker in the conventional option market. Examining each aspect of the put and call broker's task is also an excellent way of discovering how the conventional option market works.

A put and call broker's basic function is to bring buyers and writers of conventional options together. Typically, both the buyer and writer are customers of NYSE member firms. Usually the buyer will be a customer of one firm and the writer a customer of another firm. The put and call broker's role is to act as a broker's broker, as an intermediary between the firms representing buyer and writer.

For a variety of reasons most NYSE members have been happy with this arrangement, and only a few joined the Put and Call Brokers and Dealers Association themselves. The put and call broker's spread is a charge which a stock exchange member might find difficult to collect from the customer if the brokerage firm performed the option trading function in-house. Also, the put and call broker handled many of the details of a conventional option trade in return for his fee. Because most NYSE members did not do enough option business to justify employing an option specialist prior to the establishment of the CBOE, they had relied heavily on the put and call broker's expertise.

Before the era of negotiated commissions, one of the greatest incentives to use an independent option house was that a NYSE member firm ordinarily obtained more stock commission business from an option house than was generated on options bought and sold by the firm's own customers. This extra commission business was from the stock transactions of retail clients of the put and call house and from the stock trading of the option firm. This business was usually divided among NYSE member firms roughly in proportion to the amount of business they directed to the option house.

In addition to the basic task of bringing buyers and writers of conventional options together, the put and call broker performs a number of other services. Some option firms act as dealers and make markets in options on certain stocks. When a potential buyer or writer is anxious to trade an option on a particular stock and the option firm is unable to find the other side of the transaction, some dealers will buy or write the option for their own account in the expectation that they will be able to find the other side of the contract in the relatively near future. Many of the "special options" that used to be advertised in *The New York Times*, *The Wall Street Journal*, and *Barron's* had their origin in the put and call dealer's market-making activity.

Apart from functions related to negotiating the terms of the trade, the put and call broker plays an important role in the mechanical aspects of a conventional option transaction. Specifically, the put and call broker arranges for the conversion of puts into calls and makes certain that the endorsement or performance guarantee by the NYSE member firm representing the option writer is in the proper form. Finally, the Put and Call Brokers and Dealers Association publishes standard option contract forms and sets policies for the adjustment of option striking prices or expiration dates if changes are required.

Conversion is the process of transforming a put into a call or a call into a put. Conversion is frequently necessary because buyers are interested primarily in call options, while conventional option writers often prefer to write straddles. Though the put and call broker arranges for conversions, the actual conversion is done by a small number of NYSE member firms. As the reader will understand after reading Chapter 4, Section D, conversion is not a complex process. However, conversion is sufficiently esoteric that most participants in the option market are content to leave it to the put and call broker and the NYSE member firm which runs a conversion account.

All options traded through members of the Put and Call Brokers and Dealers Association are endorsed by a NYSE member who guarantees that the option will be honored. The option buyer and writer are usually unknown to one another. To eliminate the need for personal credit checks and to remove most of the credit risk from the transaction, the endorsing firm guarantees that the writer has met NYSE or more stringent requirements for the deposit of collateral to guarantee his performance on the option contract. Even if the writer should fail to perform, the NYSE member firm itself guarantees fulfillment of the option contract. In fact, the contract which the option buyer receives is a contract with the endorsing firm, not with the option writer.

In spite of the failure of numerous firms over the years, all option contracts endorsed by NYSE member firms have been honored. As good as this record is, the conventional option endorsement process is obsolete and will probably be replaced in time by a central clearing and endorsement process like that used for listed options. For the time being, the put and call broker makes the endorsement system work. If a brokerage house is in trouble and the buyer's broker is nervous, the put and call firm can help switch the endorsement to a stronger house, usually without the knowledge of either the option buyer or the option writer.

Standard conventional put and call contracts similar to those published by the Put and Call Brokers and Dealers Association appear in Figure 3-1. These contracts spell out the basic adjustments of the striking price for cash dividends, rights, and warrants (the striking price is reduced by the amount or value of the distribution) and for stock splits, stock dividends, and reverse splits (both the striking price and the number of shares subject to option are changed so that the option buyer's net position is unaffected).

Although the contract form does not spell the procedure out in detail, should a merger occur during the life of the option contract, the buyer has the right to purchase or sell the package of securities issued in exchange for the optioned stock on terms equivalent to those stated in the option contract. For example, if the option contract is a call on 100 shares of stock at $20 per share and the optioned stock is exchanged in a merger for 50 shares of stock in a new corporation, the holder

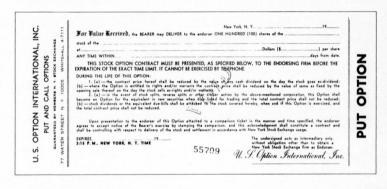

Figure 3-1. Sample conventional option contracts.

of the option has the right to buy 50 shares of the new corporation's stock at $40 per share.

The Put and Call Brokers and Dealers Association determines how option contracts should be settled when an unexpected event makes the exact terms of the contract impossible to meet. For example, when the NYSE closed on certain days during 1968 to permit brokers to catch up with their paperwork and in 1977 because of a New York City power blackout, the Association ruled that options scheduled to expire on those days would not expire until 3:15 P.M. on the next trading day. Perhaps the most difficult problem is caused by a suspension of trading in the stock which is the subject of an option contract. In such cases, the holder of the option must give notice of exercise before the contractual option expiration date; but the actual exercise of the contract is deferred until trading in the stock resumes.

Another notable function of the put and call broker is the repurchase of an option from the investor. If the option is trading in the money, the transaction occurs at intrinsic value net of applicable stock commissions to permit the customer to obtain a long-term capital gain on the option purchase. The NYSE member firm which represents the option buyer will deliver the option and will receive the commissions from the purchase and sale of the underlying stock. If the option holder is a retail customer of the option house, part of the commission will go to an NYSE member. If the owner of an out-of-the-money option wants to avoid letting the loss on that position go long-term, the option dealer will buy it for a nominal sum, usually $1.

The option houses that function primarily as brokers' brokers have been largely eliminated. The only conventional option houses which seem likely to survive as independents are those which have made a fast transition to active trading of listed options. The most successful option houses appear to have adopted two complementary strategies. First, they have continued to act as brokers' brokers for listed options, providing trading and clearing services to other firms. In addition, they have attempted to develop a public customer business of their own. Success of the latter strategy is critical to their long-term survival as independent firms.

The outlook for the independent put and call broker may be bleak, but the conventional option market is by no means dead. Listed trading in standardized options on a limited number of stocks will never satisfy the needs of all option writers and buyers. Several changes are inevitable, however. The days of enormous transaction costs are gone. Work is under way on primary and secondary trading and clearing techniques that will improve the efficiency and lower the operating costs of the conventional option market. The vested interests of some option market participants in maintaining high transaction costs have delayed implementation of an efficient central market for conventional options. When low-cost, centralized trading is finally adopted, the volume of conventional option activity will probably be much greater than at any time in the past.

Unless and until the structure of the conventional option market is revamped, this segment of the option business will not prosper. This advertisement from *The Wall Street Journal* for November 26, 1975, describes the situation perfectly:

**NOTICE TO REGISTERED
BROKER - DEALERS**

Some memberships in the Put and Call Brokers and Dealers Association, Inc. which sold as high as $17,000.00 before CBOE, are now available for approximately $1,000.00.

Late in 1977 there was only one active firm affiliated with the Put and Call Brokers and Dealers Association. Several non-members also dealt in conventional options.

C. THE SIGNIFICANCE OF THE CHICAGO BOARD OPTIONS EXCHANGE

This section focuses on the major innovations introduced by the CBOE that have revolutionized option trading. The text focuses on the economic and investment significance of the differences between listed and conventional option markets. Table 3-2 at the end of this section provides an item-by-item comparison of the two markets.

Three of the most important changes instituted by the CBOE are

1. Standardization of the striking price and the expiration date of the option contract
2. Fungibility or interchangeability of option contracts which eliminates the direct tie between option writer and buyer and facilitates the development of a secondary market in options
3. Sharply lower net transaction costs and an organized secondary market

Because the practices initiated by the CBOE have been adopted by other options exchanges in the United States and by exchanges in other countries as well, the discussion which follows is generally applicable to all listed option trading.

The importance of standardized option terms in the development of a secondary market in option contracts cannot be overemphasized. Standardization facilitates secondary trading because the number of distinct contracts a buyer or seller must evaluate is reduced. In contrast to the conventional option market where it is possible to buy or write an option with practically any striking price or expiration date, the terms of contracts available on the exchanges are more limited. The striking price of a listed option always ends in $5, $2.50, or $0 unless a stock dividend or other capital change occurs after trading in the option begins. If American Telephone and Telegraph is selling at $51 a share at the time options for a new expiration month are being listed for trading, the new AT&T option will have a striking price of $50 per share. If the stock price closes above $52.50, the exchange will add $55 contracts for each expiration date beyond 60 days. Barring stock dividends, splits, or other capital changes, it will be impossible to buy or write an AT&T option on the exchange with a striking price between $50 and $55 per share.

In addition to standardization of striking prices, the exchanges have standardized expiration dates. The expiration date is the Saturday after the third Friday in the month. While most options expire in January, April, July, and October, some underlying stocks have options expiring in February, May,

August, and November cycles, and a few use March, June, September, and December cycles.

Fungibility or interchangeability is a second important characteristic of listed options necessary for the development of an active secondary market. Fungibility means substitutability or equivalence. Each listed option with a common expiration date and striking price is interchangeable with any similar listed option. In contrast, a conventional option is a direct contract between a particular writer (or, rather, his brokerage firm) and a particular buyer. One conventional option contract is not substitutable for another, even if the terms are identical. As a result of the direct tie between buyer and writer, it is frequently difficult for the owner of a conventional option to sell or exchange the option privilege for a price in excess of the intrinsic or exercise value of the option. Just as importantly, it is impossible for a conventional option writer to terminate his obligation except through direct negotiation with the buyer of the specific contract he wrote.

With listed options, either party can usually close out a position that no longer meets his needs without undue sacrifice. The buyer and writer in a listed option transaction have no direct connection. Each has a contract only with The Options Clearing Corporation which is the issuer of listed options. The option buyer relies on the Clearing Corporation to make good on the contract. The writer's obligation is an obligation to the Clearing Corporation, not to the buyer his broker happens to meet on the exchange floor. Either the option buyer or the writer can close out his position by simply reversing the initial transaction. For a more complete explanation of the relationship between the Clearing Corporation and the other parties to an option contract, the reader should examine the relevant sections of The Options Clearing Corporation prospectus.

A third important characteristic of listed options is their relatively low transaction cost. As will be seen in Section D of this chapter, the total transaction cost of any listed option trade is substantially lower than the transaction cost of a similar conventional option trade. Lower transaction costs have an important effect on trading volume and market liquidity. As the spread between the premium paid by the buyer and the premium received by the writer grows smaller, the number of transactions will tend to grow larger. If the option premium paid by the buyer is $500 and the amount received by the writer, net of transaction costs, is only $400, a writer who was willing to accept a net premium of $425 and a buyer who was willing to pay a premium of $475 would be excluded from the market. On the other hand, if the spread were narrower, both the buyer and the writer could be accommodated and the total volume of option transactions would increase. Relatively low transaction costs have been an important factor in the high trading volume of listed options.

In addition to these three major features of listed options, there are a number of other characteristics which have contributed to their success. In contrast to the conventional option market, listed option striking prices are not reduced to compensate for the payment of cash dividends. Less frequent and more significant changes like stock dividends, stock splits, and similar distributions are handled in the same way for conventional and listed options. Apart from simplifying published trading summaries, not reducing the striking price for cash dividends is probably consistent with the preferences of option market participants. Typically, the option buyer does not value a modest reduction of the striking price very highly. The option writer may, however, see his ability to retain the dividend as an important feature of the listed option contract. Though the difference is frequently minor, the method of handling cash dividends affects the relative value of conventional and listed options on the same underlying stock.

Another important feature of listed options is that they are far more flexible instruments than conventional options and can be used in a wider variety of transactions. Because both writer and buyer can close out positions relatively quickly, trading and investment strategies which require the use of options for only a short period of time are feasible. Strategies which depend on an investor's ability to buy or sell additional options as time passes are facilitated by a secondary market.

The prices at which listed option transactions actually take place are published daily. Published prices and known commission rates assure both buyer and writer of a fair market. While we are not aware of any widespread abuse of the relative obscurity of conventional option dealer spreads, the mere fact that daily trading summaries are published in the newspapers removes some of the mystery and, quite frankly, some of the suspicion from the option market.

Though we seem to have left the era when the financial soundness of much of the securities industry was called into question, most option buyers will have more confidence in the endorsement of The Options Clearing Corporation than they would have in the option endorsement of most NYSE member firms. Appropriate or inappropriate though this difference in the investor's level of confidence may be, it is nonetheless a factor in some option transactions. The fact that the actual risk of accepting endorsements has been nil does not prevent reliance on these endorsements from being a potential problem in the over-the-counter option market.

In some respects, one of the most important innovations pioneered by the CBOE is the introduction of certificate-less clearing. Except in unusual cases where an option trader insists on evidence of the transaction in addition to a brokerage firm confirmation slip, The Options Clearing Corporation does not issue an actual option contract or certificate. This feature of listed option trading reduces the amount of paperwork and eliminates the physical movement of securities, in this case option contracts, between brokerage firms. The Options Clearing Corporation has sharply reduced the time required to clear a transaction and, as the brokerage community gains additional experience with certificate-less trading, the cost of clearing a transaction should decline. The CBOE was a pilot project not only for organized trading of option contracts but also for the introduction of certificate-less trading to the securities markets. On the basis of results to date, we can say that both features of the pilot project are unqualified successes.

Table 3-2. Comparison of Conventional and Listed Options and Markets

	Conventional	Listed
Type of options traded	Calls, puts, combination options	Calls, puts, combination orders permitted
Striking price	Any price buyer and writer negotiate	Standardized price ending in $5, $2.50, or $0
Expiration date	Any date buyer and writer negotiate	Saturday after the third Friday in the designated expiration month
Expiration time	3:15 P.M. eastern time	5 P.M. eastern time
Last date and time option can be sold	Same as expiration date and time	2 P.M. central time 3 P.M. eastern time on the business day immediately prior to the expiration date
Adjustment for cash dividend	Striking price reduced on ex-dividend date	No change in striking price
Adjustment for stock dividends, stock splits, and reverse splits	Both striking price and number of shares covered by options are adjusted to reflect the capital change	
Adjustment for rights or warrants issued to common shareholders	Striking price reduced by the value of the rights or warrants	
Limitation on purchase or sale of options on one stock	None, but limits have been proposed	1,000 contracts on the same side of the market (e.g., long calls *and* short puts); limit applies to all expiration dates
Unit of trading	One contract is an option on 100 shares of the underlying stock before any adjustments	
Method of option price determination	Buyer and writer negotiate through put and call broker	Central auction market
Secondary market	Limited; special options advertised in newspaper	Very active secondary market
Buyer's recourse to obtain performance on option contract	Primary responsibility for performance belongs to the endorsing broker who may be any member of the NYSE	The Options Clearing Corporation is the primary obligor guaranteeing the writer's performance

Table 3-2. Comparison of Conventional and Listed Options and Markets—*(Continued)*

	Conventional	Listed
Evidence of ownership	Bearer certificate	Broker's confirmation slip
Method of closing out transaction when stock sells above striking price	Option may be exercised by buyer or sold to put and call broker who exercises the option and sells the stock	Exercise is rare; contract is usually closed out in a closing purchase–sale transaction
Transaction costs	High	Moderate
Commission structure	Basic charge is negotiated by put and call broker as a spread between premium paid by buyer and premium paid to writer	Negotiated commission rates since May 1, 1975
Stocks on which options are available	Almost any stock	Over 200 selected stocks in the United States and a growing list of stocks elsewhere in the world.
Pricing information	Brokers publish indicated premiums to buyers or writers	Actual transaction prices published daily
Procedure for exercise	Buyer exercises by notifying endorsing broker	Buyer's broker notifies The Options Clearing Corporation, which selects writers essentially at random
Extensions	Available if writer agrees	Not available
Tax treatment	Identical; see Chapter 5	
Margin requirement: call buyer	100% of the option premium	
Margin requirement: covered writer	No margin required beyond that needed to carry stock position	
Margin requirement: uncovered writer	Minimum requirement is related to price of stock with adjustment for amount of premium received and amount by which option is in or out of the money. Margin requirements should be checked in detail with each brokerage firm. See Appendix A for minimum requirements in detail.	

D. FACTORS AFFECTING THE VOLUME OF OPTION TRADING

For many years, the volume of option trading in the United States has exceeded securities option trading activity in all other countries combined. The birth of listed option trading promises to expand option activity well beyond historic levels.

It is interesting to consider why options have attained this degree of success in the United States. A cynic might argue that the entire securities market in the United States is larger than markets abroad; consequently, we should expect more option trading as well. Although good statistical information is not available, the level of option trading in the United States appears to be several times as great as any proportionate relationship to trading in underlying shares would suggest. There are several explanations, unrelated to size, for the success of option trading in this country. If these explanations are correct, option trading in the United States is just entering its period of greatest growth.

An important historic fact behind the development of the option market is the constructive regulatory environment in the United States. Close scrutiny of option markets by the Securities and Exchange Commission, the National Association of Securities Dealers, and, more recently, the options exchanges might suggest a constraint on speculative fervor and therefore less interest in options. Actually, close regulation probably encourages option trading. During a highly speculative period, option activity will be high under virtually any regulatory conditions. When speculative activity wanes, however, options may be written or purchased on something approaching a rational basis. Although some observers would argue that option prices, as opposed to values, are rarely rational, both buyer and writer will be interested in the market structure within which the option is traded. Unless his speculative urges are overwhelming, a buyer wants to feel that he has access to the same sources of information as the option writer, that the market will not be manipulated, and that the writer will honor the option contract. The writer would like similar protection. Both parties take comfort in the fact that the vigilance of the SEC, the NASD, and the major exchanges has largely eliminated the illicit market practices that were so prevalent during the first third of this century.

Although the features of the option contract are probably less important than the strength of the regulatory process, the American stock option contract is inherently more attractive than its European counterpart. Before the introduction of listed option trading, European securities options were exercisable only on the date of expiration. The American option is exercisable at any time prior to the expiration date as well. In practice, most American options are exercised within a week of expiration, but the restriction that an option can be exercised on only one day does reduce a buyer's flexibility. The length of the period during which the contract can be exercised and the health of the regulatory environment interact; the European contract increases the option holder's vulnerability to any manipulative activity which might be concentrated on the day his contract expires.

Building on the framework created by the constructive regulatory atmosphere and the variable exercise date, the listed option has added several new dimensions. One of the most important features of exchange trading of options is that it provides a secondary market for contracts which are no longer attractive to the original purchaser or writer. If a listed call has performed as anticipated, the buyer can probably resell it at a price which will yield a premium over the intrinsic value of the call. If the option had been purchased over-the-counter, the buyer might not be able to get more than the option's exercise value. Likewise, the writer can terminate the listed option obligation if it becomes advisable to do so. Writing the call no longer locks the writer in for the life of the contract.

Probably the single most significant contribution of listed option trading to the expansion of the option market is that it sharply reduces the cost of a transaction. Both the writer and the buyer of a call can fare better on an exchange than with a conventional call. If commission and other transaction costs are too large, they act as a deterrent to trading. Commissions on the exchange are low enough that the buyer can

Table 3-3. Comparison of Transaction Costs: Conventional vs. Listed Option Markets

Assumptions:

Buyer buys 10 calls at $500 each with a $50 striking price. Stock rises to $60 where buyer sells or exercises calls, receiving $1,000 per contract before costs. Writer initially buys 500 shares of stock or enough to cover one-half of his obligation. All figures are expressed on a per contract basis with commissions calculated on the assumption that the transaction consists of 10 contracts.

BUYER'S POSITION	Conventional	Listed
Premium paid by buyer	$ 500.00	$ 500.00
Commission to buyer's broker	12.50	12.70
Cost to buyer to establish position	$ 512.50	$ 512.70
Gross proceeds from selling call ($60−$50) × 100 shares	$1,000.00	$1,000.00
Listed option commission		(17.20)
Round-trip stock commission on sale of options	(107.06)	
Transfer taxes	(5.00)	
Subtract: Cost to establish position	(512.50)	(512.70)
Net profit to buyer	$ 375.44	$ 470.10

WRITER'S POSITION:	Conventional	Listed
Premium paid by buyer	$ 500.00	$ 500.00
Option commission paid by writer to his broker	(12.50)	(12.70)
Put and call broker's spread (est.)	(75.00)	
Net premium to writer	$ 412.50	$ 487.30
Cost of repurchasing call from buyer	$1,000.00	$1,000.00
Add: Listed option commission		17.20
Purchase commissions initial stock position	30.13	30.13
Sale commission initial stock position		33.58
Purchase commission additional stock called	33.58	
Sale commission on stock called	50.83	
Transfer taxes	5.00	2.50
Subtract: Net premium received	(412.50)	(487.30)
Profit on stock owned	(500.00)	(500.00)
Net loss to writer	$ 207.04	$ 96.11
Net profit to buyer	$ 375.44	$ 470.10
Subtract: Net loss to writer	(207.04)	(96.11)
Net profit to investors	$ 168.40	$ 373.99
Total transaction costs	$ 331.60	$ 126.01
Less:	(126.01)	
Difference in transaction costs: Conventional vs. listed calls	$ 205.59 per contract	

consider purchasing options for a relatively small expected move in the stock. The writer has reasonable assurance that the commission cost to close out the transaction will not consume most of the premium. The lower transaction cost leads to more active trading and, consequently, to more liquid markets. The example chosen for Table 3-3 illustrates a typical difference between transaction costs for a listed option and those for a conventional option. The actual difference in a particular case always depends on what happens to the price of the stock and what the parties do to close out their respective sides of the contract.

Nonetheless, examination of the table reveals that the costs of the conventional option transaction are, in this case, more than $2\frac{1}{2}$ times as high as for the comparable listed option transaction. In fact, commissions and other charges paid by the two parties to the conventional option trade are equal to about two-thirds of the total option premium paid by the buyer. If one assumed that the transaction involved *one* call rather than ten, the costs would consume an amount nearly equal to the entire premium. With transaction costs of this magnitude, neither buyer nor writer can realistically expect superior performance unless premiums are grossly out of line with any measure of fair value.

NOTES TO TABLE 3-3:

1. If the writer had written conventional straddles instead of two calls against each round lot owned, he would have fared better but the *total* transaction cost would have been even higher. (See Chapter 4, Section D, for an explanation of why selling straddles is similar to the position discussed here.)

2. If the stock declines, total transaction costs may drop slightly faster for the conventional option but they are always substantially higher than listed option costs.

3. Transfer taxes are based on New York residence.

4. Commissions are calculated on the basis of an initial position of 10 calls and a stock position of 500 shares bought by the writer. Stock and option commission rates are those in effect prior to May 1, 1975, on the NYSE and CBOE, respectively. These commission charges are then stated on a per call basis. The total charges are 10 times the figures listed.

E. OPTIONS MARKETS OUTSIDE THE UNITED STATES

The success of the options exchanges in the United States has been accompanied by the introduction of standardized option trading in other major financial markets. Similar options exchanges are now in operation or in advanced planning stages in Australia, Canada, Europe (Amsterdam), Hong Kong, Tokyo, Manila, Singapore, and the United Kingdom. Nearly all the world's options exchanges have adopted rules and procedures similar to those of the U.S. exchanges with minor modifications necessary to make option trading procedures consistent with the host country's regulatory framework. When reading the prospectuses and introductory pamphlets published by these exchanges, one is impressed more by the differences in option terminology than by any substantive differences in trading procedures or contract provisions. With the exception of the tax discussion in Chapter 5, nearly every section of this book is applicable to any standardized stock option trading program in the world.

Investors are just beginning to see the implications of worldwide option trading. In Chapter 5, for example, the reader will find a demonstration that a nonresident of the United States should *never* own a dividend-paying common stock in a U.S.-based company if listed options are available. With options, the U.S. withholding tax on dividends can be avoided. This fact alone should lead to relatively active trading of options on U.S. securities by nonresidents.

Problems similar to the withholding tax will probably create similar opportunities in other options markets. Foreign exchange restrictions and tax impediments to the ownership of securities of foreign companies might be partially overcome by options markets. International option exchanges may accelerate the trend to 24-hour-a-day trading in the securities of major multinational companies.

Although it is too early to predict the ultimate importance of international option trading with any degree of confidence, it seems likely that options may help protect investors from foreign exchange fluctuations. Exchange rate fluctuations and impediments to the free flow of capital across international boundaries may also have some peculiar effects on option premium levels, particularly in Europe. An investor living in Switzerland who believed the shares of a British company were attractive might buy calls to participate in an expected stock price advance without undue exposure to possible changes in the relationship between Swiss francs and sterling. To the extent that this buying pushed premiums up, British investors would be encouraged to buy more shares and sell calls against the expanded stock position.

The effect of foreign exchange fluctuations and capital restrictions on premium levels will probably not be significant after puts fully complement the call option market. Until puts are universally available, however, call option premiums may tend to expand after the currency of the country in which the shares are traded has been weak and to contract when the currency has been strong. This foreign exchange effect on premium levels may be too small to measure under most circumstances.

Options on fixed income securities may be more important in European markets than in the United States because of the foreign exchange hedging possibilities they provide. Options on bonds and shorter-term debt instruments should permit sophisticated individuals and corporate treasurers to obtain foreign exchange protection more economically than existing currency futures markets.

4 USES OF OPTIONS: INVESTMENT POSITIONS AND STRATEGIES

A. GRAPHIC REPRESENTATION OF INVESTMENT POSITIONS

This chapter deals with the analysis of investment positions using a simple graphic method that allows one to illustrate the risk-reward characteristics of any holding. These graphs facilitate a profitability analysis of any position, whether that position consists of cash, of cash and securities, or of cash, securities, and options. The graphic approach also permits relatively easy adjustment for borrowing costs, taxes, and commissions. Using the graphic method, the reader can work out the profitability of any strategy that might be devised under a variety of assumptions about the likely course of stock prices.

Algebraic formulations are difficult for most investors to use, let alone to understand. In contrast, most investors with enough sophistication to use options can use graphs easily and effectively. Also, while it is easy to plug numbers mindlessly into a formula and get worthless results, if a graph is wrong, it frequently looks wrong.

To avoid dealing with stocks and options in the abstract, a specific set of stock and option terms and prices has been selected. Apart from the fact that this approach makes the examples comparable and, it is hoped, somewhat more meaningful, it permits the reader to combine two or more strategies. The particular option characteristics illustrated should help bridge the gap between conventional options and listed options.

Traditional discussions of option strategies and their risk-reward characteristics focus on the conventional option market, where most options are written with the striking price equal to the market price. For listed options, the market price of the stock generally differs (sometimes substantially) from the striking price of the option. In the graphs, a listed-type option with differing market and striking prices is used, but the method of making commission, dividend, and interest adjustments for both listed and conventional options is discussed. The purpose throughout the presentation is to develop an approach which the investor can use as the basis for a rational analysis of any conceivable option strategy.

To simplify the discussion, the following basic assumptions have been adopted:

1. The investor can obtain interest at a 7 percent annual rate on any monies he wishes to lend or invest in short-term debt instruments.

2. The investor will pay interest at a 9 percent rate for any borrowing from his broker or from a bank.

3. The common stock which the investor purchases or sells short or which underlies any options he may buy or write is selling at $95 a share.

4. There is available a listed call option with approximately 6 months remaining until expiration. It has a striking price of $100, and the current price of this call is $10 ($1,000 per 100-share contract).

5. There is a listed put option with terms analogous to those of the listed call. For purposes of simplifying these graphs, we assume that these puts are selling at $11 ($1,100 per 100-share contract).

Except where indicated, the profit-loss lines on the graphs have not been adjusted for dividends, commissions, taxes, interest, or opportunity costs. Though option writing generates a cash balance which can be invested by the writer, an interest credit is not added. With the exception of taxes, the nature and direction of the adjustments as they apply to the simpler investment strategies are discussed. A complex strategy can usually be adjusted by dealing separately with each component part. The basic explanation of the graphic approach does not require a detailed understanding of these adjustments. Many investors will conclude that adjustments are not worth the bother. If one excepts some adjustments for the tax impact of an investment and adjustments for transaction costs related to spreads and conventional options, this attitude is probably correct for most purposes.

The investment positions chosen for illustration are, for the most part, those discussed by Malkiel and Quandt in *Strategies and Rational Decisions in the Securities Options Market*. The author has added several positions not used by Malkiel and Quandt because readily marketable listed options, not available when their book was written, increase the range of possible positions.

Each investment position or strategy is depicted on a standardized graph. The profit-loss line on the graph shows the dollar profit or loss the investor will experience at each possible stock price approximately 6 months after the position is initiated. In the case of strategies involving options, one assumes that the options will expire in 6 months, and so the price 6 months out is also the price of the stock when the option expires. Any two strategies can be compared at any stock price by transferring the profit-loss line from one graph to the other or by preparing a new graph and imposing both strategies on that graph.

The reader may be tempted to skip over the earlier and simpler investment strategies and go directly to the particular

---

Figure 4-1. (Opposite) Each of these graphs has a shape characteristic of one or more specific strategies. The vertical axis on each graph represents profit or loss at a particular stock price. The straight horizontal line signifies zero profit. The horizontal axis measures the stock price, with the price rising from left to right. Detailed graphs will be found later in the chapter.

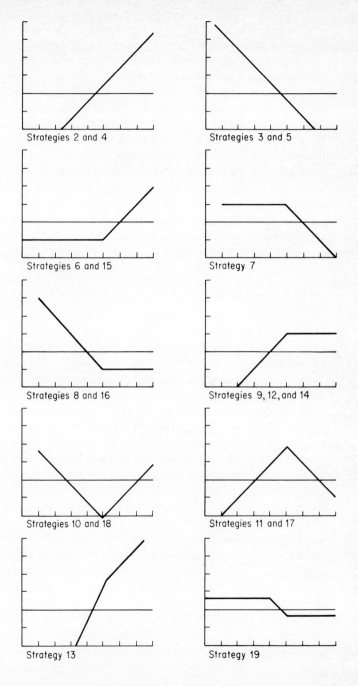

Strategies 2 and 4

Strategies 3 and 5

Strategies 6 and 15

Strategy 7

Strategies 8 and 16

Strategies 9, 12, and 14

Strategies 10 and 18

Strategies 11 and 17

Strategy 13

Strategy 19

option-related strategy which seems most interesting. We urge at least a casual examination of the simpler strategies, since the graphic display method will be of most use if its application is thoroughly understood in a variety of cases.

One of the major advantages of options is that they permit an investor to adjust his investment position to virtually any degree of bullishness, bearishness, uncertainty, or neutrality he may feel toward the market or an individual stock. The diagrams in Figure 4-1 illustrate the "shape" of a few of the simpler strategies an investor can follow to express his opinion on a stock. Under the diagrams are listed the numbers of strategies with profit-loss lines of that approximate shape. The general "shapes" can be adjusted to reflect subtly different attitudes toward a stock or the market.

Strategy 1: Cash (Purchase Short-Term Debt Securities)

This first simple graph (Figure 4-2) is important primarily because it helps explain the use of the graphic technique. The vertical axis on the chart measures the dollar profit which the investor will realize by following this strategy. The horizontal axis lists possible prices for the hypothetical stock 6 months from the day the investment is initiated.

In the example illustrated here, the investor places money in a short-term debt instrument paying, under our assumptions, 7 percent annually, or $3\frac{1}{2}$ percent over the 6-month period. On a $95 investment, the interest income for 6 months is $3\frac{1}{2}\% \times \$95$, or $3.33. As indicated by the horizontal profit-loss line, this income is totally independent of the price of any security. Though modest, the interest income is always positive.

The fact that the 7 percent interest has to be divided in half because one is dealing with a 6-month period illustrates a feature the reader should keep in mind when interpreting other graphs. To annualize profit or loss, we multiply the gain or loss at a given stock price by 2. Of course, if the period covered by the graph is not 6 months, the multiplier will be different.

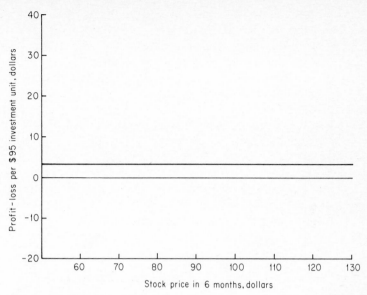

Figure 4-2. Strategy 1: Cash (purchase short-term debt securities).

Adjustment of the interest income for taxes or any transaction costs would lower the line by the amount of the adjustment.

Strategy 2: Purchase Stock

In this example (Figure 4-3) the investor purchases 100 shares of common stock at a price of $95 per share. The profit or loss is strictly a function of the price of the stock 6 months in the future. If the price of the stock falls to $70, the investor suffers a loss of $25 per share over the 6-month period. If the price of the stock rises to $110, the investor earns $15. The significant risk-reward feature of this strategy, as every stockholder knows, is that the investor's profit or loss bears a direct linear relationship to the price of the stock on the date the determination of return is made. If an investor is optimistic about the probable course of stock prices in general and this stock price in particular, he will favor this position. If he is not unreservedly optimistic, an unhedged long position in the stock is probably inappropriate. Habit, convention, and,

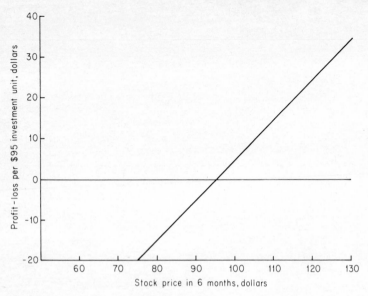

Figure 4-3. Strategy 2: Purchase stock.

perhaps, ignorance appear to be the principal reasons many investors accept this position without questioning its suitability to their risk preferences.

There are several adjustments necessary to calculate the precise profit or loss from this strategy. To adjust for dividends, the profit line is simply raised by the rate of the dividend payments. If, for example, dividend payments over the life of the investment aggregated $2, the profit-loss line would be higher by $2 at every possible stock price. In a similar manner, we can adjust for commissions on the purchase and/or sale of the shares. The purchase commission would reduce the line equally at every share price because the purchase commission is calculated at a share price of $95. A sale commission would often increase or decrease with the price of the stock. If the investor is not seriously considering sale of the shares at the end of the 6-month interval, it would probably be inappropriate to adjust for a sale commission. Adjustments for stock splits, stock dividends, and other capital changes are best made either by redrawing the graph or relabeling the horizontal axis. These changes do not affect the dollar profit.

Strategy 3: Sell Stock Short

The graph (Figure 4-4) depicting the short seller's position is the converse of the stock buyer's graph illustrated in Figure 4-3. For every point the stock rises, the buyer gains $1 per share and the short seller loses $1 per share. If the stock declines, the short seller profits to exactly the extent that the buyer loses.

Adjustments to the short seller's profit-loss line for dividends can be important. Whereas dividends increase the stock buyer's return, the short seller must pay out dividends to the owner of the stock; therefore, dividends reduce the short seller's return. Commission and other adjustments are similar for both the short seller and the buyer.

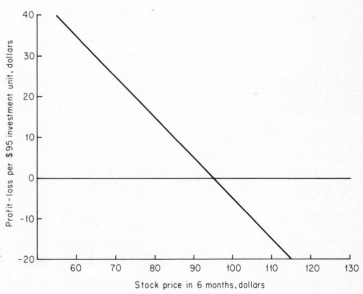

Figure 4-4. Strategy 3: Sell stock short.

Strategy 4: Purchase Stock on Margin

The principal effect of buying a stock on margin is to increase the slope of the profit-loss line so that both gain and loss, as a percent of the investor's equity, increase more rapidly as the price moves away from the original purchase price. With current initial margin requirements set at 50 percent, the approximate effect of margin transactions is to double the amount of stock an investor can carry by borrowing against his equity. Consequently, margin transactions based on this 50 percent rate will approximately double an investor's profit or loss (before interest cost) as the stock price moves away from the purchase price.

Once the investor begins to buy on margin, the adjustments he might wish to make to his profit-loss line become more complicated. The graph in Figure 4-5 assumes that the investor uses the 50 percent margin rules to carry two shares of stock instead of one with each $95 of equity. The graph has also been adjusted to reflect the cost of the money borrowed to carry half of the stock position. To make this adjustment, the

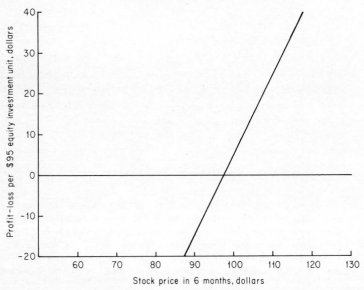

Figure 4-5. Strategy 4: Purchase stock on margin.

entire profit-loss line is lowered by the cost of the borrowed money. In this case, the investor borrows $47.50 per share owned at a 9 percent interest rate for 6 months. This borrowing reduces his profit or increases his loss for the 6 months by $4.28 for each pair of shares owned, regardless of the price at which the stock sells on the day the transaction is closed out. A further complicating feature of margin transactions is that if the price of the stock drops much below $70, the investor may receive a margin call. At that time, he will have to invest more equity or allow his broker to liquidate the position for failure to meet margin requirements.

Adjustment for dividends, commissions, and capital changes such as stock splits are slightly complicated by the margin transactions, but if these adjustments are approached one at a time, there is no insurmountable difficulty in making them.

Strategy 5: Sell Stock Short on Margin

Selling stock short on margin is not quite the converse of buying stock on margin. The slope of the profit-loss line (Figure 4-6) for the doubled stock position is increased from the basic short selling case as it is when stock is bought on margin, but there is usually no interest charge for borrowing money to carry part of the position. The margin required for a short sale serves only to guarantee that the short seller will meet his obligation if the stock rises. Money does not have to be borrowed to meet this requirement.*

---

* Investors are sometimes puzzled that a broker charges interest when a margin account shows a credit balance as a result of a combination of margin purchases and short sales. The reason for the interest charge is that the owner of the shares which the investor borrowed to sell short is entitled to the use of the money generated by the sale. Thus, though the investor's account shows a credit balance, the proceeds of the short sale usually do not offset the debit balance. Section D of this chapter explores the economics of short selling in more detail.

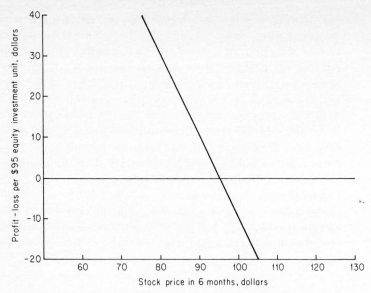

Figure 4-6. Strategy 5: Sell stock short on margin.

On 50 percent margin, dividend and other adjustments are double the magnitude of the 100 percent equity short selling case.

Strategy 6: Purchase a Call

When the investor purchases a call, the profit-loss line is no longer a straight line passing through the price of the stock on the day the purchase was made. In the case illustrated (purchase of a $10 call with a striking price of $100) the investor loses the entire investment if the call expires with the stock selling below the striking price of $100 per share. Furthermore, the investor does not even begin to make money until the price of the stock exceeds the striking price *plus* the option premium paid for the call. In this case, $100 (striking price) plus $10 (option premium) equals $110 (break-even point). If the price of the stock on the expiration date rises to $120 per share, the buyer of a call will have approximately doubled his initial investment. If the stock price rises 10 more points to $130 per share, the call buyer will have tripled his investment.

The principal advantages and disadvantages of owning a call option should be clarified by the diagram (Figure 4-7). Although he loses his entire investment if the stock sells below the striking price when the option expires, the investor's maximum risk exposure is limited to the amount of the option premium. This is true regardless of how low the price of the stock may drop. On the positive side, the call buyer participates in any advance in the price of the stock above the striking price. His profit increases point-for-point, no matter how high the price of the stock may rise over the life of the option.

Possible adjustments to the graph can be either quite simple or very complicated. For example, the commission adjustment on a listed call is relatively easy to make. The call purchase commission simply lowers the line by a constant amount at every possible price. If the call expires worthless, there is no sale or exercise commission, but if the option has value at the time the transaction is closed out, the sale commission increases as the value of the call increases. Commission adjust-

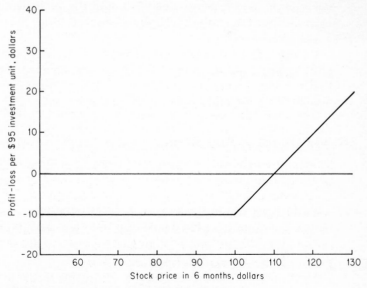

Figure 4-7. Strategy 6: Purchase a call.

ments for conventional options are more complex. Purchase commissions will ordinarily be nominal, and there will be no sale commission if the option expires worthless. If the conventional option has value, the call buyer will ordinarily have to pay a round-trip stock commission when he sells the call or exercises it and sells the stock. One side of this round-trip commission will be based on the $100 striking price of the call, and the other side will be based on the market value of the stock at the time the call is exercised or sold.

Just as the commission adjustment is different, a dividend is treated differently with conventional and listed options. In the case of listed options, there is no adjustment to the striking price for cash dividends. With conventional options, the striking price of the option is reduced on the ex-dividend date by the amount of any dividend paid. This has the effect of moving the diagonal line on the graph to the left by the amount of the dividend. If the dividend is, as we assumed before, $2 over the life of the option, the striking price of a conventional call will be reduced to $98. Thus the call, neglecting for a moment the effect of commissions, would have value at any stock price above $98, and the profit would be increased (or the loss reduced) by $2 at every price above the adjusted exercise price.

If a stock dividend is paid or a stock split declared, both the striking price and the number of shares are adjusted, but the dollar profit or loss is unchanged. These adjustments are similar for listed and conventional options.

Strategy 7: Sell or Write a Call

The graph in Figure 4-8 illustrates the position of the "naked" or uncovered call option writer. The uncovered writer gets to keep all of the call premium if the buyer of the option does not exercise it. The "naked" writing position will be profitable as long as the price of the the stock does not rise above the writer's break-even point: $100 (striking price) plus $10 (call premium) equals $110 (break-even point).

Most adjustments are similar to those made by the call buyer. In the case of a conventional or over-the-counter option,

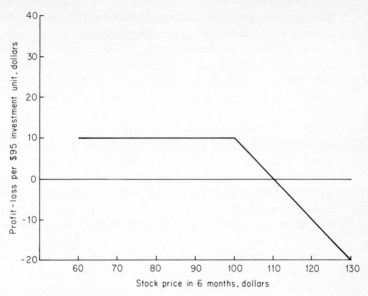

Figure 4-8. Strategy 7: Sell or write a call.

the writer will have to pay a round-trip commission equal to a purchase commission based on the price of the stock at the time the call is exercised plus a sale commission based on the striking price. If the call is listed, the commission adjustment is much more modest, since the uncovered writer can close out his obligation by repurchasing the option contract on the exchange. The commission is based on the price of the call at the time the repurchase transaction occurs.

Any dividend adjustment will depend on the rules of the market in which the call is traded. In the conventional option market the striking price would be reduced by the amount of any dividend. The striking price of a listed call is unaffected by a cash dividend. As indicated earlier, both the striking price and the number of shares subject to option are adjusted for stock dividends and splits.

The premium received by the option writer is available to him as soon as the transaction clears. He can invest it in Treasury bills or use it to reduce the debit balance in his margin account. At the interest rates we have assumed, the

$10 premium from the uncovered call would save the investor with a debit balance about $0.45 in interest charges over the life of the call (9 percent interest on a $10 reduction in borrowing for 6 months). Adjusting for this interest credit would improve the writer's profit by $0.45 at every stock price.

The risk position of the "naked" call writer is unique. He can never gain more than the amount of the call premium, yet his possible loss in the event of a runaway stock is enormous. The loss could easily be four or five times the amount of the option premium. In spite of this risk, "naked" writing can be an extremely effective strategy when used intelligently. If an investor feels strongly that a particular stock is going to decline but does not anticipate that the decline will be of such magnitude that a short sale will be conspicuously profitable, he might elect to write "naked" calls. As long as his commitment to this strategy is not substantial relative to his resources, the profitability can be excellent, and the "naked" writing position can actually reduce the overall level of risk (or variability of return) in the portfolio. The way in which this apparently high-risk strategy can reduce risk will be clear when we examine Strategy 17, which deals with the option hedge.

Strategy 8: Purchase a Put

In some respects, purchase of a put is the reverse of buying a call. Unless the put buyer is able to sell his put or exercise it at a time when the price of the stock is *below* the striking price, he can lose his entire investment. To the extent that the price of the stock drops precipitately, the buyer of a put participates point-for-point in any *decline* below the striking price. In the example illustrated in the graph (Figure 4-9), the put is profitable at any price below $89 (the striking price minus the option premium), neglecting the effect of commissions.

Adjustments are analogous to the adjustments discussed for the buyer of a call. If a conventional put has value at maturity, the put buyer will have to pay a round-trip stock commission. One side of this double commission will be based on the

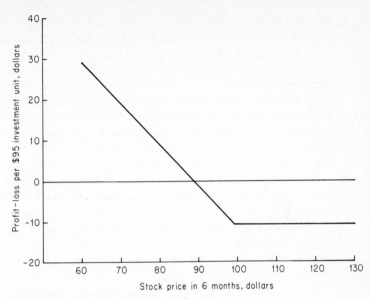

Figure 4-9. Strategy 8: Purchase a put.

striking price, the other side on the market price of the stock at the time the put is closed out. As in the case of a conventional call, the striking price on a conventional put will be reduced by the amount of any cash dividend paid on the stock. While the reader would be well advised to check this point carefully before engaging in a transaction, the striking price of a put written for conversion into a listed call or created by reversal of a listed call would probably not be reduced by the amount of a dividend. Some adjustment for any dividend would probably be made, however.

Strategy 9: Sell or Write a Put

Just as the writer of "naked" calls receives 100 percent of the premium if the stock is selling below the striking price when the call expires, the seller of "naked" puts receives 100 percent of the put premium if the stock is selling above the striking price when the put expires. The "naked" put seller's reward declines as the price of the stock falls below the striking price.

In the example illustrated in Figure 4-10, the seller of the "naked" put actually begins to lose money when the stock price falls below $89.

The motivation of the writer of "naked" puts is usually different from that of the writer of "naked" calls. In general, the writer of "naked" calls sees this strategy as an alternative to short selling. A "naked" put writer is frequently a potential investor in the underlying stock who would like the price of the stock to decline so that he can buy it more cheaply. He is often not trying to profit from the option premium itself. The put writer's avowed goal is to buy the stock at a lower net price. If the put is exercised, his cost on the stock is reduced by the amount of the put premium. The option premium is his consolation in the event that he does not get an opportunity to buy the stock.

The adjustment of a conventional "naked" put contract is similar to the adjustment of a conventional "naked" call contract. The net proceeds to the seller of the option are decreased by round-trip commissions if the put is exercised.

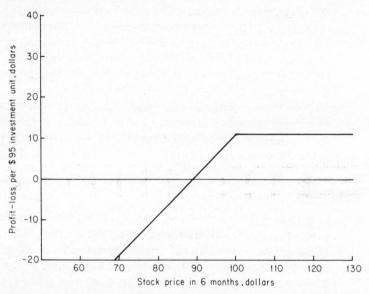

Figure 4-10. Strategy 9: Sell or write a put.

If, however, a "naked" put writer is writing the put in an attempt to lower the effective purchase price, it may be appropriate to disregard the commission adjustment on grounds that the relevant alternative would be to buy the stock outright at the market price. The striking price of a conventional put is reduced by the amount of any cash dividend. However, if the writer of the "naked" put is selling the option to a converter for conversion into a listed call, the commission and dividend adjustments may be materially different, and should be checked carefully. All other adjustments are analogous to the adjustments on calls, including any interest credit for the use of the premium.

Strategy 10: Purchase a Straddle

As illustrated by the graph in Figure 4-11, the buyer of a straddle is in an intriguing position. Like other option buyers, he can lose no more than 100 percent of the amount he invests in the straddle, but he can lose that much only if the price of

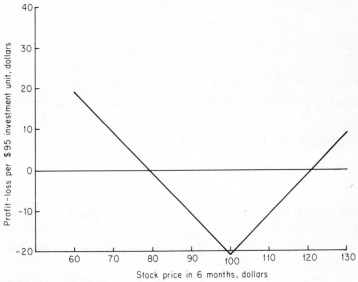

Figure 4-11. Strategy 10: Purchase a straddle.

the stock on the expiration date of the options is exactly equal to the striking price, or so close to it that sale or exercise of at least one side of the straddle does not justify the outlay of some commissions.

Just as it is hard to lose the entire premium paid for a straddle, it can also be hard to make a profit. In spite of the fact that the investor has paid substantial option premiums for both the put and call sides of the straddle, at least one of them is nearly certain to expire worthless. Consequently, the stock has to move substantially, either up or down, before the straddle buyer recovers his investment, let alone makes a profit. In the graph the break-even point on the up side is $100 (striking price) plus $11 (put premium) plus $10 (call premium), or $121 (break-even point). On the down side the break-even calculation is similar: $100 (striking price) minus $11 (put premium) minus $10 (call premium) equals $79 (break-even point).

Purchase of a straddle makes sense when the investor is convinced that a stock will make a dramatic move but is uncertain whether the move will be up or down. Once the stock price passes the break-even point in either direction, the investor participates point-for-point in any further advance or decline in the price of the stock.

The adjustments to the graph portraying a straddle are similar to the adjustments for a call and a put. The important point is that *both* the appropriate adjustments for a put *and* for a call must be made because the straddle *is* a put and a call.

Strategy 11: Sell a Straddle

Writing "naked" straddles was not a common strategy before listed put trading began, but when used with care it can be very effective. Ordinarily the writer of a "naked" put or call has some thoughts about the direction a stock is likely to move during the life of the option. The seller of a "naked" straddle, on the other hand, is making a bet on the magnitude of the move. His point of maximum profitability is the striking price of the options which make up the straddle. At that price neither side of the option will be exercised. As the price of the stock on the expiration date moves away from the striking price, the profit to the writer of the uncovered straddle declines. In the example illustrated on the graph (Figure 4-12) the seller of the straddle will earn a profit over a $42 range of stock prices from $79 on the low side to $121 on the high side. In writing the straddle he is betting that, on the day the option expires, the stock will be selling within this range and, he hopes, close to the center of it.

The adjustments necessary to make this graph represent the actual cash flows are simply the adjustments necessary for the two components of the straddle, the put and the call. If the options are conventional, any dividend paid over the life of the options moves the whole triangular shaped formation to the left by the amount of the dividend because the striking prices on both the put and the call are adjusted downward. Since both sides of the straddle are rarely exercised, each leg of the triangle must be adjusted by commission charges based on the closing commission requirements of the option that will have intrinsic value on the expiration date.

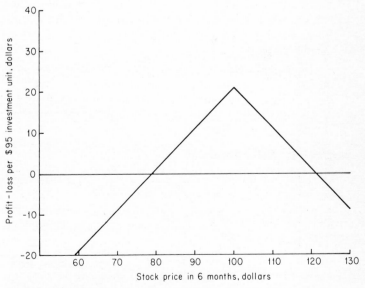

Figure 4-12. Strategy 11: Sell a straddle.

Selling a "naked" straddle can be a sensible strategy when the investor feels strongly that the underlying stock will not move significantly in either direction over the life of the option. Another common strategy with many similar investment characteristics is the option hedge, usually constructed using listed options. The option hedge is discussed as Strategy 17.

Strategy 12: Purchase the Stock and Sell a Call

This strategy, illustrated by the solid line in the graph (Figure 4-13), is the classic posture of the covered call writer. The covered call writer buys 100 shares of the underlying stock and writes one call contract using the stock position as collateral. The call premium provides a degree of protection should the underlying stock decline during the life of the option. In return for this downside protection, the covered writer's profit is limited, in this case to $15 per share over 6 months, no matter how high the stock price rises. At any stock

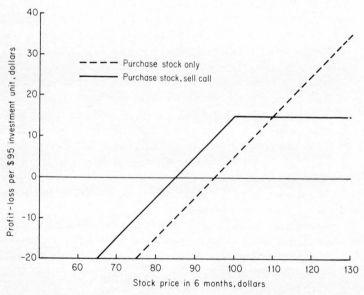

Figure 4-13. Strategy 12: Purchase the stock and sell a call.

price in excess of $110 per share the writer would have been better off not to have written the call, as indicated by the intersection of the solid line and the dashed line which represents Strategy 2, owning the stock without writing a call.

The commission and dividend adjustments are a combination of the adjustments necessary to analyze the basic stock ownership position (Strategy 2) and those necessary to analyze the uncovered call writer's position (Strategy 7). When these strategies are combined, certain adjustments cancel out. For example, if the call is a conventional call, no dividend adjustment will be necessary if the call is exercised because the adjustment in the striking price exactly offsets the dividend received by the writer as owner of the stock.

The motivations of covered writers are diverse. An investor may own a long-term position in the underlying stock which, for tax reasons, he is reluctant to sell even though he is not optimistic about the near-term price action of the stock. Rather than incur a large tax liability, he writes options to partially insulate himself from what he feels is a significant downside risk. In the event that this investor's appraisal of the stock proves incorrect and it rises over the life of the option, he does not have to deliver his long-term low-cost stock. If the call was written on an exchange, he can repurchase the option, terminating his writer's obligation and realizing a short-term capital loss on the option. If a conventional option is exercised, the writer can purchase new shares in the open market and deliver them against the call, keeping his long-term position in the stock intact. Any investor who buys stock in this manner to deliver in lieu of his long-term, low-basis position should try to structure the transaction to avoid making a "wash sale" which will prevent him from deducting the loss on the transaction. The wash sale rules are discussed in some detail in Chapter 5, Section A.

In contrast to the writer who uses long-term, low-basis stock as collateral, some writers write calls only on stocks they like and are willing to hold. This approach may seem peculiar because by writing the option, these investors are precluded from obtaining more than a limited profit if the stock rises as they anticipate. If the stock rises above the striking price, these writers are sure to earn the option premium. When earned consistently, option premiums can provide a highly satisfactory return. The major risk in adopting this strategy is that the premium may limit the return when the stock rises by substantially more than it reduces the loss when the stock declines.

A third group of writers will write covered options only when they feel the option premium is high relative to the fair value of the option. This group is usually relatively neutral toward the stock, yet can have a strong opinion that the option is overpriced. The merits of this approach will be clearer after we have examined the evaluation of option contracts in more detail.

Strategy 13: Purchase the Stock and Sell a Put

The investor who sells a put on a stock he already owns will participate fully in any upside move as a result of his long position in the stock. (See Figure 4-14.) In addition, he will receive the amount of the premium paid by the buyer of the

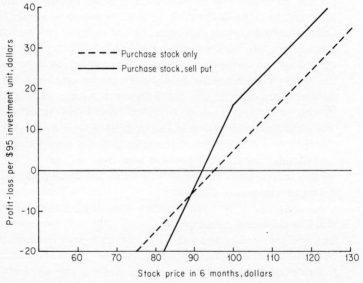

Figure 4-14. Strategy 13: Purchase the stock and sell a put.

put. On the other hand, he doubles his leverage on the downside. Evaluating the position at expiration, for every point that the stock drops below the striking price, the value of this investor's position will drop by two points, one point from the decline in value of the stock he owns long and one point from the decline in value of the stock that will be sold to him by the holder of the put.

The adjustments for this combined strategy are simply the sum of the adjustments which the owner of the stock and the "uncovered" seller of a put would make, a combination of Strategies 2 and 9.

The motivations of an investor adopting this strategy may seem somewhat obscure. Usually, this investor has a very constructive attitude toward the underlying stock. In fact, by selling the put he is expressing a willingness to double his position. By selling a put rather than simply purchasing the stock outright, the investor is trying to have the best of all possible worlds. If the stock rises as expected, he will participate in the rise through the increase in the value of his stock holding. The put will not be exercised, and the premium will be pure profit. If the price of the stock declines, he will find himself the proud owner of twice as much stock as he owned before. Thanks to the premium received for writing the put, his effective cost on the additional stock purchased will be $89 per share, a saving of $6 over the $95 market price at the time the transaction is initiated.

On the negative side, this strategy can be dangerous if an investor's resources are limited. The collateral value of his stock position will be declining at the time he is called upon to buy additional shares. Unless an investor's feelings on a stock are particularly strong or unless he wishes to engage in a program of compulsory averaging down, writing puts against long positions in a stock is probably not a sound strategy if it is pursued very aggressively.

Strategy 14: Purchase the Stock and Sell a Straddle

This position illustrates a strategy that used to be adopted by writers of conventional options. The demand for options is primarily a demand for calls, but because the premium income is larger and because of certain tax benefits under the former tax law, option writers often preferred to write straddles. The put side of the straddle was usually converted into a second call.

The apparent attraction of writing straddles collateralized by a long position in the underlying stock should be clear from the diagram which shows this strategy imposed upon the graph of buying the stock alone. (See Figure 4-15.) Over a price range of some \$42—\$21 on each side of the striking price—the investor is better off adopting this strategy than owning the stock alone. He will show a profit at any stock price above \$87 per share. Should the stock sell above the striking price, his profit will be a substantial \$26 per underlying share for the 6-month period, or double that amount when annualized.

The only significant weakness in this strategy is apparent if the price of the stock declines sharply. For every point that the stock declines below the striking price, the covered straddle writer is in essentially the same position as the writer of a put

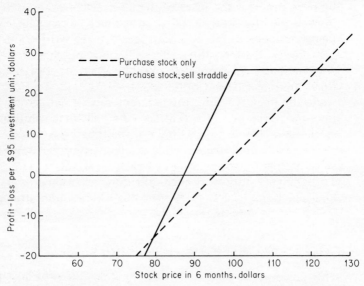

Figure 4-15. Strategy 14: Purchase the stock and sell a straddle.

who also owns the underlying stock. The value of his position decreases by one point on the stock he owns and one point on the stock that will be sold to him by the owner of the put side of his straddle. The risk characteristics of this position are identical to those experienced by a covered call writer using a margin account to obtain leverage.

Strategy 15: Purchase the Stock and Purchase a Put

This is usually considered to be an insurance or risk-reduction strategy. When he buys the put, the investor is ensuring that his loss can be no more than the amount of the premium on the put less the amount by which the put is selling in the money. On the up side, once the price of the stock passes the striking price, the investor who adopts this strategy will participate point-for-point in any increase in the price of the stock. (See Figure 4-16.)

Adjustments to this position can be made by combining the appropriate adjustments for being long the stock (Strategy 2) with the adjustments for owning the put (Strategy 8).

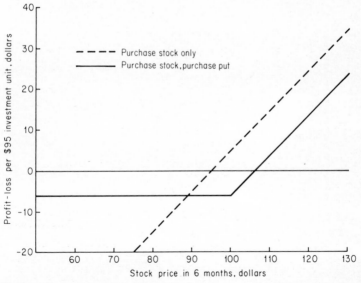

Figure 4-16. Strategy 15: Purchase the stock and purchase a put.

The investment rationale for this strategy is virtually identical to the rationale used to justify the purchase of a call; in fact, the shapes of the profit-loss lines are identical. The downside risk is limited; yet, after deduction of the put premium, the upside potential is unlimited. Though tax factors and investment policy restrictions may complicate the decision, this strategy will usually be less attractive than the alternative of investing most of an individual's cash in high-yielding debt securities and buying a call to give the same upside exposure.

Strategy 16: Sell the Stock Short and Purchase a Call

As in the case of Strategy 15, the option serves as an insurance policy, limiting the investor's risk. Here the call protects the investor from a major upward move in the price of the stock (Figure 4-17). If this configuration of possible gains and losses appeals to him, the investor should look into the possibility of buying a put and keeping any unused cash in short-term

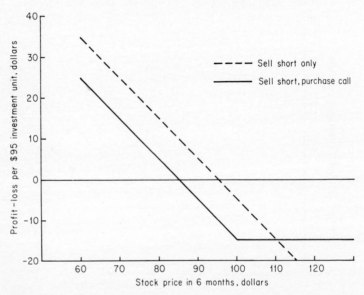

Figure 4-17. Strategy 16: Sell the stock short and purchase a call.

debt instruments. Buying the put will always be a cheaper way of achieving this risk-reward relationship.

For a variety of reasons, most importantly the high transaction costs of conventional options, Strategies 17, 18, and 19 are practical only with listed options. If any of the proposals to lower the transaction costs of conventional options and create a secondary market are adopted, the applicability of these strategies would expand.

Strategy 17: Set Up an Option Hedge

The investment posture illustrated here consists of a long position in the underlying stock used as collateral for writing two calls. The number of calls written in an option hedge is less important than the fact that the calls cover more shares than the investor owns and that the profit-loss line on the graph peaks at the striking price and begins to decline as the stock rises further (Figure 4-18).

The reader will recognize in this diagram the shape of the

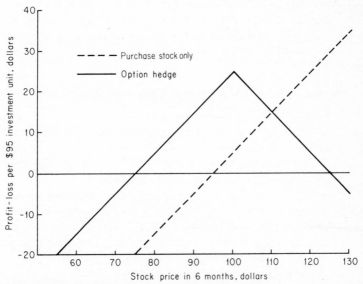

Figure 4-18. Strategy 17: Set up an option hedge.

graph developed for Strategy 11, the sale of an uncovered straddle. As in the cases of previous strategies, there is more than one way to achieve this tent-shaped risk-reward structure. Because it offers the investor a chance for a long-term capital gain, the option hedge may be preferable to writing a straddle. In addition, it may be possible to defer any long-term capital gain on the stock position by continuing to write options against the stock as option positions expire or are closed out. The investor may also find the option hedge easier to "unwind" than the "naked" straddle. On the other hand, if an investor has excess capital losses or has no intention of holding the stock beyond the expiration date of the options, he will usually find writing straddles more attractive because commissions will be lower.

The most important feature of the option hedge and the straddle is that peak profitability is achieved at the striking price of the options, and the striking price is usually close to the present stock price. To the extent that the future stock price is likely to be close to the present price (or the striking price), the most profitable point is also one of the most probable. The option hedge is one of very few investment positions that provides a respectable profit if the stock stands still. This feature makes it useful in reducing the investor's exposure to market risk.

Strategy 18: Set Up a Reverse Option Hedge

Figure 4-19 illustrates a reverse option hedge consisting of a short position in the common stock, offset by a long position in two calls on that stock. As in the case of the option hedge, the number of calls purchased will depend on the risk-reward preferences of the investor. In contrast to the option hedge, which is based on the expectation that the stock price will be stable, the reverse option hedge will be profitable only if the stock moves dramatically in either direction. In the same way that an option hedge is comparable to writing a straddle, a reverse option hedge is comparable in terms of its risk-reward characteristics to buying a straddle.

Whereas it was argued that the option hedge was frequently

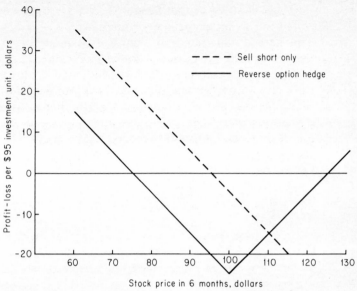

Figure 4-19. Strategy 18: Set up a reverse option hedge.

preferable to writing a "naked" straddle, transaction cost and tax considerations ordinarily make purchase of a straddle preferable to the reverse option hedge, if puts are available on reasonable terms. If listed puts are trading on the underlying stock, buying a straddle will be preferable to the reverse option hedge for most investors.

The holder of the reverse hedge has to pay out the proceeds of the short sale to the lender of the stock. The price paid for a listed put will at least partially reflect the equivalent of interest on the proceeds of the short sale. This point will be clarified in Section D of this chapter.

Strategy 19: Set Up a Listed Option Spread

The listed option spread is a hedged strategy consisting of a long position in one option and an offsetting short position in another option. Ordinarily both options will be listed options, though some spreads have been done using a conventional option as one side of the spread. The possible variety of spreads is so great that Section E of this chapter will be devoted to this investment phenomenon.

The spread illustrated in Figure 4-20 assumes that the investor buys the $10 option with the $100 striking price used in the previous graphs. To set up the spread, the investor writes an option having the same expiration date, but a striking price of $90, that is selling for $16, that is, $1,600 per 100-share contract. The profit-loss line shows a profit if the stock declines and a loss if the stock rises.

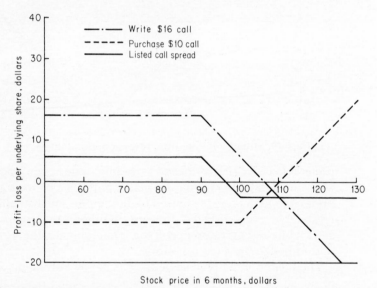

Figure 4-20. Strategy 19: Set up a listed call spread.

In addition to the relatively long-term spread illustrated here, some investors find very-short-term spreads in expiring options attractive; others attempt to set up arbitrage spreads to take advantage of temporary price disparities; and still others set up bullish spreads that are most attractive when the stock rises. Each spread has different investment characteristics; these will be discussed in detail in Section E of this chapter.

By this time, it should be clear that with options an investor can structure the risk-reward characteristics of an individual investment position or his entire portfolio in virtually any way he chooses. In fact, by combining long and short positions in stocks and options, it is possible to almost completely eliminate market risk from a diversified portfolio. To understand one of the many ways in which this can be done, the reader need only visualize half of his portfolio in option hedges and the other half in reverse option hedges or straddles. If he has sufficiently diversified his stock positions, *his rate of return will be independent of the direction of stock price movement.* By setting up diversified hedged positions, the portfolio manager can use options to *virtually eliminate market risk.*

Obviously, controlling portfolio risk is only half the answer. To make the machinations described here worthwhile, the investor needs to obtain a superior return on investment in relation to risk exposure. The next few sections will focus on the trade-off between risk and reward and on the improvement of investment results through the intelligent use of options.

B. THE ROLE OF OPTIONS IN INTELLIGENT PORTFOLIO MANAGEMENT

One reason options are avoided by many investors is that the successful use of options requires more attention and analysis than most people devote to their portfolios. Much of the aura of complexity which surrounds options is due to a tendency to view them as unique or unusual investments. It is far more useful to relate the risk-reward characteristics of options to those of stocks and bonds than to emphasize the differences between options and other investment vehicles. The idea that "highly leveraged" options fit into the same risk-reward hierarchy as corporate bonds or common stocks can be difficult for many investors, including some experienced option traders, to accept at first. Nonetheless, most investors find options easier to understand when they examine them in terms of their impact on total portfolio risk.

The purpose of this section is to demonstrate that the intelligent use of options requires evaluation of option contracts combined with measurement and control of portfolio risk. This section is directed at the investor who attempts to analyze investment positions in terms of *risk* and *reward*. Such an investor is sensitive to the trade-off between opportunities to obtain high rates of return and the increased risk of loss which usually comes with such opportunities. Those who view investments in this framework can improve their decision-making process, and perhaps their results, by understanding the risk-reward characteristics of stock options.

Options will never be appropriate for every portfolio. On the other hand, the use of options is frequently and inaccurately dismissed as speculative and unsuitable for any conservatively managed account. Decisions to use or to avoid options should be based on careful analysis of the usefulness of options in attaining an investor's objectives. Too frequently, such decisions are based on an erroneous perception of what options can or cannot contribute to the management of a portfolio.

1. Risk-Reward Characteristics of Options

To illustrate the risk-reward characteristics of options, we have chosen Strategy 12 from the previous section—covered writing of a call option—for more intensive analysis. In Figure 4-21, a modified version of Figure 4-13, the ownership of shares of common stock is designated by the solid line (A-A'). The ownership of common stock, combined with the sale of a call option on that underlying stock, is designated by the broken line (B-B'). As in the earlier diagrams, the vertical axis represents the profit or loss from each of these positions at a particular stock price on the day the option expires. The horizontal axis represents the price of the stock on that day.

As in the earlier examples, the stock is purchased at $95 per share. The shareholder who does not sell the call option participates point-for-point in every increase or decrease in the price of the stock. His profit is theoretically unlimited on the up side and limited only by a stock price of zero on the down side.

The alternative strategy of covered call writing, illustrated by the broken line, is based on the sale of a call option against the stock position. The hypothetical call option used in the

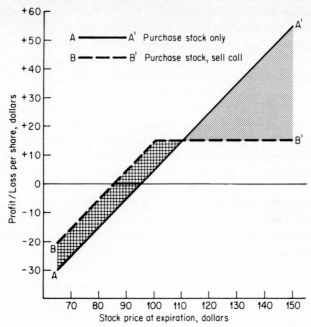

Figure 4-21. Comparison of profit/loss: long stock position vs. covered writer position.

diagram has a $100 striking price and a life of about 6 months from the time it is sold. The writer obtains a $10-per-share premium. Any loss on the long stock position will be reduced by the $10 per share obtained from the option.

The covered call writer's position does have some disadvantages. If the price of the stock rises above $110 per share (the striking price plus the call premium), the investor would have been better off not selling the call. In return for a degree of downside protection, he has given up the opportunity to participate in any rise in the price of the underlying stock above $110 per share.

In the diagram, the downside protection provided by the option premium received is designated by the cross-hatched trapezoidal area to the left of the intersection of the two profit-loss lines. The upside opportunity given up by the covered call writer is represented by the shaded triangular area to the right of the intersection of the two lines.

Figure 4-21 highlights several features of covered call writing. Note that the seller of the covered call option *reduces the variability of his return on investment.* If the stock rises sharply, the return on the stock position will be reduced by the amount of any loss on repurchase of the option. If the stock is called away at a price of $100 per share when the market price at the time of exercise is much higher, the investor may experience a sizable opportunity loss. If the stock declines, the loss will be reduced by the amount of the premium collected. Regardless of the direction in which the stock price moves or how far it moves, *covered call option writing reduces the variability of the return from a portfolio of equity securities.* The importance of this point is hard to overemphasize.

Risk reduction does not come without cost. Whereas the covered call writer *obtains protection against loss,* he *surrenders the opportunity for unlimited appreciation.* Only if the risk-reduction value of the premium *exceeds* the potential capital gain he forgoes can the investor expect to improve the risk-adjusted total return from a portfolio through call-writing transactions. Because the covered call writer makes a profit when the stock rises and reduces his loss if the stock declines, there is a widespread but erroneous belief that selling covered call options is the closest thing to a perfect investment strategy that has been devised. Unfortunately, as Milton Friedman is so fond of quoting, "There is no such thing as a free lunch."

If the value of the premium received is too small relative to the value of the opportunity for appreciation given up, the covered writer will obtain a substandard return on investment over a period of time. When the value of the premium received equals the value of the opportunity forgone, after adjustment for risk, the option is said to be *fairly priced.* When the value of the protection is inadequate, the option is *underpriced.* When the premium is more than adequate to compensate for the capital appreciation opportunity given up, the option is *overpriced.*

To appreciate the importance of the size of the option premiums in determining investment results, the reader should compare Figures 4-21 and 4-22. In Figure 4-22 the option premium received by the covered call writer is only

$1, not the $10 assumed in the earlier diagram. With this very low premium for a 6-month option, the cross-hatched area representing the downside protection afforded by the premium is much smaller, and the shaded area depicting the upside opportunity loss is considerably larger. A change in the size of the option premium affects the size of *both* areas, with obvious implications for investment results. If any reader needs a demonstration that covered call writing is not a simple technique that almost magically "adds to the income" of a portfolio, Figure 4-22 should provide that demonstration. Actually, as we will see momentarily, *covered call writing is more likely to reduce portfolio returns than it is to increase them.*

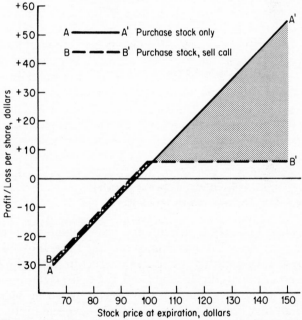

Figure 4-22. Comparison of profit/loss: long stock position vs. covered writer position with low option premium.

2. The Risk-Return Trade-Off

Perhaps the significance of overpriced and underpriced options and their effect on investment results can be brought into perspective best by an examination of Figure 4-23. This diagram represents the expected risk-return trade-off characteristics of a variety of investment opportunities. The vertical axis (Y) measures the investor's expected annual return on investment for different investment opportunities. The horizontal axis (X) measures the degree of risk associated with a particular investment. Risk is expressed as the standard deviation (or variability) of the rate of return.

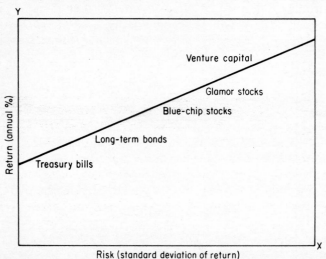

Figure 4-23. The risk-return trade-off.

Treasury bills show essentially no variability of return relative to the yield anticipated at the time the bills are purchased. Though the interest rate structure as a whole can move up or down, the Treasury bill rate is fixed for the life of each bill at the level the investor accepts when he buys the bill. If an investor wishes to increase his expected return, he can purchase long-term corporate bonds. Because of changes in the market value of bonds due to interest rate fluctuations and the risk of default by some borrowers, the return from an investment in bonds for a particular time period may be greater or less than the risk-free rate of return on Treasury bills. Most investors will not be willing to hold long-term bonds unless they have the *expectation* of a higher rate of return than they would be able to obtain from Treasury bills. The same argument holds for any other investment. If an investor buys common stocks, he will generally require a higher expected total rate of return than he would be willing to accept from long-term bonds or Treasury bills. To compensate for the risk to principal and the consequent variability in the return on investment, the investor in venture capital projects will require an even higher expected rate of return.

Like any other investment vehicle, options fit into this risk-reward structure. As we saw in Figure 4-21, selling a call option against a stock position reduces the variability of the rate of return on investment. Thus, selling a call will have the effect of reducing portfolio risk levels. If the call option an investor sells is neither overpriced nor underpriced, sale of the option will also have the effect of *reducing the expected return on investment* because the overall risk of the portfolio will be reduced. By definition, *sale of a fairly priced option will simply move the risk-return position of a portfolio downward and to the left along this line.* On the other hand, purchase of an option will increase the variability of the expected return from a portfolio. An investor who buys a fairly priced call option demonstrates willingness to accept greater variability of return in exchange for the expectation of a higher average rate of return.

If the prospective option investor remembers nothing else from this section, he should keep in mind that selling call options will tend to move the expected risk-reward position of a portfolio down and to the left along the risk-reward trade-off line of Figure 4-23, whereas the purchase of call options will tend to move the expected return up and to the right. Theoretically, it is possible to reduce the risk level of a portfolio of glamor stocks to the risk level of a portfolio of Treasury bills through the sale of an appropriate number of call options. In practice, commissions and other trading costs make it difficult to maintain such a low risk level with options. Within reasonable limits, however, it is possible to use options to adjust the risk posture of a portfolio rather closely to an individual's risk preferences.

The opportunities for risk modification which options provide are extremely important, but they are not the principal reason for using options. It is possible, if option premiums are too high or too low relative to their fair value, to structure a portfolio which provides a *higher expected return per unit of risk* than any portfolio of conventional securities lying along the risk-return trade-off line. If a call option is *overpriced* and an investor sells that option, the risk-reward structure of the portfolio will move not only to the left along the risk-return line but also *above* the line. If the investor starts with Treasury bills or other short-term debt instruments and *buys underpriced* call options with a portion of his assets, it is possible to achieve an expected rate of return *above* the line while obtaining a degree of risk equivalent to the risk associated with owning a portfolio of long-term bonds or common stocks.

In contrast to the seller of overpriced call options, the investor selling underpriced calls will be reducing his return *more than proportionately to the reduction in risk.* This investor would generally be better off reducing the risk exposure of a portfolio by selling a portion of the stock and investing the proceeds in bonds or some other lower-risk investment rather than accepting inadequate option premiums. The risk-return position of a portfolio will fall below the risk-reward trade-off line in Figure 4-23 if underpriced options are sold against stock positions or if overpriced options are bought.

Selling a call option in a diversified equity portfolio will *always* reduce risk, as measured by the variability of the expected total return on the portfolio. Selling the option will *not* always (or even usually) enhance the overall rate of return. *By consistently selling overpriced options and/or buying underpriced options as part of a program of risk management, an investor can break away from the risk-reward trade-off line.* Few serious investors will use options for any reason other than to enhance the rate of return per unit of risk.

3. Variations in Option Premium Levels

An obvious reaction at this point might be "It's all very well to suggest that the investor should sell overpriced options and buy underpriced options. Assuming the market for options is an efficient market, it is likely that options will be fairly priced most of the time." There is no simple answer to this challenge, but a partial answer is suggested by the diagram in Figure 4-24.

Figure 4-24 shows a monthly index of listed option premium levels since shortly after the beginning of listed option trading on the Chicago Board Options Exchange. The mechanics behind the calculation of the index are not particularly important for our purposes here, but they will be outlined in Chapter 9. What is important is that the index roughly approximates the degree of price variation in a "typical" option contract with the striking price and market price equal. The index indicates that a typical premium was just under 1.0 on the index, or the approximate equivalent of $4 for a 6-month option on an "average" $40 stock at the end of April 1974. The index rose to about 1.75, or the rough equivalent of about a $7 premium for the same option in November 1974. In early 1978 the index was consistently below 0.70 or the equivalent of less than $3 for the "typical" 6-month option on a $40 stock.

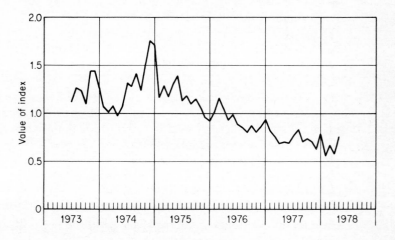

Figure 4-24. An index of listed option levels. (Base period stock price volatility: October 1968–September 1972 = 1.0)

The index is based on premium levels of options on 14 of the first stocks listed on the CBOE. The fluctuations in option premium levels for individual stocks or the fluctuations for the most overpriced or most underpriced options on a specific stock show even more dramatic changes. It is not at all unusual for premium levels on some stocks to vary by a factor of 2 or 3 over the course of a year. Given the magnitude of these premium fluctuations, opportunities for portfolio risk adjustment and return enhancement through the purchase and sale of options are obviously extensive.

4. Option Evaluation and Portfolio Management

Individuals, institutional investors, brokerage firms, and college professors have invested thousands of hours and millions of dollars in sophisticated computer programs designed to determine when option premiums are too high or too low relative to their fair value. The techniques and mechanics of option evaluation merit the attention of all serious investors. Chapter 7 will explore option evaluation in greater depth. Our focus here, however, is an examination of how options fit into the process of portfolio management, not the merits of particular evaluation models.

Most individuals and portfolio managers who use options take one of two approaches to the use of options. Some investors focus strictly on the fundamental or technical outlook for the underlying common stock and, on the basis of their fundamental or technical analysis, construct either a bullish or a bearish investment position using options or stock and options. Investors accustomed to conventional analytical and portfolio management approaches frequently pay little heed to computerized evaluation of option contracts.

In marked contrast to those who focus strictly on their investment attitude toward the underlying common stock, there is a sizable group of investors who focus strictly on computerized option evaluation. This group believes that no analytical technique can forecast stock price direction but that an investor can consistently make money selling overpriced and buying underpriced options. Overpricing and underpricing will be consistently determined by complicated computer programs.

Who is correct? Both. And neither. The author agrees with the conventional investor who says it is ridiculous to sell an overpriced naked call option on IBM if there are sound reasons for believing that IBM's stock will rise in price over the life of the option. The author also agrees with the computer evaluation advocate who argues that one should not buy that option. Fortunately, the approaches are not as contradictory as they may seem.

A portfolio manager or an individual investor can integrate conventional stock selection techniques with computerized option evaluation. The resulting portfolio would be carefully designed to reflect a desired degree of risk exposure. Each position in the portfolio would reflect the best analysis of the outlook for the particular stock in question and would integrate that analysis with evaluation of the option contract. For example, a covered writing position in IBM would be appropriate if the option was overpriced and the investor felt the stock was going up. Because selling the option reduces the risk associated with a long position in IBM, the investor should *buy more IBM stock* as a covered writer than as an owner who was not using options.

Fundamental analysis should also have an impact on the computerized evaluation of the option contract. Nearly all the more sophisticated option evaluation models base their calculation of the fair value of an option on five factors:

1. Time remaining until expiration

2. Money market interest rates

3. The size and pattern of dividend payments on the underlying stock

4. The relationship between the current stock price and the striking price of the option

5. The expected volatility (range of price movement) of the underlying stock

All these factors except future stock price volatility can be easily observed and appropriate values supplied to the computer. Most users of computerized option evaluation models derive a stock price volatility estimate from the past volatility pattern of the underlying stock. While historic stock price volatility data are important, an intelligent portfolio manager or individual investor will temper his use of historic data with judgments based on fundamental analysis of the stock. The behavior of IBM and its related options in late 1975 illustrates the importance of fundamental analysis in the development of volatility estimates.

The stock price volatility that seemed appropriate for IBM prior to settlement of the Telex antitrust case was slightly higher than the long-term historic volatility of IBM, reflecting (among other things) the antitrust uncertainty and the relatively high volatility of IBM's common stock in late 1974 and early 1975. The day after the Telex settlement was announced, by which time the stock had had an opportunity to react to the news, we lowered our volatility estimate for IBM to approximately the average long-term historic volatility for the stock. In our view, a major uncertainty in the outlook for IBM had been removed. There was now reason to believe that IBM's volatility would more closely parallel the historic norm because there almost certainly would be no major antitrust settlements or decisions for at least a year. The "market" apparently agreed with our analysis. The premium level of the IBM options, as measured by a technique similar to that used in deriving the index illustrated in Figure 4-24, dropped sharply after the initial rise in the underlying stock. Actually, the premium levels on IBM options dropped by much more than the clearer antitrust outlook and the price rise seemed to justify. The IBM options, which had been significantly overpriced during the summer of 1975, appeared quite underpriced by year-end.

Unlike many users of options, the author and his associates do not believe that any option strategy is inherently superior to any other. At times option premiums on particular stocks are so high that it makes no sense to purchase these options. At other times premiums are so low that it is impossible to justify a covered writing position on any rational basis. If an investor is flexible in his choice of option strategies, there will almost always be attractive investment opportunities based on the use of options.

5. The Analysis of Risk

While evaluation of the expected profit from buying or selling a particular option can be complex, analysis of the risk impact of an option position on a portfolio is straightforward. To appraise the risk position quantitatively, the investor must translate each option into a risk equivalent position in the underlying stock. If the option contract used in the example in Figure 4-21 moves up or down in price by one-half point for each one-point change in the price of the underlying stock, that option contract is the risk equivalent of 50 shares of the stock. The dollar gain or loss from a long or short position in that option will be approximately one-half the gain or loss from movement in a corresponding long or short position in a round lot of the underlying stock. If an investor wants to establish a position that is the risk equivalent of owning 100 shares of this stock, he can do so in any one of three ways:

1. Buy 100 shares of stock.
2. Buy 2 options (50 shares equivalent × 2 contracts = 100 shares).
3. Buy 200 shares of stock and sell 2 options [200 shares − (50 shares equivalent × 2 contracts) = 100 shares].

The fraction of a point by which an option price is expected to change when the underlying stock price changes by a full point is called the *neutral hedge ratio*. The concept of the neutral hedge ratio and the notion of options as stock equivalents are basic to the informed use of options. They will appear repeatedly throughout this book.

Any option or option and stock position, no matter how complicated, can be readily translated into the risk equivalent of a specific number of shares or a dollar investment in the underlying stock. If this analysis is undertaken for the entire portfolio, it is a surprisingly simple matter to convert all positions into stock equivalents. Once this is done, the portfolio can be analyzed using the techniques of conventional portfolio management to appraise diversification and market risk exposure. Obviously, the fraction of a point that an option price will change for each one-point move in the stock will vary as the option nears expiration and as the relationship between the option striking price and the stock price changes. Consequently, the investor must analyze the risk structure of a portfolio frequently to be certain that the risk exposure to a particular underlying stock has not changed beyond acceptable limits. In turbulent markets the risk exposure to a particular stock may change significantly in a short period of time. The alert and flexible investor can usually maintain adequate diversification and appropriate overall market risk exposure even when the market is unsettled.

Some skeptics dismiss options as more suitable for short-term traders than for long-term investors. While it is true that option contracts have a limited life, an investor can use options to maintain a fairly stable exposure to a particular stock. Using options can be completely consistent with a policy of holding positions for long-term investment. On the other hand, options make it more difficult to use the long-term investment argument as an excuse to avoid decisions. Options encourage an investor to reexamine his attitude toward a stock at frequent intervals.

C. REASONS FOR USING OPTIONS— AND SOME MISCONCEPTIONS

As the various investment positions were examined closely in Section A, some of the motives that might lead an investor to adopt a particular strategy became apparent. The purpose here is to expand upon and evaluate the reasoning used by investors to justify their various uses of options in the light of the risk-reward discussion of Section B. While most strategies make sense under certain assumptions or circumstances, the rationale leading investors to adopt a particular strategy might be incomplete or erroneous.

1. Buying Options

Most option buyers say that they purchase puts and calls to increase their leverage when they expect a significant move in the stock. Because the purchase of options permits investors to control more shares of stock than they could possibly control under any realistic set of common stock margin requirements, options can provide more return on the investor's dollar than any other method of investing in securities with the obvious risk of a total loss. The 100 percent cash requirement applied to the purchase of puts and calls, and certain rules which prohibit individuals or groups acting in concert from buying more than a certain number of options, limit the individual's ability to leverage and pyramid an investment. Thus, while the option buyer cannot imitate the great speculators of the 1920s, the leverage obtainable through options is still substantial.

Many of the same investors who emphasize the importance of leverage on the upside in the case of calls, or on the downside in the case of puts, also focus on the importance of an option's ability to limit the investor's risk. Any buyer of a put or call knows the maximum loss possible at the time the option purchase is made. This limited-risk feature of options has apparently begun to appeal to a few institutional investors. Intrigued by the potential of a speculative stock, yet concerned for their fiduciary and quasi-fiduciary responsibilities, a very few institutional investors have begun to take advantage of the limited-loss feature of options. Rather than invest $100,000 in the securities of a particular corporation, the institution will invest $10,000 in call options and put the remaining $90,000 in short-term debt instruments. Interest on the short-term debt will typically cover about one-third of any possible loss on the calls. If the stock price advances sharply over the life of the options, the portfolio participates in this advance. On the other hand, downside risk is strictly limited to the amount of the option premium. This use of options will probably expand as institutional investors become more comfortable with options.

The purchase of options to construct a kind of synthetic

convertible bond actually fits the risk-reward requirements of an institution far better than the more typical institutional strategy of covered call writing. To the extent that an investor's goal is to limit portfolio risk exposure, the combination of short-term debt and a long option position has a maximum risk equal to the amount paid for the options. The covered writer's risk is reduced by the amount of the option premium received, but the markets of the early seventies suggest that this is not always enough protection. A quick review of the graphs in Section A should convince the reader that it is the option buyer whose risk is always known and limited to the premium he pays. The option writer, whether or not he also has a position in the stock, can incur very large losses. The popular view of the option buyer as a risk taker will change slowly as a new type of buyer appears.

A relatively small number of options are purchased to hedge short or long positions in the underlying common stock. Perhaps the major reason hedging with options has not enjoyed more popularity is that, as we saw in the previous section, buying a call to hedge a short position is functionally equivalent to buying a put. Likewise, buying a put to hedge a long position is functionally equivalent to buying a call. Most investors find it less costly, and less complicated, to purchase the put or the call outright, rather than construct the hedge.

2. Writing Options

Over the years option writers have developed a number of explanations and rationalizations for the basic strategies of writing calls, puts, and straddles against positions in the underlying common stock. A very common justification for option writing is that it permits writers to generate additional "income" on their investment portfolio. While this notion may have developed from the fact that most expired option premiums used to be taxed as ordinary income to option writers, it is important that writers not lose sight of the fact that they are giving up certain rights in return for this additional "income." For example, the writer of a covered call is giving up the right to participate in any appreciation in the underlying stock beyond a price equal to the striking price of the option plus the amount of the call premium.

Given the limited resources and relative lack of sophistication of some option buyers, many observers would expect their analysis of an option position to be superficial. Option writers, however, have long been considered among the most sophisticated participants in the securities markets. To the extent that these investors *really* view their option premiums as additional "income" that accrues to them without significant obligation, their reputation as sophisticates is in danger. Rational analysis, at a minimum, consists of careful examination and weighing of what the investor is giving up in return for what he is receiving. This minimum standard is sometimes more easily satisfied by the option buyer than by the writer, who frequently must evaluate a position in the stock as well as any option he may write. The fact that rational analysis is complicated is no excuse not to undertake it, however.

If an option premium is too low, the writer who consistently writes such options will find that, despite all his additional "income," his net worth is declining or, at best, growing very slowly. The option premiums he receives during periods when the stock rises will be inadequate to make up for his losses when the price declines. Because the covered call writer agrees to limit his return on the up side, he must earn enough from the option premium to protect his capital during periods when the stock drops.

A classic explanation for writing options is that the investor writes calls in an attempt to hedge his long position in the stock. Frequently, this investor is concerned about the safety of his long position because he expects the stock to decline, yet he does not want to incur a capital gain tax liability by liquidating the position. He may anticipate a modest, temporary decline which would permit him to obtain an option premium with minimal risk of having the stock called away.

Occasionally, an option writer will argue that he is writing calls in the hope of selling his securities at a higher effective price than is presently available. This can be a sound strategy if the investor is happy holding the securities at current or lower price levels and yet would be willing to liquidate the position at slightly higher prices. The chance to sell stock at a higher effective price through receipt of a call premium is appealing. The writer must be certain, however, that the superficial appeal of this argument is not a substitute for careful analysis of both the stock and the option-writing opportunity. If the premium is inadequate to cover the risk of a decline in the stock price, this rationale for option writing becomes questionable and the stock should probably be sold outright.

A more subtle weakness of the "sell a call to sell the stock at a higher effective price" argument is that the act of selling a call *today* may actually prevent an investor from liquidating the stock position at the target price *tomorrow*. An example might be helpful in illustrating this point. An investor holding the hypothetical $95 stock of Figure 4-21 might decide to sell the hypothetical $10 option with a $100 striking price because he would be satisfied to sell the stock for $110 per share. If the stock ran to $110 soon after the call was sold, this investor *could not realize a net price of $110 for his position* because the call would be selling at, say, $16. If the whole position were closed out, he would realize a net price of $104: $110 on the stock less a $6 loss on the call. If he did not close out the position and the stock subsequently dropped to $75, he would have missed the chance to sell at $110, and the opportunity for profit would have been missed.

An argument similar to the "sell the stock at a higher price" thesis motivates certain writers of puts who argue that they write puts in an attempt to lower their effective purchase price. If this writer of puts is correct in thinking that the stock is attractive for purchase, he may be ahead to buy it outright. The put premium would be inadequate compensation for missing the chance to purchase a stock that doubles. Only a careful evaluation of the put premium and the investor's expectations for the stock permit an appropriate decision.

3. Risk Modification and Option Evaluation

By far the most important rationale for the purchase and sale of option contracts is that, unlike other securities, they provide the investment manager with virtually unlimited flexibility in the risk management of a diversified portfolio. This argument was rarely heard prior to the creation of the listed option, but it has attracted many adherents and should eventually dominate discussions of diversification and portfolio theory as well as option discussions. Using options, an investor or a portfolio manager can accept or lay off risk as he sees fit. Neutralization of market risk alone would be considered a worthwhile objective by many investors. Options provide the opportunity not only to neutralize risk but to obtain a superior return as well.

Contrary to popular belief, not every option writer is guaranteed a 15 percent annual return on his money, nor is every option buyer a lamb being led to the slaughter. Listed options are traded in a reasonably efficient market. If option premiums are higher than fair value, enough writers will be attracted to push premiums down. If premiums are too low, buyers will be attracted. In spite of this mechanism, there is a fairly wide range of prices within which a particular option contract might sell. If he buys options that are underpriced and writes options that are overpriced, the investor can probably achieve a superior return and simultaneously adjust market risk exposure.

Because the investor using options can adjust his risk parameters in virtually any way he chooses, the individual option contract should be purchased or sold only if it offers the prospect of superior reward. In this context, the dominant factors in determining a strategy should be the investor's thoughts on the investment merits of the underlying stock and an estimate of the fair value of specific option contracts. While rational evaluation of option contracts is not a simple task, as we shall see in our discussion of option evaluation, the investor who ignores the importance of option value in structuring whatever option-related strategy he may undertake is virtually assuring himself of mediocre long-term results at best.

Although option evaluation is stressed here, the value of any other analytical process an investor may rely on is not disputed. Whether he feels a stock will go up because it broke out on a chart or because he has done exhaustive fundamental research, the investor should still not ignore option evaluation. Recognizing that his analysis could be wrong and assuming that the investment in question will be only part of his total portfolio, the investor might be ahead if he buys the stock and writes overpriced call options instead of buying the same options outright. The covered writing strategy expresses the investor's bullishness on the company's prospects, and the overpriced option works for the investor rather than against him. If he buys the overpriced call option, the investor can control more shares with the same investment, but if his judgment on the stock is only average, the risk-adjusted expected value of the call would be less than the purchase price. In the covered writer's position, an overpriced option will give the investor a superior return with average stock judgment. Similar arguments apply in reverse if the investor expects a stock to decline. Buying an underpriced put is better than writing an underpriced call. Option evaluation can stack the odds in an investor's favor, even if his stock judgment is only average.

None of the arguments examined in this section as reasons for buying or writing an option is adequate without an appraisal of the fair value of the option contract. The option buyer who pays too much and the writer who accepts too little are fighting the investment battle with one hand tied behind their respective backs.

A persistent focus on option evaluation is not an argument that the investor should scan the exchange closing prices each day in search of temporarily overpriced or underpriced options. After the investment merits of a stock have been carefully evaluated, a rational investor will seek those options which are consistently overpriced for writing strategies or those which are underpriced for strategies requiring option purchases. Not every investor can be an arbitrageur and profit from small discrepancies in the pricing of options. Every investor can, however, avoid making transactions at prices that give the arbitrageur his opportunities.

Option evaluation is a complex process. We will examine it in detail after we look at some other uses of options, the tax treatment of option transactions, and option participation by various investors.

D. THE INVESTMENT SIGNIFICANCE OF LISTED PUT OPTIONS

This section examines the investment characteristics of exchange-listed put options within the framework developed in the earlier sections of this chapter. This framework reflects the belief that options should be used *only to improve the risk-reward characteristics of a portfolio*. Risk-reward improvement in the construction of a portfolio may be achieved systematically by appropriately using option evaluation and by treating both put and call options as common stock risk equivalents.

Most of the detailed examples used in earlier sections have been based on call option strategies. This focus on calls reflects the interest of most option users and the fact that an option to buy seems to be easier to comprehend than an option to sell. While many investors will never use puts, an investor will never fully understand calls without some knowledge of the relationship between calls and puts. Starting with a review of the basic features of a put, this section relates puts to calls, discusses the economics of short selling, and notes why certain investors should be active participants in the put market.

An exchange-listed put option is a negotiable contract traded on a national securities exchange. The writer or seller of a put receives a certain sum of money, termed the *option premium*, from the put buyer. In return for this premium, the buyer gets the right to sell the put writer 100 shares of a stated common stock at a fixed price, the *striking price*. This right can be exercised at any time prior to the expiration date of the option. The striking price and the number of shares covered by the put contract are subject to adjustment in the event of a stock split, stock dividend, or similar capital change but are not adjusted to reflect ordinary cash dividends.

1. Basic Risk-Reward Characteristics of the Put Contract

Examining a possible transaction with the aid of a pair of diagrams should help clarify the risk-reward features of the put contract. Someone who *buys* an option to *sell* (a put) will not exercise that option unless the actual market price falls below the striking price. Consequently, the buyer of a put who holds the option until the expiration date will lose the entire premium paid for the put option unless the stock falls below the striking price. As the stock drops further below the striking price, the put buyer will begin to recover the premium paid and eventually earn a profit. The *writer* of a put will not be required to buy stock unless the market price of the stock falls below the striking price. The writer retains the entire premium if the stock price remains above the striking price.

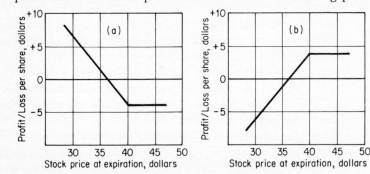

Figure 4-25. Comparison of profit/loss: buyer of put (*a*) vs. writer of put (*b*)

Figure 4-25 shows the risk-reward positions for investors on both sides of a put contract with a $40 striking price and a $4 option premium. In Figure 4-25*a* the put buyer's profit-loss position is shown as of the date of exercise or expiration. The buyer loses the entire $4 premium if the stock price stays above $40 per share because the right to sell at $40 is worthless if a higher price is available on the stock exchange. The put buyer begins to recover premium as the stock drops below

$40 and fully recovers the premium at the break-even price of $36 per share.

If the put buyer can buy stock on the market at $36 and deliver it to the writer of the put contract at a price of $40, the difference of $4 exactly equals the put premium before commissions. Below $36, the put buyer profits point-for-point as the stock continues to decline because the stock can be purchased at the lower price and sold to the writer of the put at $40. The put buyer's profit per share is equal to the $40 striking price less the sum of the $4 premium and the price at which the stock is ultimately purchased.

Figure 4-25b, the put writer's profit-loss line, contrasts with Figure 4-25a. The put writer's profit is the put buyer's loss, and vice versa. If the stock sells above $40, the put writer keeps the entire premium. As the stock drops, the put writer will still be required to buy stock at $40. The put writer's loss per share, like the put buyer's profit, is equal to the $40 striking price less the sum of the $4 premium and the price at which the stock can be sold after the put is exercised.

Anyone who has examined the graphic representations of call option profit-loss positions in Section A of this chapter will recognize in Figure 4-25b the same general shape that characterizes the covered call option writer's profit-loss position. The covered call writer, like the put writer, has a fixed profit if the stock is above the striking price on the date the option expires. The covered call writer also has a measure of downside protection, represented by the option premium. The profit-loss diagrams for the put writer and the covered call writer look the same because, *in most important respects, they are the same.*

2. Conversion: The Key to Analyzing Puts

A thorough understanding of puts requires an understanding of the conversion process. Through conversion, calls can be transformed into puts, and puts transformed into calls. Most of the confusion surrounding puts will be eliminated if the investor keeps in mind that the sale of a put option, margined by a Treasury bill or similar short-term debt instrument, should be the approximate risk-reward equivalent of a covered call writing position using the corresponding listed call option (i.e., the call with the same striking price and expiration date as the put). Likewise, a long position in a listed put option is approximately equivalent to a long position in the corresponding call and a short position in the underlying stock.* Understanding the conversion process (the mechanism which makes these two pairs of positions equivalent) is critical to an understanding of the appropriate uses of puts.

Figure 4-26 is a modification of the covered call writer's risk-reward diagram in Figure 4-21. The modifications introduced here are the sale of a put option and an adjustment for dividends. The ownership of shares of common stock is designated by the solid line *(A-A')*. The ownership of common stock, modified by the sale of a call option on that underlying stock, is designated by the broken line *(B-B')*. *The sale of a put collateralized by a short-term debt instrument is shown as a dotted line (C-C').* The vertical axis on the diagram measures the profit or loss from each of these positions at a particular stock price on the day the option expires. The horizontal axis shows a possible range of stock prices on that day.

These profit-loss lines are adjusted for dividends paid on the stock but not for transaction costs or interest earned on the collateral used to margin the put position. If interest earned on the collateral were added or an interest charge to carry the stock position were subtracted, *B-B'* and *C-C'* would be virtually identical.

In the examples, the stock is selling at $95 per share when the positions are initiated. As indicated in Section B of this chapter, the shareholder who simply buys the stock *(A-A')* participates point-for-point in every increase or decrease in the price of the stock. This investor's profit is theoretically unlimited on the up side and limited only by a stock price of zero on the down side.

Covered call writing, illustrated by line *B-B'*, is simply the sale of a call option against the stock position. The call option used in this example has a striking price of $100 and a life of

---

* Later this statement will be qualified in a way that has important implications for the valuation of puts and their use in structuring a portfolio.

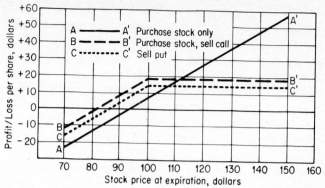

Figure 4-26. Comparison of profit/loss: covered call writing vs. put writing. (Note: Line B-B' reflects the payment of two $1.00 per share quarterly dividends on the underlying stock. Line C-C' does not reflect interest earned on the collateral posted to carry the put position. If the interest was added, B-B' and C-C' would be virtually identical.)

6 months from the time it is written (sold). The writer obtains a $10-per-share premium, which provides a degree of protection against loss if the stock declines. Any loss on the long stock position will be reduced by the $10 per share obtained by selling the option. The maximum profit in this case is equal to the call premium received ($10) plus the amount by which the striking price exceeds the price at which the stock is purchased ($100 − $95 = $5). If the stock rises, the obligation to repurchase the call or deliver the long stock position limits the investor's profit to a maximum of $15 per share plus dividends, no matter how high the stock price climbs.

The seller of a put option contract is obligated to buy the underlying stock from the holder of the option at a fixed price per share at any time during the life of the option. In the example given, the put writer has agreed to buy the stock at a price of $100 per share at any time during the next 6 months in return for a premium of just over $13.50 per share.

The profile of the put writer's profit-loss line is identical to that of the covered call writer's profit-loss line. The put writer experiences diminishing profit or, as the dotted line drops below the zero profit line, increasing loss as the price of the stock moves below the put's striking price. The loss to the put writer on stock that must be purchased at $100 per share, or, alternatively, the loss from closing out the obligation by repurchasing the put will grow as the stock declines. We know that any profit earned by the covered call writer is limited to the premium received, plus dividends, plus or minus any difference between the purchase price of the stock ($95) and the striking price of the option ($100). Likewise, the potential profit to the writer of the put is limited to the amount of premium received. Any expected dividends and any difference between the striking price of the option and the market price of the stock will be reflected in the premium the writer of a put receives.

In Figure 4-26, the only difference between lines B-B' and C-C' is the fact that C-C' does not include interest earned on collateral needed to carry the put writer's position. Another, perhaps better, way of expressing this difference is to say that B-B' does not reflect the opportunity cost of carrying the long stock position. Market factors related to the supply of, and demand for, puts and calls may also affect the relative pricing of the two types of options. Before we examine some of these factors, the introduction of a formula for put-to-call conversion is in order.

The positions graphed in Figure 4-26 assume that the underlying stock pays a $1 dividend quarterly and that the annualized yield on low-risk, intermediate-term debt securities is 7 percent. Using these data on dividends and interest rates and employing a general conversion formula, an investor will be able to calculate the approximate value of either a put or a call with a given striking price and expiration date when the price of the corresponding call or put is known. The conversion formula expressed in terms of the present value of a put is

$$Pp = Pc - Ps + D + \frac{S}{1 + nr}$$

where Pp = price of a put
Pc = price of a corresponding call with identical striking price and expiration date

S = striking price of the options
Ps = price of the underlying stock
n = life of the options expressed as fraction of a year
r = intermediate-term interest rate on Treasury bills or high-grade commercial paper*
D = present value of all dividends expected to be paid before expiration of the options†

Substituting specific values for the example from Figure 4-26 in this equation gives the following:

$$Pp = \$10 - \$95 + \$1.97 + \frac{\$100}{1 + (0.5 \times 0.07)}$$

$$= \$13.59$$

This value of $13.59 for the put was used in plotting the graph in Figure 4-26. Apart from tax and commission considerations (which will occasionally lead to material differences) and neglecting for the moment the possibility of early exercise of the put, the investor who deposits collateral earning interest at a rate of 7 percent and sells this put for $13.59 will have an identical profit-loss position to that of the investor who buys 100 shares of the underlying stock at a price of $95 and sells the corresponding call option for a $10 premium.

This formula is called the *conversion equation* because some investment firms, popularly known as "converters," have used it to convert puts into calls and calls into puts when writers prefer to sell one type of option and buyers want the other type. Once listed puts are trading on all option stocks, the equation will be used primarily *to determine the most efficient way to take a position.* Because the risk characteristics of the covered call writer's position are nearly identical to those of the put writer's position, an investor's return may be improved by taking one of these positions in preference to the other and

---

* For some investors the appropriate rate may be the interest rate a broker charges on debit balances. Learned papers can be written (and undoubtedly will be) on the selection of an appropriate interest rate.
† Note that the *present value* of the anticipated dividends will be slightly less than the actual dividend payment.

earning a small arbitrage profit if the prices of the two options differ from the appropriate relationship. Arbitrage opportunities based on conversion relationships between puts and calls *may* be consistently available to certain investors. Understanding these possible arbitrage opportunities will be easier if the reader first understands the calculation of stock risk equivalents for simple stock and option positions.

3. Conversion and the Calculation of Risk Equivalents

In Section B of this chapter we introduced the idea that it is possible to translate any listed call option position into a risk equivalent position in the underlying stock by calculating the fraction of a point by which the price of the option will change if a one-point move occurs in the underlying stock (the neutral hedge ratio). *Specifically, if the price of an option changes by one-half point when the price of the underlying stock changes by a full point, then that option, over a reasonable period of time and a range of stock prices, will behave in essentially the same manner as 50 shares of the underlying stock.* If a call changes in price by one-quarter point for each one-point move in the stock, the option will behave like 25 shares of stock.

The same concept holds for translating put options into stock equivalents. Because the put writer's position is the risk equivalent of covered call writing, *the number of equivalent shares represented by a put is equal to 100 minus the number of equivalent shares represented by the corresponding call.* If a call behaves like the equivalent of 25 shares of the stock, by moving one-quarter point for each one-point move in the stock, then a position in the analogous put contract will be the equivalent of 75 shares (100 shares minus 25 shares). The buyer of the put is "buying" the risk equivalent of a 75-share short position in the stock because, through the conversion mechanism, buying a put is the risk equivalent of buying the analogous call (plus 25 shares) and selling the underlying stock short (minus 100 shares).

Complex option positions are usually less attractive than relatively simple ones because transaction costs rise as the complexity of the position increases. The risk-reward characteristics of complex positions can also be difficult to evaluate. An investor may find that a position he meant to be bearish was, in fact, bullish. A position that is bullish at current stock prices may *become* bearish if the stock advances sharply. *The best way to keep track of a complex position is to translate each component into its common stock equivalent and total these equivalents to get the stock equivalent risk exposure of the entire position.*

Table 4-1 shows the risk equivalents of a number of simple and complex stock and option positions. The security or combination described in the left-hand column is usually the most common way to establish a position. The other securities or combinations in the same row are risk equivalents of the left-hand column. *Unusual combinations may be the most efficient way to establish a position if they can provide the expectation of an arbitrage-type profit. The opportunity for arbitrage will arise*

Table 4-1. Risk Comparability of Investment Positions

1. Buy 100 shares	Buy a call Sell a put	
2. Buy a call	Buy 100 shares Buy a put	
3. Buy 200 shares Sell two calls	Sell two puts	Buy 100 shares Sell a put Sell a call
4. Sell a call	Sell 100 shares short* Sell a put	
5. Buy a put	Sell 100 shares short* Buy a call	
6. Sell a put Sell a call	Buy 100 shares Sell two calls	Sell 100 shares short* Sell two puts
7. Buy a put Sell a call	Sell 100 shares short*	
8. Buy a put Buy a call	Sell 100 shares short* Buy two calls	

NOTE: The security or combination in the left-hand column is usually the most common of several possible ways of establishing an investment position. If all puts and calls are assumed to have the same striking price and expiration date, the positions in each row have equivalent risk characteristics. Positions marked with an asterisk involve a short sale of the underlying common stock and are unattractive for most investors.

if the market mechanism does not force put and call prices into conversion parity adjusted for the possibility of early exercise of the put.

4. The Economics of Selling Short

Some ways of establishing risk equivalent positions are marked with an asterisk in Table 4-1. The asterisk indicates that these choices will almost certainly be less efficient than the other choice or choices on the same line. The inherently less efficient choices involve selling the stock short.

A short seller makes a profit if the stock sold short can be repurchased later at a lower price. The reason selling the stock short leads to a less efficient position is that any interest income earned on the cash proceeds of a short sale belongs to the shareholder who loans his stock to the short seller. *This interest income does not benefit the short seller.* In calculating the value of a put through the conversion equation, the buyer of a put gets credit for interest earned on the proceeds of the short sale that is *implicit* in calculating the price the buyer should expect to pay for the put.

Because the treatment of the proceeds of a short sale is important to an understanding of put and call price relationships and because most investors are not thoroughly familiar with the mechanics and economics of selling short, a brief digression is in order. Once an investor understands the debits and credits to the short seller's brokerage account, it will be clear that, *if listed puts and calls are available on a stock, it will rarely make sense for entities other than certain brokerage firms to sell the stock short.*

When a brokerage firm customer buys stock on margin, the customer's account is charged interest on the amount of any debit balance. The debit balance in the account is *not reduced by the proceeds of a short sale.* To deliver shares sold short, the seller must *borrow* stock from someone who owns it. The stock *lender* continues to receive any dividends on the stock. These dividends are paid by the short seller. The stock lender's account is also credited with cash equal to the market price of the stock loaned. The cash can be invested in a short-term debt instrument to earn interest for the stock lender.

If the stock rises after the short sale, the brokerage firm will debit the short seller's account for the amount of the rise and will transfer the funds to the stock lender's account. If the stock price falls, the transfer will be reversed. This process is called *marking the accounts to the market*. The stock lender not only continues to receive dividends on the stock and participates fully in any increase (or decrease) in the value of the stock holdings but also earns interest on a short-term debt instrument equal in value to the stock loaned.

Actual stock loan arrangements are usually more complicated than these brief paragraphs suggest, and a variety of costs will reduce the stock lender's return. Nonetheless, an investor will be better off taking a position that gives at least partial credit for the interest earned on the proceeds of an actual or implicit short sale. Usually any position using listed put and call options that does not involve an actual short sale will provide partial or full implicit interest credit.

Table 4-1 indicates that a would-be short seller of stock can establish an equivalent risk position by purchasing a put and selling a call. Readers who find this equivalence hard to understand should use the data from the conversion example in this section to construct a diagram analogous to Figure 4-4, in Section A. Constructing graphs or using the equivalent positions from Table 4-1 like substitution exercises in a high school trigonometry class will permit simplification of the most complex option positions. When complex positions are analyzed in this manner and, even more importantly, when option positions are translated into stock equivalents on the basis of the relationship between stock price and option price changes, misunderstandings about the risk characteristics of options will begin to disappear.

If there is a relative "shortage" of puts and the price of the puts is higher than indicated by the conversion equation (after adjustment for early exercise), arbitrage-type transactions should force the prices approximately into line. *This arbitrage can occur even if no one actually sells the stock short.* Put premiums must reflect at least part of the interest credit from the implicit short sale because an investor who wants to take a long position in the stock can reverse the position of the short seller by selling a put and buying a call. *If puts are overpriced relative to their adjusted conversion value, a sizable group of investors who would otherwise buy the stock will find selling a put and buying a call to be a more efficient way of taking the equivalent of a long stock position.*

There may be modest but persistent overpricing of puts relative to predicted values until investors become more familiar with the writing side of the put transaction. Some investors will obtain superior returns by taking advantage of this disparity. *All investors will risk inferior returns if they use options without careful attention to option evaluation, adjusted conversion parity, and the equivalent positions listed in Table 4-1.*

One final observation on the impact of the option market on short selling is in order. Any investor who is accustomed to reviewing the short interest in a stock or who is engaged in stock loan activities should anticipate a change as a result of the introduction of puts. After a brief period of adjustment, the availability of both puts and calls on a stock should sharply reduce the short interest and, consequently, the stock loan demand for the shares. Unless an institution is already engaged in stock lending, it probably does not make sense to expend the effort needed to inaugurate a stock loan program now.

5. Who Should Use Listed Puts?

Both puts and calls on a given stock usually will be either overpriced or underpriced together, but valuation disparities will be common. There should be opportunities for superior results if an investor combines the three facets of intelligent option portfolio management:

1. Careful analysis of the risk characteristics of each investment position and of the total portfolio

2. Systematic integration of option evaluation into the portfolio management process

3. Attention to the relative rewards associated with each of the risk equivalent ways to take a position

The introduction of puts expands the third facet and increases the complexity of the decision-making process. Fortunately, the results can be worth the extra effort.

Most of the explanatory and educational material on puts published by the exchanges and others views the put writer as someone who hopes to purchase stock at a price below the market price at the time the put contract is sold and the put buyer as someone who expects the stock price to decline dramatically. As we have seen, the risk position of the put writer is analogous in every respect (except, perhaps, tax treatment) to the position of the covered writer of the corresponding call option. Likewise, the buyer of a put has a risk position similar to that of an investor who buys a call and sells the underlying stock short.

It is obvious that the buyer of a put is bearish and that the seller of a put is bullish on the underlying stock. However, the fact that it is possible to translate these option positions into stock equivalents means that the decision to sell a put as an alternative to establishing a covered call writing position or the decision to buy a put rather than to sell a naked call should depend on the investor's tax situation and the relative evaluations of the options. The reader may begin to suspect that this analysis of the appropriate use of listed puts by various types of investors will differ markedly from other discussions of this topic.

The material which follows is based in part on the assumption that if puts sell at a price different from the price predicted by the conversion formula adjusted for early exercise, the actual price of the put will be *above* the predicted price. Certain types of investors can take advantage of such disparities more easily than others.

The subsequent discussion reflects tax interpretations expressed in the revised CBOE booklet *Tax Considerations in Using CBOE Options*, in the American Stock Exchange booklet *Tax Planning for Listed Options*, and in the House Ways and Means Committee staff report on the Mikva bill (H.R. 12224). No investor should rely on this discussion for tax advice, however. Investors should consult either a professional tax practitioner or an authoritative tax service before entering into any of the positions described. While some of this material might ordinarily have been covered in the general tax discussion in Chapter 5, taxes can play such an important role in the decision to use puts that a certain amount of tax analysis seems appropriate here.

a. *Short Sellers.* There are two potentially attractive ways to take a bearish position if listed puts and calls are available: buying puts and selling uncovered calls. (As noted above, actually selling the stock short will almost never be attractive to the typical investor.) Other things being equal, the purchase of a listed put offers two potential advantages over the uncovered sale of a listed call. First, the put buyer's risk is limited to the amount of premium paid for the put contract. In practice, however, the theoretically unlimited upside risk from the sale of a naked call is of only minor concern to the vigilant short seller. The short seller has no intention of letting the stock run away on the up side and will cover some or all of the naked call position if the stock moves up strongly. Second, if a put is owned for more than the required holding period before being sold, the buyer can obtain a long-term capital gain. Unless the exchanges decide to list options with more than 12 months of life at the time of the original listing, it will no longer be possible to obtain a long-term capital gain on any long option position. Consequently, the criterion for choosing between buying a put and selling a naked call will be simply a determination of the overvaluation or undervaluation of the options.

If the price of a put is in line with the price of the analogous call, an investor who finds a call option to be underpriced will find the corresponding put option to be underpriced as well. Likewise, if the call is overpriced, the put will be overpriced. If the put and call are both overpriced, selling the call will be the most efficient way to express one's bearish sentiments. If the put and call are both underpriced, buying the put will be more efficient. If both seem fairly priced and the put does not sell at even a slight premium to adjusted conversion value, the limited risk associated with owning a put makes buying it preferable to the uncovered sale of the call.

While the overpricing or underpricing of the options should be the primary criterion for choosing between buying a put and selling an uncovered call, the short seller, even more than most investors, will want to monitor the stock equivalent risk exposure of a position. Though a long put position may give the same bearish exposure as a short call position at the time one position or the other is established, the passage of time and, most importantly, changes in stock prices can affect the degree of bearishness of a position. Specifically, a long put position will become more bearish (i.e., more profitable per point of decline) as the stock drops and less bearish (i.e., the loss per point will become progressively smaller) as the stock price rises. On the other hand, a short call position will become less profitable per point of decline as the stock declines and will lead to a greater loss per point of price advance as the stock price rises. If the stock price is unchanged, the short call position will become extremely profitable, and the long put position extremely unprofitable, as the value of the options erodes with the passage of time.

These patterns of changing "bearishness" in the two ways of establishing a "short" position have several obvious implications for the short seller. First, if a large movement in stock prices is anticipated, the investor should always be a buyer of options—in this case, puts. If the anticipated stock price movement is small, the investor should always be a seller of options—in this case, uncovered calls. Second, the position may have to be adjusted as time passes and as stock prices change to keep the stock equivalent risk exposure within appropriate limits. For example, if the stock declines as anticipated, the long put position may become more bearish or the short call position less bearish than desired. The investor *may* want to consider modifying the position to bring the degree of bearishness into closer alignment with the original position.

b. *Investors with Capital Loss Carry-Forwards.* Even with passage of the Mikva bill, which makes any gain or loss on an option-writing position a short-term capital gain or loss, the covered writer of a call can still obtain a long-term capital gain on a long position in the underlying stock. The writer of a put can never obtain a long-term capital gain. The put writer will have a short-term capital gain or loss, depending on the investment results of his position.

The change in the tax law, lower commission costs, and the likelihood of at least a slightly unbalanced demand from buyers of puts create a situation whereby any investor with a sizable capital loss carry-forward will probably find the sale of a put at least as attractive as the covered sale of a call.

c. *Nontaxpaying Investors.* The manager of tax-exempt funds or any nonresident of the United States who is exempt from domestic taxation on capital gains may find the sale of puts preferable to the covered sale of calls. A tax-exempt institution will pay no taxes on gains from either position, and yet the commission costs on the sale of a put will almost certainly be lower. The possibility of an extra premium due to a relative shortage of put writers could provide an added return.

Certain nonresidents may, under some circumstances, have an added advantage because their collateral (and the proceeds from the sale of the put) could be invested in a security not subject to dividend or interest withholding. Dividends earned on stock held as part of the covered call writing position would usually be subject to tax. This possibility will be explored further in Chapter 5, Section D.

One caveat is in order for any fiduciary contemplating the sale of puts as an alternative to covered call writing. The Comptroller of the Currency and various state insurance commissioners have ruled that covered call writing can be an acceptable investment strategy for national banks and appropriately domiciled insurance companies. These rulings provide a measure of comfort to any fiduciary contemplating a covered call writing program. As equivalent as the risks are, however, *one should not assume that selling puts will be similarly acceptable to these or other regulators.* This issue will be discussed at length in Chapter 6.

At the very least, any fiduciary selling puts should maintain careful records showing that sale of a put at the time such transaction was made was clearly preferable to sale of the corresponding call against a long position in the underlying stock. Though it would probably be possible to reconstruct such records in the event of a legal challenge, reconstruction might prove more costly than maintaining the records from the beginning. Furthermore, the fact that the alternative of covered call writing was systematically checked and found to be less desirable than selling puts would seem to provide some ammunition for the defense if litigation occurred.

d. *Corporations.* Section 246(c) of the Internal Revenue Code requires that a corporation desiring to take advantage of the 85 percent intercorporate dividend deduction must establish a 15-day holding period in any common stock before entering into a contract to sell that stock or buying a put option. If the holding period is not established, any dividends received do not qualify for the 85 percent deduction. While the Internal Revenue Service has issued a private ruling that selling a call does not obligate the investor to sell the stock (see page 140), the issue is far from settled.

The most obvious way to deal with the problem presented by Section 246(c) is to wait 16 days after a stock is purchased before selling a call or buying a put. To the extent that a corporation's directors will approve, buying dividend-paying common shares in one company and buying puts or selling uncovered calls on the stock of a similar company is another possibility. A less obvious way to avoid problems with the holding-period requirement is to buy a combination of straight or convertible preferred stock positions and use puts and calls to adjust portfolio risk appropriately. A particularly intriguing idea is the use of put and call options on interest-sensitive common stocks to reduce the risk to principal in a preferred stock portfolio. The potential for such interest rate hedging will be discussed in Chapter 5, Section D.

6. Early Exercise of Puts

Sellers of calls are familiar, sometimes distressingly so, with the phenomenon of early exercise. Though other factors occasionally lead to early exercise of calls, the most common cause is the call buyer's desire to obtain a dividend paid on the underlying stock. Consequently, early exercise is most common when the call is in the money and there is a relatively short time period between an ex-dividend date and expiration of the option.

Sellers of puts must be prepared for early exercise under a different set of circumstances. Specifically, the seller of a put that is in the money (i.e., the stock is selling significantly *below* the striking price) will frequently experience early exercise *after* the stock goes ex dividend if the option has a relatively short remaining life. Whereas sellers of calls find early exercise a problem when the dividend is sizable and the call is in the money, sellers of puts will find early exercise a problem when future dividends will be small or nonexistent and the put is in the money. Early exercise of in-the-money puts will be a particular problem in less volatile stocks. A moment's reflection will suggest that early exercise of puts may become quite common in bear markets and during any period when interest rates are high.

The reasons behind the early exercise of a put are related to the earlier discussion of the economics of short selling. The total investment return to the holder of *any* security consists of the algebraic sum of any periodic dividend or interest payment and any capital gain or loss. Frequently, there will be no dividend due on the underlying stock during the remaining life of a put. Consequently, the holder of a deep-in-the-money put will not benefit from a stock price reduction on an ex-dividend date. The holder of this put will be carrying the equivalent of a short position in the stock. Only if the put is bought *below* intrinsic value will the buyer of the put get credit for the proceeds of the implicit short sale. On the other hand, if the put is selling below its intrinsic value, an arbitrageur can profit by exercising it and reinvesting the cash received in a security with a higher expected total return. A deep-in-the-money put is an unstable position.

Call writers have learned that the buyer of a call has absolute control over who will receive a particular dividend on the underlying stock. The call buyer may exercise this control to deprive a call writer of the dividend. The owner of a put exercises similar control over who will receive a dividend. Ordinarily, the holder of a put will choose to "receive" dividends or get "credit" for them in the form of a probable decline in the stock price on the ex-dividend date. If there will be no dividends during the remaining life of an in-the-money put option, it can sell at or slightly below intrinsic value. There will probably be a greater tendency to exercise in-the-money puts than in-the-money calls because, in effect, *the carrying cost of a long position can be eliminated by exercising the put.* With exercise more likely, the willingness and ability of a brokerage firm to take positions to facilitate customer trades will be even more important to the writer of puts than to the writer of calls. The effect of early exercise on the value of a put can be significant. This complex topic will be explored in Chapter 7.

7. The Effect of Puts on Option Premium Levels

Conventional wisdom holds that a dramatic influx of option writers, encouraged by passage of the Tax Reform Act of 1976, will drive premiums to such low levels that it will be impossible for a writer to obtain an adequate return on investment. The low level of option premiums during most of 1976 and 1977 is cited as evidence supporting this notion.

Evidence to be presented in Chapter 10 suggests that the low level of option premiums during this period was due primarily to the low volatility or narrow trading ranges of individual stocks and to the stability of the overall market. Lower interest rates than those which prevailed during the first few years of listed option trading also have contributed to an apparent reduction in option premiums. While it will be some time before the effect, if any, of the 1976 tax legislation on option premium levels can be quantified, it is doubtful that this legislation has been more than marginally significant in its effect on premium levels.

Structural considerations (such as restrictions on certain institutional investors' ability to buy options and the introduction of puts) play only a modest role in setting option premium levels. If it has any effect, the introduction of puts may tend to increase premium levels. The effect on premium levels of put trading should offset any indiscriminate writing by institutional investors.

Just as the impact of institutional writing on premiums is the first issue raised during most general discussions of options, the first question asked when puts are discussed is generally: "I can see the attraction of buying puts, but who will want to write puts?" As has been amply demonstrated, there are good reasons to be on either side of the put contract, just as there are good reasons to be on either side of the call contract. Much of the preceding discussion is based on the premise that the buy side of the put transaction will have broader initial appeal than the sell side. There is, furthermore, an aspect of put trading that *might* lead to an expansion of option premiums in the same manner that widespread "dumping" of calls by institutions *might* lead to a reduction in option premium levels.

The analysis of option positions in terms of underlying stock equivalents helps clarify the idea that trading in puts might lead to an expansion of option premiums. The serious investor who buys underpriced call options as part of an investment program does not buy them for leverage but as an attractively priced substitute for a risk equivalent amount of the underlying stock. Assume for a moment that the listed call options available on a stock are underpriced. An investor wishes to take a 100-share stock equivalent position through purchase of some of these underpriced options. Further, assume that the call option which the investor wishes to use is the risk equivalent of 50 shares of the underlying stock. This means that the investor will buy *two* of these call options to provide the risk equivalent of a 100-share position in the underlying stock.

If listed puts are available, the investor can take a 100-share stock equivalent position in other ways. Just as each call option is the risk equivalent of 50 shares of stock, a long position in a put with the same striking price and expiration date is equivalent to a short position in 50 shares of the stock. If the options are sufficiently underpriced, the investor may wish to take the 100-share risk equivalent position by buying *four* calls and *two* puts. Each of the calls will be the risk equivalent of a 50-share long stock position, and each of the puts will be the equivalent of a 50-share short stock position. Owning four calls gives the investor an equivalent position of 200 shares long, and owning two puts is the risk equivalent of selling 100 shares short. The net risk equivalent position is 100 shares long.

Because listed puts permit this alternative way of taking a 100-share stock equivalent position, put trading may lead to an expansion in option premium levels. Clearly, taking a 100-share risk equivalent position by buying four calls and two puts provides substantially more demand for options than the simple purchase of two calls. In effect, because puts can be converted into calls, and calls into puts, the alternative way of taking the position leads to an effective demand for six calls: four directly and two through the conversion mechanism.

Obviously, this example can be carried to ridiculous extremes. In a sense, the purchase of six calls and four puts or eight calls and six puts would also be the risk equivalent of 100 shares of the underlying stock. When large dollar investments in options are translated into relatively small stock equivalent positions, the notion of options as stock risk equivalents begins to get a bit tenuous. Within reason, however, it is clear that a market in listed put options will *tend* to increase the demand for *all* types of options and *may* lead to a rise in premium levels.

In the long run, the level of option premiums on most stocks will be determined by the recent price volatility of the underlying stock. An influx of institutional sellers or the introduction of trading in listed puts will have, at most, a peripheral effect on premium levels.

E. LISTED OPTION SPREADS

Most experienced users of options would agree that many investors who do not use options could benefit from the effective integration of options into their investment program. These same experienced users of options would also agree that *most* of the investors actively engaged in option spreading would be better off if they had never heard of the option market. To argue that spreading *never* makes sense would dramatically overstate the case. Yet the individual investor who trades fewer than 10 option contracts at a time and who pays full retail brokerage commissions cannot presume to compete with market makers on the exchange floor whose commission costs are nominal. When the investor faces such distinct disadvantages, a prudent policy would be to bow out of this phase of the option market and leave it to the professionals, who have the time, the inclination, and the profit incentive to pursue it.

An attractive listed option spread is an opportunity to purchase one option and simultaneously sell another option of the same class on the same underlying stock with the expectation of an arbitrage-type profit. The expected profit arises from the fact that the option purchased is undervalued relative to the option sold.

The option market, by and large, is extraordinarily efficient in pricing one option relative to another on the same underlying stock. The option market appears to be much less efficient in pricing all these options relative to the underlying stock. In other words, when one option on a stock is underpriced, typically the other options on that stock will also be underpriced. Investors will find more opportunities to exploit discrepancies between options and the underlying stock than discrepancies among the various options on that stock.

There are exceptions to the generalization that all options on a particular stock will tend to be appropriately priced relative to one another. Because of these exceptions, the experienced investor may want to try a few spread transactions. Successful spreading requires a solid understanding of the underlying stock and access to an option evaluation model that makes dividend adjustments and shows the appropriate price relationships between options of the same class.

Spreading opportunities appear most frequently in newly listed or newly active options. Established, actively traded option classes usually have a large number of market makers who are prepared to pounce on any temporary valuation disparity. Even in active option stocks, however, a large institutional order to "roll over" one option into another may lead to a valuation discrepancy which the individual investor can exploit.

Another source of spreading opportunities is the misuse by other investors of option evaluation models. While the simple models used by some investors do not adjust for dividends at all, most reasonably sophisticated option models assume that every company pays a regular quarterly dividend equal to the last dividend payment. If a company has an irregular dividend policy or pays a large year-end extra, the opportunity for profit in a spreading transaction can be worthwhile, though rarely earthshaking.

1. Tax Considerations

Spreading originally became popular with individual investors for two reasons. First, spreading was generally perceived to offer a potential tax advantage before the 1976 tax changes. During the early years of listed option trading any gain or loss on option writing was considered to be an ordinary gain or loss for tax purposes. Any gain or loss on an option purchased was a capital gain or loss, short-term or long-term, depending on the holding period of the option position. The short (6 months) holding period for long-term gains, the difference in tax treatment between the buying and writing positions, and the fact that forcing exercise when a writing position was profitable could occasionally convert an ordinary gain into a short-term capital gain caused spreading to appeal to a variety of investors. The appeal was greatest to investors in high tax brackets who could benefit from the long-term capital gains treatment on long option positions or who had capital loss carry-forwards which they could at least attempt to "convert" into ordinary losses.

The second reason spreading became so popular in the early days of listed options was that spreading frequently generates enormous commissions. An actively traded spreading account can easily incur an annual commission bill equal to the equity in the account. While no statistical computations are available, a substantial fraction of all brokerage firm option compliance problems have originated in active spreading accounts. With the passage of the Tax Reform Act of 1976 and the restraining influence of brokerage firm legal and compliance staffs, there is much less emphasis on spreading today than there was in the early years of listed options.

Paradoxically, most of the spreading promotional activity going on today still relates to some of the tax features of spreading. The most aggressively marketed approach to spreading since late 1976 involves the formation of a small brokerage firm to support the activities of one or more floor traders on an option exchange. High-tax-bracket investors are offered limited partnership interests in the specialized brokerage firm with the implied assurance that losses (short-term capital or ordinary) will be realized immediately and that long-term capital gains will be realized in future years.

The tax idea behind this promotion is that a brokerage firm has 30 days in which to decide whether a position should be assigned to its trading account or to its investment account. If a position is placed in the brokerage firm's trading account, any gain or loss on that position becomes an ordinary gain or loss because the brokerage firm is in the business of trading securities and because its trading gains or losses are much like the inventory profits or losses of a merchant. If a position is allocated to the investment account, any profit or loss becomes a capital gain or loss. The brokerage firm is offered this choice to reduce the chance that it will amass huge, nondeductible capital losses. When brokerage firm tax treatment is combined with the opportunity to use option spreads to realize losses in the current year and defer gains to subsequent years, the superficial tax appeal of this limited partnership investment becomes apparent: If all goes well, the limited partners should have losses to deduct in the near term, while gains can be deferred to future years and, perhaps, converted into long-term capital gains. Although most legal and tax advisers doubt the legitimacy of a brokerage firm limited partnership organized primarily for tax purposes, the idea has been marketed aggressively in an environment in which most tax shelters have been eliminated or reduced in attractiveness.

Although miniature brokerage firms established as a tax-avoidance device probably will not provide the desired tax results, some investors may still benefit from the tax-timing possibilities of listed option spreads. If an investment position is undertaken with the expectation of profit and not solely for tax purposes, option spread transactions may be used to defer gains from one year to the next. The precise requirements for tax deferral with spread transactions have not been spelled out by the Internal Revenue Service; however, on the basis of rulings applied to other arbitrage and quasi-arbitrage transactions, we can say that earning a pretax profit is the best insurance against an attack by the IRS. Even if an actual profit is not earned, the transaction would probably stand up if there was a meaningful investment reason for taking the position, apart from any tax-reduction opportunities. If an investor sets up option spreads with little risk exposure and negative expected returns apart from tax features, an alert IRS agent might call the transactions a sham. Indeed, similar arguments have been made against commodity tax spreads in a recent IRS ruling.

Using spreads as part of a diversified stock and option portfolio should raise no tax questions if the tax-deferral aspects of the spread are supplementary to other investment goals such as portfolio diversification and risk adjustment and where the spread has at least a modest expected pretax profit. A satisfactory investment basis for a spread which will defer income to a subsequent year would be that the option purchased was undervalued relative to the option sold. While such spreads are not routinely available, they arise with sufficient frequency to make using them worthwhile to certain high-tax-bracket investors.

2. Some Rules for Profitable Spreading

In addition to the preceding discussion of spread transactions motivated partly by tax considerations, a basic discussion of the various types of spreads and of some general rules for finding attractive spreads seems in order. The examples used here are all call spreads, but analogous put spread positions are also possible, and their analysis follows similar lines—with an occasional perverse twist.

Table 4-2 covers a variety of different call spread transactions. Though the most common types of call spreads are mentioned here, this table and the accompanying discussion are by no means exhaustive of the possibilities. In constructing Table 4-2, it was assumed that an underlying stock sells at $43 per share and that one of the option exchanges lists January, April, and July expirations of $35, $40, and $45 striking price call options. Each of these nine options is designated with a letter (A through I) at the top of Table 4-2. Beneath this section of the table is a listing of nine basic call spreads. The first column lists the most common name given a particular spread (the variety of names for each type of spread is limited only by the imagination of the individual naming it). In the second column an example of each spread is given. For example, a vertical bull call spread might be established by buying (or going long) a January $40 striking price call option and selling (or going short) a January $45 striking price call option. In a vertical bull call spread the expiration date is the same on each option, but the striking price of the option sold is higher than the striking price of the option purchased. The third column shows times at which this particular type of spread might be especially attractive. Ideally, the conditions described in this column should be combined with an unusually favorable pricing discrepancy between the options used. This last column should be viewed as an "all other things being equal" statement because relative underpricing of the option(s) purchased or relative overpricing of the option(s) sold could make some of these positions attractive in a different environment.

The vertical bull call spread will usually be most attractive when all the options on a particular underlying stock tend to be overpriced. When all options are overpriced, out-of-the-money options will tend to be overpriced *relative* to in-the-money options on the basis of expected profits to a writer.

The second spread listed in Table 4-2 is the vertical bear call spread. In the example given, the investor purchases the January $45 striking price call option and sells the January $40 striking price call. This is simply the reverse of the vertical

Table 4-2. Definitions of Call Spread Positions

Striking Price	January	April	July
45	A	B	C
40	D	E	F
35	G	H	I

Name of Spread	Example	When to Use*
1. Vertical bull	Long D, short A	Options overpriced
2. Vertical bear	Long A, short D	Options underpriced, short sale
3. Horizontal, or calendar	Long C, short A	Options underpriced or timing adjustment
4. Diagonal bull	Long E, short A	Near-term options overpriced
5. Diagonal bear	Long B, short D	Near-term options overpriced, short sale
6. Variable vertical	Long 1D, short 2A	Options overpriced
7. Variable diagonal	Long 1E, short 2A	Near-term options overpriced
8. Butterfly, or sandwich	Long 1A, short 2D, long 1G	Never
9. Unmarginable calendar	Long B, short C	Timing adjustment, options overpriced

* Assumes stock selling at $43 per share.

bull spread. Just as the vertical bull call spread is most attractive when options are overpriced, the vertical bear call spread is most attractive when options are underpriced. If options are underpriced, the vertical bear call spread can frequently be an attractive alternative to a short sale or to the sale of an underpriced uncovered call option. If both options are underpriced, the expected profit on the January $45 striking price call purchased usually will be greater than the expected loss on the January $40 striking price call sold. The resulting expected net profit will reduce or, perhaps, eliminate the penalty associated with selling an underpriced call option. Unlike the short seller or the seller of a "naked" call, the vertical bear spreader can lose no more than $5 per underlying share less the net difference in premiums at the time the position is initiated. Of course, he can make no more than the net difference in premiums.

The third type of spread listed in Table 4-2—the horizontal, or calendar, spread—is frequently avoided by professional option traders on the grounds that they find it extremely difficult to make money with this kind of spread. Their reasons for rejecting the position are easy to understand. The only way an investor can earn a material profit with a calendar spread is if the stock is selling very close to the $45 striking price at the time the short option expires. If the stock has stayed very close to $45 during the period the position is held, the premium on the July $45 striking price option which the investor owns may have eroded more than originally expected, reflecting the lack of volatility in the underlying stock.

The investor's position is even less favorable if the stock moves dramatically away from the striking price. If the stock rises to $50 or $55 per share just before the January option expires, for example, the January option will sell at its intrinsic value, and the premium over intrinsic value of the July option will shrink as the distance between the striking price and the market price of the stock increases. There is a point, typically not very far from the striking price, beyond which the erosion of premium over intrinsic value on the January option will be less than the erosion of the premium over intrinsic value of the July option. In summary, the investor finds it difficult to profit materially from a calendar spread no matter what the stock does. If the stock moves dramatically, the premium over intrinsic value on the long option evaporates. If the stock does not move, the premium on the long option still evaporates because the underlying stock appears to lack volatility.

Persuasive as it may seem, this argument overstates the case against calendar spreads. Though no one has published a statistical study to document it, there is widespread acceptance of the idea that a stock will tend to sell close to the striking price of one of its options as an expiration date approaches. To the extent that there is any validity to this belief, calendar spreads probably make more sense than the case against them suggests. Furthermore, if option premiums are low when the position is established, calendar spreads can make more sense than they would if premium levels were high. If the option purchased as the long side of the spread already has an extremely low premium, there is little chance of unusual premium erosion if the stock price stagnates until the short option position expires. On the other hand, if the stock should experience a high degree of volatility, there is always the chance of a modest expansion in the relative premium of the long option as a consequence of the higher volatility of the underlying stock.

These considerations are unlikely to persuade a large number of investors that horizontal, or calendar, spreads are the ideal investment, and nothing of that sort is intended. The point to be made is that calendar spreads can be more useful than they are generally believed to be. During a period of low option premiums they can be an attractive strategy in their own right, and they are the principal strategy used in timing adjustments to defer a gain from current to subsequent tax years.

The diagonal bull call spread, the fourth type listed in Table 4-2, is illustrated by the purchase of an April $40 striking price option and the sale of a January $45 striking price option. It might be described as expressing longer-term bullishness on the outlook for the underlying stock, combined with a feeling that the near-term picture may be dull. This type of spread makes the most sense during periods when near-term options are overpriced relative to longer-term options. This relationship will occur most frequently when a sharp drop in the price of the underlying stock leads to an expansion of near-term premiums without a corresponding expansion in longer-term premiums.

The diagonal bear call spread, the fifth type listed, is illustrated by the purchase of an April $45 striking price option and the sale of a January $40 striking price option. Like the diagonal bull, this type of spread is usually most attractive on an evaluation basis during periods when near-term options are overpriced, usually as a result of a sharp drop or rise in the price of the underlying stock.

The variable vertical spread—in Table 4-2, the purchase of one January $40 striking price option and the sale of two January $45 striking price options—can be either bullish or bearish depending upon striking price–market price relationships, time to maturity, and, most importantly, the ratio of options sold to options purchased. The variable vertical call spread is currently one of the most popular types of spread transactions, probably because it lends itself to a spurious type of "analysis" which focuses on the price parameters within which or beyond which the investor will earn a profit. Many of the rules of thumb proposed for evaluating variable spreads are Byzantine in their complexity and totally lacking in validity. In Chapter 7 we will have more to say about the parametric analysis that is often applied to variable spread positions.

The vertical variable spread is usually most attractive when options are overpriced. The out-of-the-money options sold will typically be more overpriced in dollar terms than an at- or in-the-money option.

The variable diagonal spread illustrated in Table 4-2 by the purchase of an April $40 striking price call option and the sale of two January $45 striking price call options is similar in most respects to the variable vertical spread. Like the diagonal bull spread, this position is most attractive when near-term option premiums have expanded relative to long-term option premiums.

The butterfly, or sandwich, spread is the option trader's

equivalent of the Holy Grail. The ideal butterfly spread is a position which every would-be spreader seeks but which few, if any, find. In the ideal butterfly spread, the money received for the options sold will be equal to the amount paid for the options purchased. To illustrate, in the example used in Table 4-2, the options purchased are the January $35 and the January $45, and the options sold are two January $40. The risk-reward characteristics of this position are reflected in Figure 4-27 on the assumption that the amount paid for the options purchased equals the amount received for the two options sold. From this diagram it is obvious that if commissions are ignored, the investor cannot lose money on this position. If the stock sells below $35 per share, all options will expire worthless. If the stock sells between $35 and $45 per share, the gain on the $35 option owned will exceed any loss on the two $40 striking price options sold. Above $45 per share, any loss on the two $40 striking price options is exactly offset by the combined gains on the long $35 and $45 striking price options. At a stock price of $40 per share on the date of expiration, the butterfly spreader will have a handsome five-point profit, and, commissions aside, at no price will a loss be experienced.

The problem with this seemingly ideal strategy is that the trade simply cannot be executed on the terms suggested in Figure 4-27. While some closing option price relationships published in the newspaper may suggest that a riskless butterfly is possible, the investor who asks his broker to execute such a trade will be disappointed. Unless the investor or the broker can *leg* into the position (see Glossary), the profit-loss line is likely to be lower than it appears in the diagram in Figure 4-27. If the profit-loss line is dropped still further by a commission adjustment, the illusive attractiveness of the butterly spread evaporates. The investor establishing and subsequently liquidating a butterfly position is exposed to round-trip transaction costs on three different options. Even with negotiated commissions this is a substantial price to pay. The statement in Table 4-2 that a butterfly spread should never be established is extreme, but the investor who accepts this advice will save himself and his broker enough wasted effort to make up for any possible missed profits.

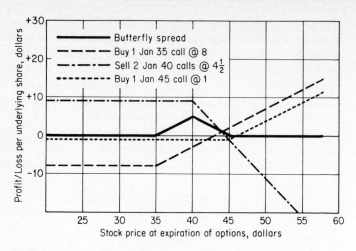

Figure 4-27. A butterfly spread and its components.

The last type of spread listed in Table 4-2 is the unmarginable calendar spread. This is represented in the table by the purchase of an April $45 striking price call and the sale of a July $45 call. This type of spread is used primarily for timing adjustments and for obtaining arbitrage profits from price disparities. It can help an investor plan the realization of gains and losses to minimize taxes and to obtain spreading profits when longer-term options are overpriced relative to near-term options.

The major problem with this spread is that it requires an enormous collateral deposit as margin. Occasionally the relative price of two options will reflect not only their value in terms of the probable behavior of the underlying stock but also the margin requirement faced by the seller of the options. To the extent that a large number of investors attempt to defer gains from the current year to subsequent years through ordinary calendar spreads, there may be a tendency for the longer-term options to be overpriced relative to the near-term options. The investor who has substantial collateral (perhaps in the form of municipal bonds, since a credit rather than a debit balance is created) can take advantage of this temporary valuation discrepancy. Furthermore, the decision to use an unmarginable calendar spread suggests that an investment purpose accompanies any tax motivation behind the investment strategy.

3. Transaction Costs

Perhaps the greatest problem with spreading is the extraordinarily high transaction costs which the investor incurs. The most frequent answer to this criticism of spreading is that with negotiated commissions a broker can reduce the commission impact if a spread makes good economic sense. This answer is fallacious for two reasons. First, more than half of the transaction cost in a typical option trade is not the broker's commission but the trading spread between the bid price and the asked price on the option exchange. When a broker goes to the exchange floor to execute a trade, the option might be quoted $4\frac{3}{4}$–5. This quote indicates that the option can be sold at $475 and purchased at $500. This $25 spread must, in effect, be paid by all market participants when a round-trip transaction is executed. While the commission that the broker adds to, or subtracts from, the transaction price is negotiable, the trading spread will always be there. If an investor wants to buy this option, he will have to pay $5 per underlying share. If he wants to sell it, he will receive only $4.75 per underlying share.

The second problem which the "commissions can be negotiated" argument fails to recognize is that the brokerage firm's floor broker and/or its upstairs trading desk will devote the time and attention to an order that the commission charge justifies. If commissions are cut sharply, a complicated option order may be ignored. Even worse, if strict limits are not imposed by the investor, the order may be executed poorly.

Given all the handicaps he faces, the average investor with no more than his wits and a weekly advisory service to guide him should probably avoid spreading. Unless an investor has some very specific tax problems, there are better ways to make money in the option market. Because spreading can be useful in timing the realization of gains and losses, the topic will come up again in Chapter 5, Section D.

F. SHORT-TERM TRADING OF LISTED OPTIONS

There are two principal groups of active short-term traders of listed option contracts. The first group consists of professional traders and arbitrageurs who attempt to take advantage of temporary disparities between and among the prices of options, related convertible securities, and the underlying common stock. Arbitrage activity can be based on elaborate calculations or on an intuitive feel developed over years of experience. Through their efforts, professional traders and arbitrageurs make the market fairer and more efficient for the second large group of active traders, the general public.

In contrast to the full-time arbitrageur, the nonprofessional trader is more likely to have a stronger opinion on the probable direction of the market or the stock underlying an option than on the suitability of a particular option price–stock price relationship. Individual investors are usually attracted to option trading by the leverage inherent in option contracts or by the relatively low trading cost. If an individual anticipates a sizable near-term move in a particular stock or in the general market, he can control more shares by buying or spreading options than in any other way. Furthermore, transaction costs may be lower in the options market than if a position is taken directly in the stock.

Although the purpose of this section is to provide some suggestions to the active option trader, a few disclaimers are in order. The author has never claimed an ability to predict short-term swings in the overall market or the short-term price behavior of an individual stock. Although many people do claim such ability, and a few even appear to have it, a skeptical attitude toward such claims is probably a healthy one for any investor to adopt. These paragraphs reflect no judgment concerning anyone's claim to trading ability, nor do they give advice on how to acquire it. The intent is simply to point out a few ways in which the active short-term option trader can improve the odds.

Other things being equal, the short-term trader with access to a rational option evaluation model and an understanding of how it works should try to write options that are overpriced and buy options that are underpriced. Unless his conviction is unusually strong, he should try to find another way to participate in any expected move before taking a position that is at variance with the relationship between the fair value of an option and its market price. Though option evaluation can highlight opportunities, most traders will use it to help them avoid unsatisfactory situations or to help them select a particular option contract to trade once they have decided on the direction in which they expect the particular stock or the overall market to move.

One of the worst mistakes a short-term trader can make is to buy an option simply because it is underpriced or to sell it simply because it is overpriced. No option evaluation model predicts the direction of price movement of the underlying stock. It is possible to go a step further than the basic evaluation model, however, and suggest the type of option contract that the active trader should consider. The trader who is writing uncovered calls in anticipation of a decline should usually try to write calls that are in the money. This strategy generally maximizes downside leverage per dollar of margin required and may slightly reduce transaction costs. A short-term trader who is a buyer should generally select calls which are slightly out of the money and which have a short remaining life. The premiums on these calls will be small, and the potential is excellent for a large percentage gain if the trader's expectations for the underlying stock are correct. Similar rules apply to the short-term trader using puts as part of his investment strategy.

If option evaluation indicates that a particular sector of the option market is temporarily overpriced or underpriced, the trader might find it possible to concentrate activity in that sector. Relevant sectors might include long-term options versus short-term options, options deep in the money versus options out of the money, or options on volatile stocks versus options on conservative stocks. The trader using option evaluation to concentrate activity in particular sectors of the market will usually find that most disparities have a tendency to disappear over time. If they disappear while he has a position, he will obtain an arbitrage profit in addition to any other profit he achieves.

With the possible exception of a particularly attractive listed option spread, the short-term trader should avoid complex hedging strategies because they increase costs. The favorable margin treatment accorded a spread can increase downside leverage if the trader expects a substantial and rapid decline in the stock price. However, the cost of an unsuccessful spread should be weighed against the strength of the trader's conviction. To put the cost in perspective, round-trip commissions on an unsuccessful spread can *easily* exceed the initial margin posted.

Finally, more than any other participant in the option market, the short-term trader needs to watch his portfolio risk exposure. The best technique for doing this is to convert each option position into stock equivalents as described in Sections B and D of this chapter. If a position appears too large on the basis of the translation into stock equivalents, it is too large a commitment on any basis, even if the dollar value of the option position seems reasonable. Every set of guidelines for traders ever published contains an admonition to the trader to be fully aware of the risks he is taking and to make certain that they are consistent with his resources. In the option market the only meaningful way to make this kind of calculation is to translate option positions into stock equivalents.

These suggestions may or may not appeal to the short-term trader who has strong convictions. However, if one's convictions are less than overwhelming, these ideas should be of help.

5 TAX TREATMENT OF OPTION TRANSACTIONS

This chapter begins with a discussion of the tax treatment of options from the respective viewpoints of the option buyer and the option writer; then it proceeds to a discussion of special tax problems for entities other than individual investors. These general discussions are followed by a section highlighting some specific investment opportunities which are based in part on the tax treatment accorded option transactions. The final section discusses tax considerations affecting the liquidity of listed option markets.

A. TAX TREATMENT OF OPTIONS FROM THE VIEWPOINT OF THE OPTION BUYER

Table 5-1 permits the option buyer to evaluate the tax impact of the purchase of an option under virtually any circumstances. To use this table, the investor need only examine the column labeled *Description of Transaction* and choose the caption which describes the particular case. More complicated transactions than those described in the table occur frequently in option trading. These complex transactions can usually be broken down into simple segments, and the tax treatment of each segment may be determined by an examination of the table.

An individual investor who uses the table carefully and follows the procedures described below to avoid "wash sales" will have few tax problems with options. However, the table is not meant to serve as a substitute for a qualified tax adviser or an annotated copy of the Internal Revenue Code. Any investor who engages in more than an occasional option transaction should consult a professional tax adviser and be familiar with Sections 1091, 1233, and 1234 of the Internal Revenue Code and related regulations and rulings. A tax adviser should also be consulted to be certain that the treatment suggested here is applicable to a particular taxpaying entity and that more recent legislation, regulations, and rulings are not pertinent.

Several features of Table 5-1 require more detailed explanation than that provided on the table itself:

1. The designations *short-term* and *long-term*, which are used extensively in the tables refer to periods of less than 12 months and 1 day and of 12 months and 1 day or longer, respectively. A distressing number of taxpayers neglect to wait the extra day necessary to secure long-term capital gains treatment for their profits. As a result of the extension of the long-term capital gains holding period by the Tax Reform Act of 1976, an investor cannot presently obtain a long-term capital gain through the purchase of an exchange-listed option. Because the option exchanges will probably recognize the desirability of adding option contracts with an original life of more than 1 year, the table covers these long-term options.

2. The table was constructed from the point of view of an individual taxpayer who is not a dealer in securities. Under some circumstances a corporation, a member of a partnership, or some other entity will receive different tax treatment. Section C discusses some of these different tax treatments.

3. A relatively minor caveat is that any sale of an option contract to register a loss must be made to an unrelated person. The sale of a worthless option to an unrelated buyer for a nominal amount is a perfectly acceptable way to keep a short-term loss from going long-term. If the buyer of an option happens to be the investor's mother,

Table 5-1. Tax Treatment from Option Buyer's Viewpoint

Description of Transaction	Tax Treatment of Option Premiums			Effect on Common Stock Holding If Any	Comments (Also See Text)
	Holding Period of Option	Nature of Gain or Loss	Timing of Recognition of Gain or Loss		
I. Buy put					
A. Having owned underlying stock less than 12 months and 1 day					
1. Sell put	Short-term	Short-term capital gain or loss	Date of sale of option	Holding period of stock is eliminated for purposes of long-term gains by purchase of put. Any gain on stock is long-term 12 months and 1 day after put is sold. Any loss on stock is long-term 12 months and 1 day after stock was purchased.	This is a change from an earlier IRS position that if a put was sold (as opposed to exercise or expiration), the short sale rule did not apply
	Long-term	Long-term capital gain or loss			
2. Exercise put	Immaterial	Cost of put is deducted from proceeds of sale of stock	Date of exercise	Any gain on common stock is short-term. Any loss will be long-term if the date of exercise is more than 12 months and 1 day after purchase of the stock.	
3. Let put expire	Short-term Long-term	Short-term capital loss Long-term capital loss	Date of expiration	Holding period of stock for purposes of determining long-term gain begins on date of expiration of put. For purposes of determining loss, holding period begins on day stock was purchased.	

Table 5-1. Tax Treatment from Option Buyer's Viewpoint (Continued)

Description of Transaction	Tax Treatment of Option Premiums			Effect on Common Stock Holding If Any	Comments (Also See Text)
	Holding Period of Option	Nature of Gain or Loss	Timing of Recognition of Gain or Loss		
B. Then buy underlying stock one or more days later					
1. Sell put	Short-term	Short-term capital gain or loss	Date of sale of option	If stock is sold for a gain, holding period starts on day option is sold. If stock sold at loss, holding period starts on day stock was purchased	
	Long-term	Long-term capital gain or loss			
2. Exercise put	Immaterial	Cost of put is deducted from proceeds of sale of stock	Date of exercise	Gain on common stock is short-term after deducting cost of put from proceeds. Loss will be long-term if stock held more than 12 months and 1 day.	
3. Let put expire	Short-term	Short-term capital loss	Date of expiration	For purposes of determining taxation of gain, holding period of stock begins on day put expires. If a loss, holding period begins on day stock was purchased.	
	Long-term	Long-term capital loss			
C. Buy underlying stock on same day and identify put as intended to be used with this stock position					
1. Sell put	Short-term	Short-term capital gain or loss	Date of sale of option	If stock is sold for a gain, holding period starts on day option is sold. If stock sold at loss, holding period starts on day stock was purchased	
	Long-term	Long-term capital gain or loss			
2. Exercise put	Same as stock	Cost of put is deducted from proceeds of sale of stock	Date of exercise	Loss is short- or long-term depending on holding period from date of purchase.	

Transaction					
3. Let put expire	Same as stock	Add cost of put to basis of stock	Date of sale of stock	Gain or loss on sale of stock is short- or long-term depending on holding period.	Holding period of stock starts on day stock and put are purchased. Note recognition of put loss is deferred until stock is sold.
D. Do not own related stock during life of put					
1. Sell put	Short-term	Short-term capital gain or loss	Date of sale of option		
	Long-term	Long-term capital gain or loss			
2. Let put expire	Short-term	Short-term capital gain or loss	Date of expiration		
	Long-term	Long-term capital gain or loss			
II. Buy call					
A. Sell call	Short-term	Short-term capital gain or loss	Date of sale of option	Purchase of call can cause wash sale.	Short sale of stock does not affect holding period of call. Long-term loss on call can be avoided by exercising call and selling stock even if call has been owned more than 12 months and 1 day.
B. Exercise call	Immaterial	Cost of call added to purchase cost to determine basis of stock	Date of sale of stock	Purchase of call can cause wash sale. Holding period of stock starts on day call is exercised.	Note that recognition of gain or loss on call is deferred until stock is sold.
C. Let call expire	Short-term	Short-term capital loss	Date of expiration	Purchase of call can cause wash sale.	
	Long-term	Long-term capital loss			
III. Buy straddle or other combination option	Same as separate put and call	Same as separate put and call		Same as separate put and call.	
IV. Adjustment of striking price or number of shares for dividends or other capital changes					On conventional options cost of straddle is allocated 55% to call and 45% to put unless there is a substantial reason to allocate in another way. No effect on income, gain or loss, or tax basis.

however, the Internal Revenue Service will not allow recognition of the loss.

4. To the extent that an option transaction changes the tax basis or holding period of the underlying stock owned by an investor, the change applies only to the number of shares represented by the option. For example, if the investor buys 1,000 shares of a stock and, within 12 months, buys five puts, the holding period is interrupted on only 500 shares of stock.

5. The most frustrating feature of the tax code for many investors is Section 1091, which sets down the wash sale rule. This rule provides that if an investor acquires (a) substantially identical securities or (b) an option permitting the acquisition of substantially identical securities within a 61-day period beginning 30 days before the sale of securities and ending 30 days after the sale, no deduction for any loss realized on that sale is permitted.

In simpler language, the purpose of the wash sale rule is to prevent the investor from selling a security and repurchasing it almost simultaneously, realizing a short-term loss and reducing the tax basis for possible long-term capital gains treatment of any future profit. The investor does not lose the deductibility of the wash sale loss forever. The loss is added to the investor's basis for the substantially identical assets or options acquired during the 61-day period. The holding period of the original assets is added to the holding period of the assets acquired during the wash sale period, making fast action imperative to avoid letting any short-term loss go long-term.

The investor will avoid trouble with the wash sale rule by following several rather straightforward rules:

1. Never purchase a common stock, convertible bond, convertible preferred stock, warrant, or option on the securities of any company if one has realized a loss on the sale of equity securities of that company within the past 31 days.

2. Never purchase the stock, an option on the stock, or convertible securities of a company within about 35 days of the time a position one already holds in the securities of that company will go long-term for capital gains tax purposes. This policy will permit the investor to realize a short-term loss on the position about to go long-term, if that becomes necessary, without closing out the newly purchased position.

These simple rules are slightly more restrictive than the tax code requires with respect to losses realized on the sale of some convertible securities, but it is probably best to err on the side of caution. Since it is impossible to reflect all the nuances of the rule in this brief chapter, the reader is referred to the Internal Revenue Code and Regulations. As the reader will note from Table 5-2, on the wash sale rule, *any loss realized from the sale or repurchase of an option is never a wash sale loss under current law.* This is a distinct advantage in complex option transactions, but the investor should be alert to possible changes in this situation.

Table 5-2. Wash Sale Reference Table

Way in Which Loss Is Realized / Possible Contaminating Transaction within 61-Day Wash Sale Period	Buy Option (Opening or Closing Purchase Transaction)	Write Option (Opening or Closing Sale Transaction)	Buy Common Stock or Convertible Security	Sell Common Stock or Convertible Security
Sell stock	WS	OK	WS	OK
Sell convertible bond	U	OK	U	OK
Sell convertible preferred stock	U	OK	U	OK
Sell warrant	U	OK	U	OK
Cover short sale of stock	OK	OK	OK	OK
Cover short sale of convertible bond	OK	OK	OK	OK
Cover short sale of convertible preferred stock	OK	OK	OK	OK
Cover short sale of warrant	OK	OK	OK	OK
Closing purchase transaction on option	OK	OK	OK	OK
Closing sale transaction on option	OK	OK	OK	OK

NOTE: A husband and wife or a taxpayer and his closely held corporation are ordinarily considered single tax units in determining the applicability of the wash sale rule.

KEY: WS Wash sale, loss not deductible
U Uncertain, study regulations carefully or play it safe and avoid the transaction
OK No risk of wash sale under present law

Probably the best way to maintain an investment position in a specific underlying stock without running afoul of the wash sale rule is to sell the stock and simultaneously sell one or more puts to obtain a roughly equivalent bullish exposure to the stock. In this manner, a loss can be realized for tax purposes, the stock position will be effectively maintained, and problems with the wash sale rule will be avoided.

In most cases the puts sold should be in the money, but not so far in the money that exercise is likely before the necessary 31-day nonownership period has elapsed. If the stock pays a significant dividend, selling an in-the-money put about 35 days before the ex-dividend date is an ideal strategy.

There is little question that selling puts to avoid conflict with the wash sale rule will work under the present tax code. Nonetheless, investors should be alert to possible changes in the code, as this is a rather obvious way around the wash sale rule's intended restrictions on maintaining a position while realizing short-term losses.

If the advantageous tax treatment of long-term capital gains is ever eliminated, the wash sale rule may become moot except in timing the realization of losses. In Table 5-1 and in the text, it has been assumed that long-term capital gains treatment will continue to be permitted. However, some brief comments on the likely effect of various "reform" proposals on the tax treatment and investment characteristics of option positions appear in order.

If long-term capital gains cease to exist, many of the tax-oriented strategies outlined in subsequent sections will no longer be of interest. Others may be of greater interest than they are today (e.g., the technique of transferring a gain from the current year to a subsequent tax year).

High-tax-bracket investors often object that they do not benefit materially from additional short-term gains which they might realize from option transactions. As we will see in Section D of this chapter, an inability to obtain long-term gains on the option transactions themselves is probably less of a problem than most of these investors realize. Nonetheless, it is probably safe to assume that elimination of long-term capital gains tax treatment will markedly expand option trading activity, as investors who previously avoided options begin to enter the option market.

B. TAX TREATMENT OF OPTIONS FROM THE VIEWPOINT OF THE OPTION WRITER

Table 5-3, which outlines the tax treatment of options from the viewpoint of the option writer, is similar in format to Table 5-1, which shows tax treatment of option purchases. The warnings, explanations, and definitions which are offered in connection with the option buyer's tax table also apply to the writer's table.

Two topics which were discussed extensively in the first edition of *The Stock Options Manual* were the use of option writing to convert ordinary income into a long-term capital gain and the use of straddles to generate a combination of short-term capital gains and ordinary losses. Both of these aspects of the tax treatment of options were changed by the Tax Reform Act of 1976.

Virtually all the committee discussions and most of the staff memorandums prepared in conjunction with the passage of this legislation focused on the apparent tax advantage to the option writer who sold a call on a runaway stock. The specific criticism leveled at the ordinary gain or loss treatment of option-writing transactions was that an investor who bought stock and sold a call might escape taxation completely. After waiting the required holding period, the investor might be able to sell the stock for a substantial, but lightly taxed, long-term capital gain and repurchase the option to realize a fully deductible ordinary loss. Little attention was paid to the consequences of a market decline: a combination of capital losses (not fully deductible against ordinary income) and ordinary gains which are fully taxable at the time of realization.

Ironically, little public attention was paid to the possible impact of the tax treatment formerly accorded writers of straddles. If listed puts as well as listed calls had been available while the old tax treatment applied, it would have been possible to generate a combination of long-term capital gains and ordinary losses with an extraordinarily high degree of reliability.

Table 5-3. Tax Treatment from Option Writer's Viewpoint

Description of Transaction	Holding Period of Option	Nature of Gain or Loss	Timing of Recognition of Gain or Loss	Effect on Common Stock Holding If Any	Comments (Also See Text)
I. Write put					
A. Put expires	Immaterial	Short-term capital gain	Date of expiration	No effect	
B. Put exercised	Immaterial	Proceeds from sale of put reduce basis of stock purchased	Date stock acquired through exercise is sold	Reduces basis	Holding period of stock starts on day put is exercised. Note that recognition of tax effect of premium is deferred until stock is sold.
C. Put repurchased	Immaterial	Short-term capital gain or loss	Date of repurchase	No effect	
II. Write call					
A. Call expires	Immaterial	Short-term capital gain	Date of expiration	No effect if shareholder is an individual	
B. Call exercised	Immaterial	Call premiums added to proceeds of sale of stock; character of gain or loss on stock determines nature of total gain	Date of exercise if stock delivered long; date of covering purchase if stock delivered short	No effect except on lot of stock delivered against exercise	Holding period of stock extends from purchase date to exercise date if stock is delivered long.
C. Call repurchased	Immaterial	Short-term capital gain or loss	Date of repurchase	Might create wash sale in rare instances	
III. Write straddle or other combination		Same as separate put and call		Same as separate put and call	Special treatment of straddles was eliminated by the Tax Reform Act of 1976.
IV. Adjustment of striking price or number of shares for dividends, splits, or other capital changes					No effect on income, gain or loss, or tax basis.

136

Conversations with Representative Mikva, the sponsor of the option portion of this tax legislation, and with his staff and the staff of the House Ways and Means Committee suggest that they were aware of the potential for integrating the old straddle rule, ordinary income treatment of writing transactions, and long-term gains on option purchases. If the law had not been changed in late 1976, the option exchanges would have become the biggest shelter in the history of the income tax.

As a result of the tax changes, most individual taxpayers will find tax considerations in the sale and subsequent repurchase of put and call positions to be very straightforward. Any gain or loss is a short-term gain or loss, and the sale of an option has no effect on an individual's holding period or on the tax treatment of the underlying stock as long as exercise does not occur. Various corporate and other institutional investors must be concerned with some unique tax characteristics of option writing; their problems will be explored in the next section.

C. SPECIAL TAX PROBLEMS

A general option text is not the place for an exhaustive discussion of the intricacies of the tax code as they apply to special groups of taxpayers. A brief review of the major tax considerations faced by these specialized investors is appropriate, however, if for no other reason than to raise red flags for investors who might be considering an option strategy which would bring them into conflict with the tax code. This brief summary is based, in part, on the CBOE booklet, *Tax Considerations in Using CBOE Options*, written by Donald M. Tannenbaum of Oppenheim, Appel, Dixon & Co.

1. Pension and Profit-Sharing Plans

An amendment to Section 512 of the Internal Revenue Code, passed in 1976, eliminated any uncertainty as to the effect of selling options on the tax status of any tax-exempt organization. As a consequence, there are no material tax considerations for pension and profit-sharing plans desiring to engage in option transactions. There can, however, be penalty assessments under the Employee Retirement Income Security Act of 1974 against the company sponsoring the pension or profit-sharing plan. The discussion of prudence in Chapter 6, Section C, will touch on some steps that should be taken to avoid penalties and lawsuits by plan beneficiaries.

2. Other Tax-Exempt Organizations

With the possible exception of foundations, there seem to be no tax consequences related to the use of options by any tax-exempt organization. The only problem a foundation might face is related to a provision of Section 4944 of the Internal Revenue Code which indicates that any transaction by a foundation which involves the purchase of put and call options will be examined carefully to determine whether the managers of the foundation's assets were taking undue risk. The statutory test is the extent to which the purchase of options impairs the foundation's ability to fulfill its charitable purpose. As long as a foundation's total investment program meets very general standards of prudence, this tax provision should present no problems. The foundation's trustees may, however, want to take extra precautions and establish particularly careful records of the reasoning behind their investment decisions in order to avoid any possibility of criticism.

Endowments, foundations, and certain other tax-exempt investors have a unique advantage over pension funds and most other institutional investors: They can be on either side of the option contract. If options are overpriced, they can be sellers. If options are underpriced, they can be buyers. They can use puts as well as calls. The importance of this flexibility is hard to overrate.

3. Mutual Funds

The most important changes in the tax treatment of option transactions by mutual funds were made not by the 1976 Tax

Reform Act but by a section of the House Ways and Means Committee report on this legislation. In a rather unusual passage, the committee report spells out the intent of Congress on the tax treatment of option premiums received by mutual funds. Prior to 1976 it was extremely difficult for a mutual fund manager to sell options without risking the fund's tax status as a regulated investment company and, consequently, its ability to distribute interest and dividends to shareholders without first paying a tax at the corporate level. While a number of tax-related restrictions on mutual fund portfolio turnover remain in effect, mutual fund option activity is restricted more by the wording of most fund prospectuses than by the tax law. Numerous funds are now authorized by their prospectuses to undertake one or more types of option transactions.

A word of caution about one aspect of the tax treatment of mutual fund option transactions is probably in order. Recently, a number of new option-writing funds have been sold to the public. The prospectuses of these funds refer to tax opinions offered by the fund's legal counsel that 100 percent of any capital gains realized from option writing and distributed to shareholders can be treated as qualified dividends for purposes of the $100 dividend exclusion and, more importantly, for purposes of the 85 percent intercorporate dividend deduction. A large part of the marketing success of these option-writing funds appears to be due to this interpretation of the tax treatment accorded a corporate investor. Securities industry sources indicate that a substantial fraction of the shares of these funds have been sold to corporate buyers.

There is no unequivocal expression of the intent of Congress in enacting the section of the Internal Revenue Code that permits mutual fund shareholders to treat short-term capital gains from security transactions as qualifying dividends. However, a recent IRS private ruling holds that qualified dividend treatment of option premiums distributed by mutual funds will be limited to the 25 percent of gross income permitted for interest and other nondividend income.

4. Nonresidents

The major option tax issue for nonresidents prior to enactment of the 1976 tax legislation was whether it was necessary for a brokerage firm to withhold taxes on profits generated by option-writing transactions. The change to capital gains tax treatment for option-writing profits settled the withholding issue and created an extraordinary investment opportunity for nonresidents. A way in which nonresidents can "own" dividend-paying stocks without being subject to withholding will be outlined in the next section.

5. Corporations

The most important aspects of option taxation for corporate taxpayers center around Section 246 of the Internal Revenue Code and the intercorporate dividend deduction. As indicated in the discussion of puts in Chapter 4, Section 246(c) of the Internal Revenue Code requires that a corporation claiming the 85 percent intercorporate dividend deduction establish a 15-day holding period in any common stock before a put option is purchased or the holder becomes subject to a contractual obligation to sell substantially identical stock. If this holding period is not established, dividends do not qualify for the 85 percent deduction.

The IRS has issued a private ruling that the sale of a listed call does not create a contractual obligation to sell. If this ruling is not changed, it will be relatively simple for a corporation to establish an essentially riskless investment position while obtaining a fully deductible loss on securities transactions (stock and option transactions taken together) combined with an 85 percent deductible intercorporate dividend. Because the statute was written expressly to prevent such maneuvers, this ruling seems subject to change.

6. Partnerships

Until recently, private investment partnerships (hedge funds) located in New York State or New York City risked imposition of an unincorporated business tax on their entire net income if they wrote options. Even the federal change to capital gains treatment of option-writing income did not eliminate this problem. The wording of the New York State and New York City unincorporated business tax laws suggested that an investment partnership might be treated like an operating business if it engaged in anything other than passive investment transactions. There was even some concern that these taxes might be levied on the option-writing profits of individuals living in New York.

Legislation passed early in 1977 clarified the status of option-writing income. Now, option writing will not subject a private partnership or individual located in New York to the threat of the unincorporated business tax.

7. Dealers in Securities

Ordinarily, transactions by securities dealers give rise to ordinary gains or losses because securities are the dealer organization's stock-in-trade. Section 1236 of the Internal Revenue Code permits broker-dealer organizations and individuals acting as broker-dealers to designate a security position as an investment within 30 days of the trade date. The purpose of this rule is to permit full deduction of any trading or market-making losses without denying the broker long-term capital gains treatment on true investment positions.

If a securities firm trades stocks and options actively, it may be possible for it to defer the taxation of income by realizing losses early and deferring gains. Theoretically, the broker-dealer could also improve his chances to obtain a long-term gain by placing a profitable position in the investment account promptly. In reality, a lot can happen in the 11 months between the time a position is designated an investment and the date it goes long-term for capital gains tax purposes.

A number of small brokerage partnerships have been formed in an attempt to exploit the tax treatment accorded securities dealers and to serve as rather unusual tax shelters for high-tax-bracket investors. The general partners of these tax-shelter brokerage firms are usually traders working on the floor of one of the option exchanges. Limited partnership capital is contributed by high-tax-bracket investors looking for tax write-offs. The general partners receive substantial salary income and a share of the profits if the partnership earns an economic (as opposed to an aftertax) profit. The limited partners hope to reduce their current tax bills by deducting large ordinary losses as soon as possible, while deferring any gains indefinitely. Ideally, the partnership would ultimately realize long-term capital gains.

Investors are attracted to these partnerships like the proverbial moth to a flame by the lure of immediate tax deductions and the prospect of long-term capital gains on the horizon. These partnership agreements are structured to reward the general partners in the event of a significant increase in the net worth of the partnership, but the required minimum payments to the general partners, plus very high operating expenses, make the prospect of a pretax profit for the limited partners remote at best. The likelihood of net economic losses and a very high probability of tax litigation make this tax shelter extremely questionable.

8. Personal Holding Companies

Any net premium income received by an option writer was treated as ordinary income before the 1976 tax-law changes. Premiums were included in adjusted ordinary gross income but were excluded from personal holding income in the determination of whether a corporation qualified as a personal holding company. To the extent that a corporation was trying to qualify, option premiums might have created a problem. To the extent that a corporation was trying to avoid personal holding company treatment, option writing constituted an opportunity.

Under the revised tax treatment, net option premiums received are capital gains. Capital gains are excluded from adjusted ordinary gross income and from personal holding company income. As a consequence, no gains from option transactions enter into the determination of personal holding company status.

Treating options as stock equivalents in the manner outlined in Chapter 4, it may be possible to use options to structure a portfolio to achieve or avoid personal holding company status without changing the firm's investment policy. For example, if a corporation is seeking to qualify as a personal holding company and yet the directors are inclined to own low-yielding growth company stocks, most of the assets could be invested in good-quality preferred stocks, and the growth stock positions could be taken via options. On the other hand, if management wants to avoid personal holding company status but leans toward high-yielding basic industry stocks, the corporate portfolio should be invested largely in municipal bonds. The basic industry stock exposure could be obtained in the option market. Section D of this chapter even outlines a way to reduce the long-term interest rate risk of these preferred stock and municipal bond positions.

9. Section 1244 Election and Subchapter S Corporations

If a stockholder wants to treat losses as ordinary rather than capital losses under Section 1244 or to obtain the special advantages of Subchapter S status, there are limits on the types of income the corporation can receive. Income subject to these limitations includes gains from the sale of stock or securities. While the use of options might help an investor defer income from one year to the next to retain Subchapter S qualification, these corporate entities should probably avoid active participation in the options market.

D. SOME TAX OPPORTUNITIES

The notion that the Internal Revenue Code contains major "loopholes" is naïve. To the extent that some forms of investment income seem to be taxed more lightly than others, careful examination usually reveals that *pretax* returns in the tax-favored investments are below average. Nonetheless, there are opportunities to minimize taxes while obtaining desired investment results. This section explores a few of the ways in which options can help various types of investors improve aftertax returns.

The first edition of *The Stock Options Manual* devoted most of its discussion of the tax opportunities created by options to the difference between the tax treatment accorded the seller of an option and the tax treatment of other securities transactions. This focus, combined with the discussion of the special tax treatment of straddles, was the basis of most of the tax-oriented investment opportunities that were attractive at that time. Since the first edition was published, investors have gained more experience with options, tax practitioners have had more time to investigate the possibilities, and the Tax Reform Act of 1976 has changed the ground rules. The tax-saving opportunities for active users of options have expanded and grown more complex.

This section not only reviews a few of the basic tax strategies that have applied since the Tax Reform Act of 1976 but also discusses some more sophisticated tax-oriented strategies. In addition, at least a partial answer is provided to the following objection, which is expressed by many high-tax-bracket investors: Since the long-term capital gains holding period has been extended to 12 months and 1 day, it is no longer possible to obtain a long-term capital gain on an option transaction. As we will see, options can be extraordinarily useful to the high-tax-bracket investor in modifying the risk structure of a portfolio, assisting in the accumulation of long-term capital gains on other security positions, and minimizing tax payments.

1. Hedging a Preferred Stock or Municipal Bond Portfolio against Changes in Long-Term Interest Rates

Readers may note that this subsection title is one of the few places in this book where they have seen or will see the word "hedging." The term has been avoided largely because it is often used too loosely. A true hedge consists of a long position and a short position designed to offset at least one type of risk. The concept of hedging in the option market is freely applied to positions as distinct as covered call writing, spreading, or even the purchase of a call to "hedge" the risk of a short sale.

In this book the term "hedging" is used in the same sense in which it is used in the commodities markets and in common parlance. The purpose of hedging is *to reduce the risk of loss from an investment position by making approximately offsetting transactions that will largely eliminate one or more types of risk*. The specific type of hedging covered in this subsection is hedging against the risk of changes in long-term interest rates. The investment characteristics of options can be combined with the tax treatment that certain investors are accorded on income from common and preferred stocks and municipal bonds. The aftertax investment results of these hedged positions can be extraordinary relative to the small risks involved.

Because historic price data on preferred stocks are readily available in usable form, the focus of the material which follows will be primarily on hedging a preferred stock portfolio against changes in long-term interest rates. The basic principles developed here also apply to hedging a long-term municipal bond portfolio or even a portfolio of high-dividend utility common stocks against interest rate fluctuations.

Most investors who can benefit from them are aware of the tax advantages of municipal bonds. Corporate treasurers are familiar with the 85 percent dividend-received deduction available on most preferred and common stocks owned by a corporation. The reason these securities are not more widely used by investors who could benefit from them is that their prices fluctuate, sometimes dramatically, in response to changes in long-term interest rates. A corporate treasurer or a high-tax-bracket individual can be confident that the modest yield available from commercial paper or certificates of deposit will actually be realized. On the other hand, a relatively small increase in long-term interest rates can cause a decline in preferred stock, municipal bond, or utility common stock prices that will wipe out the entire return.

After exploring the magnitude of the aftertax yield advantage of preferred stock to a corporate taxpayer (the advantage of municipal bonds to a high-tax-bracket individual investor is similar), the following paragraphs will demonstrate how the exposure of a preferred stock portfolio to fluctuations in interest rates can be reduced to an acceptable level and will show that the best available risk-reduction technique appears to be hedging with listed options on interest-sensitive common stocks. It will also be demonstrated that hedging against fluctuations in long-term interest rates with GNMA futures contracts is more expensive and less predictable than using options. Skeptics are urged to compare the price action of a preferred stock portfolio with that of a "risk equivalent" common stock portfolio over a 5-year period to see how the hedge might have operated. Transaction cost data and a rough break-even analysis are also provided.

a. *The Attraction of Preferred Stock to a Corporate Investor.* To illustrate the aftertax superiority of preferred stocks for the corporate investor, *if risk to principal is ignored,* Table 5-4 compares yields typical of late 1976.

For the corporate taxpayer, aftertax returns from preferred stocks are higher than net yields on any of the other securities listed in the table, even higher than interest payments on

Table 5-4. Comparative Pretax and Aftertax Yields to a Corporate Investor (December 1976 typical yields)

	Pretax Yield, %	Net Aftertax Yield, %*	Aftertax Advantage of Preferred over Alternative Investment, %
AA utility preferred stock	8.25	7.66	—
Dow-Jones municipal index†	6.00	6.00	1.66
AA utility bonds	8.25	4.29	3.37
4-year Treasury notes	5.75	2.99	4.67
3-month Treasury bills	4.35	2.26	5.40
90-day commercial paper	4.50	2.34	5.32
1-year municipal project notes	2.50	2.50	5.16

* Assumes a basic tax rate of 48% and applies the 85% dividend-received deduction on preferred stock dividends.

† Based on 20-year bonds of 20 issuers.

completely tax-free municipal bonds. The contrast with net yields on corporate bonds, short-term municipal notes, commercial paper, or Treasury bills is even more dramatic.

Particularly significant is the more than 5 percent aftertax current yield advantage of preferred stocks over commercial paper. Corporate financial officers have been known to perform incredible gymnastics to improve the *pretax* return of a commerical paper portfolio by only 10 basis points. Preferred stocks offer the opportunity to improve the *aftertax* return by hundreds of basis points if the problem of capital risk can be solved.

b. *The Problem of Capital Risk.* The primary disadvantage of preferred stocks as a repository for corporate cash is that preferred stock prices fluctuate. The benefits of a high current yield may be largely or entirely eliminated by an increase in long-term interest rates. Because of this risk and because preferred stock transaction costs (commissions plus the trading spread) are higher than the transaction costs of short-term money market instruments, many corporate treasurers have been reluctant to use preferred stocks in cash management.

An increase of 50 to 100 basis points in long-term interest rates could produce a capital loss in a preferred stock portfolio that would take several years of higher aftertax yields to make up. Furthermore, the transaction costs associated with preferred stock trading make the break-even holding period for a preferred stock position versus a commercial paper position at least 3 to 4 months, even if long-term interest rates do not change.

c. *Hedging against Interest Rate Fluctuations.* A few financial officers have experimented with the use of Treasury bond and GNMA futures contracts to hedge interest rate risks. Others are looking forward to the introduction of options on long-term fixed income securities. While options on long-term bonds will be an important preferred stock hedging tool, *there is a way, available now, to hedge the long-term interest rate risk of a preferred stock portfolio which is more effective than GNMA futures contracts* and which may prove superior to hedging with options on long-term bonds. With this technique, interest rate risk can be reduced at a lower net cost than through GNMA futures and, perhaps, at a lower net cost than will be possible through options on long-term debt securities. The technique uses *put and call options on interest-sensitive common stocks* to offset the preferred stock price risks associated with interest rate fluctuations.

As a practical matter, no hedging technique can completely eliminate all the interest rate risks of a preferred stock position. Furthermore, factors other than interest rates affect the price of a preferred stock or of an interest-sensitive common stock. An actual or anticipated change by a rating service, adverse or favorable publicity about a utility's proposed nuclear power plant, rejection or approval of a utility rate increase application, and a change in the fundamental industry position of a nonutility company can all affect preferred and common stock prices—in ways that often cannot be adequately anticipated or hedged. Fortunately, a wide variety of studies indicate that risk factors specific to individual companies tend to cancel out in a diversified portfolio. When specific company risks have been largely diversified away, interest rate trends remain as the principal determinant of the prices of both preferred stocks and selected interest-sensitive common stocks.

d. *How Preferred Stocks Are Hedged with Options on Interest-Sensitive Common Stocks.* Diversification is appropriate in a preferred stock portfolio and in the selection of underlying interest-sensitive common stocks for the offsetting option hedge position. However, for the sake of simplicity in illustrating how the option hedging technique works, an example based on one preferred stock and one interest-sensitive common stock will be used.

Assume that an investor takes a $1-million position in Public Service Electric and Gas $7.80 preferred. Assume further that, after analyzing the relative sensitivity to changes in long-term interest rates of the PSE&G preferred and First Charter Financial common stock, the investor concludes that the price of FCF common will fluctuate in response to interest rate changes approximately four times as much as the PSE&G preferred. This relationship implies that the investor could sell short approximately $250,000 worth of FCF common stock to counteract the interest rate risk of the $1-million preferred stock position.

For a variety of reasons, actually selling FCF common stock short is less desirable than establishing a position that is the *risk equivalent* of a short sale. This risk equivalent position is established *in the options market*. It is possible to sell enough calls or buy enough puts on FCF to create an option position that will change in market value by about the same dollar amount as a $250,000 short position in the stock. Understanding this point is critical to understanding how the hedge with options on interest-sensitive common stocks works.

The desirability of translating option positions into stock equivalents to analyze the degree of market risk exposure associated with a position has been noted elsewhere. In the present example, if FCF is selling at $17.25 a share, a 4-month call option with a $15 striking price might behave like the equivalent of approximately 80 shares of the underlying stock, whereas a comparable put with a $15 striking price might behave like the equivalent of 20 shares of the underlying stock. In other words, if the stock price changes by $1, the call price will change by about $0.80, and the put price by $0.20. If a position is taken in FCF options to offset the interest rate risk of a $1-million investment in PSE&G preferred, approximately 181 calls would have to be sold or 724 puts purchased, to establish the equivalent of a $250,000 short position in FCF stock. The following calculations illustrate how the number of calls and puts is computed.

Long position   A $1-million investment in PSE&G $7.80 preferred.

Offsetting hedge   The $250,000 FCF common stock equivalent is 14,493 shares with the stock at $17.25.

Because it will change in price by about $0.80 for each $1 change in the stock price, each FCF 4-month call with a $15 striking price is equivalent in risk to about 80 shares of FCF common stock.

Therefore, the corporation can sell 181 FCF calls instead of selling the stock short; 181 calls × 80 shares equivalent = 14,480 shares equivalent.

Because each FCF put with a $15 striking price will change

in price by about $0.20 for each $1 change in the stock price, each put is equivalent in risk to about 20 shares of common stock.

Therefore, the corporation can buy 724 FCF puts instead of selling the stock short; 724 puts × 20 shares equivalent = 14,480 shares equivalent.

Before we can examine the costs of an option hedging program when calls are the only listed options available or explore the potential net cost reduction when the hedger can choose between selling calls and buying puts, we must determine how well price changes in selected interest-sensitive common stocks correlate with preferred stock price changes.

e. *Price Movements of Preferred Stocks and Interest-Sensitive Common Stocks.* Intuitively, most securities market participants would expect the prices of interest-sensitive common stocks and the prices of preferred stocks to rise when interest rates fall and to fall when interest rates rise. Furthermore, the common stocks might be expected to show greater percentage changes in price because their dividends are lower and their earnings streams as well as their price earnings and dividend multiples are sensitive to interest rate changes. For most of the common stocks usually regarded as interest-sensitive these expectations are borne out, but there are some important exceptions. The first step in the analysis is to test correlations and weed out exceptions.

No readily available index of preferred stock prices was found, and so one was devised based on the monthly closing prices of six preferred stocks listed on the New York Stock Exchange. This index became a proxy for the price behavior of a hypothetical preferred stock portfolio.

Selecting appropriate interest-sensitive common stocks was more complicated. Not all the stocks generally considered interest-sensitive react to interest rate changes in the same manner. The ideal hedging stock should respond to interest rates by moving in the same direction as preferred stocks and by a predictable relative magnitude. As a first step in identifying such common stocks, all the common stocks with exchange-traded call options that seemed to be likely candi-

Table 5-5. A Tentative List of Interest-Sensitive Stocks with Listed Options

Aetna Life and Casualty	Georgia Pacific
American Electric Power	Great Western Financial
American Telephone and Telegraph	Household Finance
BankAmerica	INA
Boise Cascade	Jim Walter
Chase Manhattan	Loews
Citicorp	Louisiana Pacific
Commonwealth Edison	Tiger International
Consolidated Edison	Transamerica
Continental Telephone	Travelers
El Paso Natural Gas	Virginia Electric
Federal National Mortgage Association	Western Union
First Charter Financial	Weyerhaeuser
General Telephone and Electronics	

dates were listed. The resulting list of 27 stocks is shown in Table 5-5.

To test the degree of interest rate sensitivity for each stock, the correlation coefficient of the common stock price with the preferred stock index for calendar year 1976 was calculated. Correlation coefficients with the preferred stock index were also run for the S&P 500 and the Dow-Jones industrials. The results of a few of these tests are shown in Table 5-6.

In general, the stocks thought to be "interest-sensitive" were more closely correlated with the preferred index than

Table 5-6. Correlation Coefficients: Prices of Selected Stock and Averages vs. Preferred Stock Index

	Correlation Coefficient with Preferred Index
Aetna Life and Casualty	.808
American Telephone and Telegraph	.935
BankAmerica	.454
First Charter Financial	.836
Great Western Financial	.933
INA	.856
Loews	.745
S&P 500	.723
Dow-Jones industrial	.450

with the broad common stock averages. With conspicuous exceptions, the correlation coefficients with the preferred index were high. The median correlation coefficient with the preferred stock index for the 27 stocks listed in Table 5-5 was .779. The coefficients ranged from a low of − .511 to a high of .977. Similar correlation coefficients were obtained when the price movements of long-term bonds and utility common stocks were compared with "interest-sensitive" common stock price movements.

Obviously, a few of these 27 stocks react to changes in long-term interest rates much differently from the way preferred stocks react. To obtain the appropriate behavior from the common stock equivalent hedge position, the 12 stocks with correlation coefficients in excess of .800 were selected for further evaluation. Two of the 12 were dropped from consideration because trading volume in their options has been too light to permit an effective and continuous hedging program. The other 10 stocks with appropriate price behavior have active options markets.

Next, an interest-sensitive common stock index based on the remaining 10 common stocks was prepared. Each stock's contribution to the index was weighted to reflect the relative magnitude of its response to interest rate fluctuations. If one stock changed in price by twice as large a percentage as the preferred stock index and another changed by four times as large a percentage, the dollar weighting of the first stock would be twice the dollar weighting of the second.

These two indexes made it possible to determine what actual results might have been achieved by hedging a preferred stock portfolio over an extended period with option positions selected to be the risk equivalent of the common stock index portfolio. Options were not introduced into this historic test because it would have been too easy to "prove" anything one wanted to demonstrate by selecting options after one knew how the stock price had behaved. If options were used without such foreknowledge, the results should closely parallel those for the interest-sensitive common stock index.

Table 5-7 shows the changes in value of a preferred stock index portfolio and the interest-sensitive common stock index

Table 5-7. Changes in Value of Preferred Stock Portfolio and Interest-Sensitive Common Stock Hedging Portfolio, Expressed as Percentage Change in Preferred Portfolio or Preferred Equivalent Hedge Position; Portfolios Rebalanced Quarterly

		Preferred Stock Portfolio, %	Interest-Sensitive Common Stock Hedge Position, %*	Quarterly Difference, %	Cumulative Difference from 12/29/72, %
1973	Q1	(2.97)	(6.90)	3.93	3.93
	2	(1.78)	(2.50)	0.72	4.65
	3	2.25	4.64	(2.39)	2.26
	4	(6.54)	(6.60)	0.06	2.32
1974	Q1	(4.45)	(1.12)	(3.33)	(1.01)
	2	(5.79)	(10.56)	4.77	3.76
	3	(7.53)	(5.89)	(1.64)	2.12
	4	1.79	5.42	(3.63)	(1.51)
1975	Q1	9.76	8.49	1.27	(0.24)
	2	(0.61)	5.68	(6.29)	(6.53)
	3	(4.89)	(5.67)	0.78	(5.75)
	4	5.24	4.14	1.10	(4.65)
1976	Q1	4.47	6.02	(1.55)	(6.20)
	2	(1.68)	(0.81)	(0.87)	(7.07)
	3	4.77	3.67	1.10	(5.97)
	4	3.88	3.86	0.02	(5.95)
1977	Q1	(2.39)	(1.69)	(0.70)	(6.65)
	2	2.86	1.76	1.10	(5.55)
	3	—	(0.16)	.16	(5.39)
	4	(3.34)	(1.14)	(2.20)	(7.59)

* Expressed as a percentage of the equivalent preferred stock portfolio being hedged.

portfolio. The changes are expressed as percentage changes in the preferred portfolio. Because the interest-sensitive common stock prices move over a broader range in response to interest rates than preferred stock prices, the dollar amount of underlying stock in the interest-sensitive common stock hedge position is considerably smaller. If the percentage changes were expressed as a percentage of the value of this portfolio, the results would be distorted.

In examining Table 5-7, several points become clear. First, the change in value of the preferred stock and the common stock hedging portfolios was in the same direction in every quarter except one over the 5-year period of the study. Furthermore, in only two cases was the difference between the changes in the two positions greater than 4 percent of the preferred portfolio in any one quarter. In both of those cases, the quarterly changes in the quarter before and the quarter after the large difference was in the opposite direction of the large difference. Apparently, even if there is a difference in the timing of responses to interest rate fluctuations, the differences seem to cancel out over a reasonable interval.

The cumulative percentage difference from the end of 1972 to the end of 1977 was only 7.59 percent using the quarterly balancing technique. This is amazing, particularly given the unstable interest rate structure which characterized most of the 5-year period. If the common stock correlations had been updated frequently, rather than simply taking correlations for one 12-month interval and applying them to the entire period, an even better correlation might have been attained.

In the final analysis, the cumulative difference of 7.59 percent should be considered a cost of maintaining the hedge. In evaluating the costs of the hedge, it is important to remember that the net yield advantage of preferred stock over commercial paper of more than 500 basis points calculated in Table 5-4 is an *aftertax* advantage. The cumulative deviation between the two positions in Table 5-7 and the transaction cost numbers to be developed later are *pretax* numbers and should be reduced accordingly. In order to be as conservative as possible, tax credits on costs and losses have not been taken into account. The cumulative difference in the behavior of the two portfolios indicated in Table 5-7 is about what one would expect to be due to the shape of the yield curve over the 5-year period examined.

f. *GNMA Futures and Other Hedging Vehicles.* In discussions of this option hedging technique with corporate treasurers, a few of them have mentioned the possibility of hedging preferred stock positions with GNMA futures contracts. This possibility was examined carefully and found to be highly unsatisfactory.

Because trading in GNMA futures did not begin until the fall of 1975, the quantity of historical data available is less than for a hedge using options on common stocks, and the

Table 5-8. Changes in Value of Preferred Stock Portfolio and GNMA Futures Hedge Position; Expressed as Percentage Change in Preferred Portfolio or Preferred Equivalent Hedge Position; Portfolios Rebalanced Quarterly

		Preferred Stock Portfolio	GNMA Futures Hedging Position*	Quarterly Difference	Cumulative Difference from 12/31/75
1976	Q1	4.47	.19	4.28	4.28
	Q2	(1.68)	(4.83)	3.15	7.43
	Q3	4.77	7.44	(2.67)	4.76
	Q4	3.88	11.17	(7.29)	(2.53)
1977	Q1	(2.39)	(10.14)	7.75	5.22
	Q2	2.86	3.73	(.87)	4.35
	Q3	—	(.59)	.59	4.94
	Q4	(3.34)	(5.70)	2.36	7.30

* Expressed as a percentage of the equivalent preferred stock portfolio being hedged.

available data are not encouraging. Using the data for 1976 and 1977, an index of 6-month GNMA futures prices was constructed. Table 5-8 was prepared in a format similar to that used in Table 5-7. In a shorter time span than that traced in Table 5-7, the maximum end-of-a-quarter deviation was 7.75 percent, and the cumulative deviation was 7.30 percent. Fluctuations from quarter to quarter were much larger than those of the interest-sensitive common stock hedging portfolio.

The coefficients of correlation with the preferred stock index for calendar year 1976 of GNMA futures, several bond and stock indexes, and the interest-sensitive common stock index are shown in Table 5-9. Clearly, the prices of GNMA futures

Table 5-9. Selected Correlation Coefficients with the Preferred Stock Index (Calendar Year 1976)

Interest-sensitive common stock index	.962*
Median of 10 individual common stocks in index	.891*
S&P 500	.723
Dow-Jones industrial average	.450
GNMA futures index	.834
Dow-Jones 10 utility bonds	.975
Dow-Jones 10 industrial bonds	.936
Dow-Jones 20 bonds (linked to old index of 40 bonds)	.911

* The higher correlation of the index is probably due to averaging out some noise-level changes in individual stock prices.

are not as well correlated with preferred stock prices as the prices of some other possible hedging vehicles are.

Actually, the GNMA index may even understate the discrepancies between the behavior of a preferred stock portfolio and an offsetting GNMA futures position for at least two reasons. First, calculations for 1976 suggest that an enormous GNMA futures position is needed to offset fluctuations in the preferred stock portfolio. The 1976 record provides much of the data on GNMA futures available. If 1976 is not representative, hedged positions based on that year's data may be extremely unstable and will almost certainly give unanticipated results. Second, a 6-month futures index masks the effect of the "carry" on prices of GNMA futures. *Carry* is a phenomenon related to the shape of the yield curve. If the yield curve is normal (i.e., if long-term rates are higher than short-term rates), prices of GNMA futures will tend to move *up toward the spot price as time passes.* Under some circumstances this effect would be minor, but on the basis of 1976 data, an investor would need to sell almost three times the value of a preferred position in the GNMA futures market to offset the effect of interest rate fluctuations. The loss on the carry from such a position could systematically reduce or even wipe out all the preferred stock tax and yield advantages.

Even apart from these considerations, GNMA futures contracts are inherently inappropriate for preferred stock hedging. GNMA certificates are like annuities in that each year some principal is returned to the investor along with the interest payment. The average maturity of a GNMA certificate is expected to be about 12 years. In contrast, neither preferred nor common stocks have fixed maturities.

The Chicago Board of Trade has recently introduced a futures contract on long-term Treasury bonds and several exchanges hope to begin trading options on long-term bonds. Table 5-9 indicates that the correlation between prices of long-term bonds and prices of preferred stocks has been quite close. Until these new markets are fully developed, the best available hedging vehicles to reduce the interest rate risk of a preferred stock portfolio will be options on interest-sensitive common stocks.

g. *Transaction Costs.* On the basis of typical transaction costs for options and preferred stocks, preferred stock positions hedged against interest rate fluctuations with listed options should provide an average aftertax yield as high as net yields on short-term municipal or commercial paper positions if the cash can be committed for as long as 6 months. If the money will be available for as long as a year, the hedged preferred stock position should be clearly advantageous, even after allowance for probable deviations from a perfect hedge. If both put and call options are available, the break-even holding period for preferred stocks should be reduced by the opportunity to earn arbitrage profits on option positions. If the use of options to hedge the capital risk of preferred stock investments leads to expanded trading activity in preferred issues, the average trading spread may be reduced. Lower preferred stock trading costs would further shorten the break-even holding period relative to competitive short-term debt instruments.

A careful examination of Table 5-10 will help the reader understand how transaction costs affect results and how the transaction economics of hedging the capital risk of a preferred stock portfolio with options compare with those of using GNMA futures contracts for the same purpose.

Section A of Table 5-10 shows the transaction costs that are typically incurred in establishing *and* liquidating a 5,000-share preferred stock position worth $500,000. The key figure is the 1.38 percent round-trip transaction cost expressed as a percentage of the amount invested. When this figure is divided by the 5.32 percent aftertax difference between the preferred stock yield and the commercial paper rate in Table 5-4, the reader will begin to understand how to estimate the break-even holding period for a preferred stock position relative to an alternative short-term investment.

Assuming a typical yield curve relationship between short-term and long-term interest rates, the average difference between *aftertax* preferred yields and *aftertax* commercial paper rates will be 4 to 4.5 percent over the next few years. Using this aftertax yield spread, the 1.38 percent round-trip preferred transaction costs, and the hedging costs calculated

Table 5-10. Transaction Cost Calculations for a Hedged Preferred Stock Portfolio

A. Preferred stock

Value of average preferred stock position		$ 500,000
Estimated trading spread (asked minus bid)	$ 2,500	
Estimated round-trip commissions	4,393	
Total transaction costs	$ 6,893	
As percentage of position	1.38%	

B. Option position

Value of offsetting position in common stock		$ 125,000

	Type of Option Used	
	Calls only	Calls and puts
Value of options used to get stock equivalent	$20,800	$21,337
Estimated trading spread (asked minus bid)	$ 832	$ 853
Estimated round-trip commissions	592	660
Total transaction costs	$ 1,424	$ 1,513
Expected arbitrage profit	—	$'3,201
Net cost (profit) from option position	$ 1,424	($ 1,688)
As percentage of preferred position	0.28%	(0.34%)
Annualized	0.57	(0.69)

C. Hedging with GNMA futures

Value of offsetting position in GNMA certificates		$1,500,000
Estimated trading spread (asked minus bid)	$ 1,406	
Estimated round-trip commissions	1,394	
Total transaction costs	$ 2,800	
Expected effect of "carry"	Unknown	
Net cost of GNMA hedge position	$ 2,800	
As percentage of preferred position	0.56%	
Annualized	1.12%	

Assumptions:
Commissions calculated at 25% discount off posted rates on all transactions.
Trading spreads: preferred stocks 0.5%
 options 4.0%
 GNMA futures 3/32

Options: calls at 10% premium for 6 months, puts at listed option conversion parity; strike equals market; calls equivalent to 60 shares, puts equivalent to 40 shares; average call premium $5; calls sold at fair value when calls only; calls sold at 15% over fair value or puts bought at 15% under fair value when both pute and calls are available.

GNMA futures: no effect of carry (see text), 6-month contract used.

in Section B of Table 5-10, gives a break-even holding period for hedged preferred stock positions of about 6 months. Obviously, converting the transaction costs to an aftertax basis shortens the break-even period. Because this analysis over-simplifies the effect of the yield curve, a break-even period of 6 months is probably about right, even with some tax adjustment on the costs. Since the hedge will not be perfect (see Table 5-7), this technique is probably not suitable for funds that are likely to be needed in less than a year.

Section B of Table 5-10 shows the cost of hedging the long-term interest rate risk of a preferred position with options on interest-sensitive common stocks. The calculation assumes that a $125,000 short equivalent position in the common stock will offset movements in $500,000 worth of the preferred. If the common stock used is less responsive to interest rates than assumed here, more options will be needed, but the average option premium will probably be lower. The numbers used here are probably appropriate for a $5-million portfolio consisting of 10 preferred stock positions and 10 offsetting option positions. If the average preferred position is smaller or larger than $500,000 or if a different degree of diversification in underlying common stocks is selected, the calculation will change accordingly.

The option transaction cost calculations are divided into two columns. The first column is applicable when calls are the only type of option available. The second column shows the effect on net hedging costs of being able to choose between calls and puts on the basis of overvaluation or undervaluation. When calls are the only type of option available, the average call transaction should take place at fair value. Any net arbitrage-type profit or loss from selling overpriced or underpriced calls should be modest. Experience to date suggests that if both puts and calls are available, an average arbitrage profit of 15 percent of the option price should be attainable by buying puts when the options on a stock are underpriced and by selling calls when the options are overpriced. The right-hand column in Section B of Table 5-10 indicates that this arbitrage-type profit may more than cover the transaction costs of the option hedging.

In Section C of Table 5-10 the net cost of hedging the preferred stock position with GNMA futures is calculated. In the example, GNMA futures with a principal value of $1\frac{1}{2} million are used to offset $500,000 worth of preferred stock. The 1976 experience makes this large position seem necessary. Although it is doubtful that the 1976 experience will prove typical, it is clear that prices of GNMA certificates tend to fluctuate less than prices of corporate securities because the former are guaranteed by the federal government and are not true long-term instruments.

The obvious conclusion to be drawn from Sections B and C of Table 5-10 is that the transaction costs of hedging with options on interest-sensitive common stocks are lower than the costs of using GNMA futures.

h. *A Possible Bonus.* Anyone who followed the 1977 developments in the municipal bond market is aware that tax-exempt yields fell sharply—not only absolutely, but also relative to yields on other fixed income securities. There appear to be two basic reasons for the change in relative yields. First, the Carter administration seemed likely to provide enough aid to municipalities to prevent a repetition of New York City's debt management problems. Second, for high-tax-bracket investors, the Tax Reform Act of 1976 markedly increased the attractiveness of municipal bonds as compared with competing investments. Many observers expect the spread between taxable and tax-exempt yields to widen permanently in response to these changes in federal government policy and tax law.

Similarly, a decline in the relative yields available on preferred stocks is possible if enough corporations take advantage of the hedging opportunities discussed here. If preferred yields decline (and prices rise) as a result of widespread hedging, the total return to the corporation that purchases preferred stock early in the hedging cycle could be extraordinary. Under certain circumstances, such a change in relative yields could lead to a profit on both sides of the hedge.

i. *Some Basic Questions.* In discussions with a few corporate financial officers, a number of questions have come up regularly:

1. How large an incremental return should we expect relative to rates on commercial paper?

2. What are the limits (lower and upper) to the size of a hedged preferred stock program?

3. What must we do to get started?

4. Is this technique suitable for investment of surplus cash from a Puerto Rican operation?

Obviously, the net aftertax increment to return relative to commercial paper will vary greatly depending on how the costs of establishing and, ultimately, liquidating the preferred position are allocated and on how effective the hedge is. With preferred transaction costs amortized over 3 years and with average results on hedging transactions, an incremental return of 300 basis points after tax seems a reasonable expectation for a $5-million preferred stock portfolio. This incremental return of 300 basis points translates into an average annual profit improvement of $150,000 on a $5-million program.

Smaller programs would incur larger transaction costs, and much larger programs might face a variety of constraints. Programs involving preferred stock holdings of less than $1 million would probably incur unacceptably high transaction costs or be inadequately diversified. The maximum size of a program is constrained primarily by option trading volume, the level of option premiums, and option position limits. Until puts are available on all option stocks, a $5-million portfolio is probably a realistic limit for a single corporate entity. When puts are available, this limit might rise to between $15 million and $20 million. With options on long-term debt instruments or Treasury bond futures contracts there would be almost no limit to the size of hedging transactions, but there might be reason for concern about the liquidity of a preferred stock portfolio that exceeded $50 million in value.

To activate a hedged preferred stock program, most corporations will need to obtain one or more resolutions from their directors. In a few cases, broad authority already granted to a finance committee might be sufficient.

Corporations may, under certain circumstances, be able to take advantage of the 85 percent dividend received credit on investment of surplus cash from Puerto Rican operations.

2. Deferring Gains or Losses and Accumulating Long-Term Capital Gains

Although the focus of this chapter is on taxes, it is important to recognize that few tax strategies make sense unless the underlying investment position is sound and appropriate. In a 1977 ruling, the IRS held that certain commodity tax spreads do not provide the tax results that investors setting up these spreads had intended. One of the basic principles behind this ruling is that an investment position which is taken solely because of possible or probable tax consequences will not give the tax results that might be obtained if the investment had been structured to provide (1) a degree of risk and (2) an opportunity for profit. These ingredients appear to be the two keys to acceptance of a tax-oriented strategy.

Unlike some of the commodity transactions which the IRS has ruled against, option spreads, covered call writing transactions, and variable option hedge transactions are rarely riskless. Risks can, of course, be controlled within what many investors will consider acceptable limits. With the exception of some complex spreads and in-the-money covered writing strategies, most option positions provide the possibility, if not the probability, of profit. An astute invester entering into a tax-oriented option transaction can almost certainly establish a position which provides an expectation of profit, not just a possible profit. If an investor can validate the expectation that, on the average, a large number of similar transactions will, after all commission costs, generate a net pretax profit, the tax consequences should prove difficult to challenge on the basis that the strategy lacks an investment purpose. It does not matter that in a particular case the optimum aftertax result might differ materially from the optimum pretax result. The important thing is that there be the possibility and, if possible, the probability of a pretax profit. The key to determining the probability of profit is intelligent option evaluation.

Chapter 4, Section E, discussed most of the basic types of option spreading opportunities, including spreads which could affect the timing of gains and losses. The calendar spread and the unmargined calendar spread were particularly noted for their usefulness in timing gains and losses. If timing activity becomes intense, investors may find that calendar spread relationships are distorted because margin requirements encourage the purchase of longer-term and the sale of shorter-term options. An investor with adequate collateral may find extraordinary opportunities in unmargined (or reverse) calendar spreads.

One type of spread not discussed earlier deserves mention in the context of timing strategies. The so-called "box spread" came into vogue during 1977 as a response to the negative IRS ruling on commodity tax spreads. The box spread consists of (1) a put calendar spread combined with a call calendar spread or (2) a vertical bull put spread combined with a vertical bear call spread. In a typical case, the box spread might involve the purchase of April puts and calls and the sale of January puts and calls. All options would have the same striking price. An alternative structure might involve vertical spreads in the same expiration month. Box spreads have all the low-risk advantages and, unfortunately, the principal tax disadvantages of the commodity tax spreads attacked by the IRS.

The box spread has very little risk exposure to movement in the underlying stock and virtually no possibility for material profit after commissions and the bid-asked spread on each of four option contracts. If all four positions were taken simultaneously, it would be impossible to set up a box spread with the expectation of net economic (or pretax) profit.

The problem that box spreaders create for themselves is the same problem that commodity spreaders face. The box spread position is taken solely for tax reasons. It has no economic justification. Fortunately, many strategies are available which combine the desirable characteristics of (1) limited risk, (2) the desired tax-timing effect, and (3) the possibility, even the probability, of a net economic gain.

Instead of setting up a box spread, an investor might combine a calendar call spread on one stock and a calendar put spread on a different stock. One of the spreads could be modestly bullish, and the other modestly bearish, to offset some of the related risk on two stocks of similar companies. If the investor is patient when setting up the positions, each spread might provide the expectation of an arbitrage or valuation profit from a modest discrepancy between the values of the options. There is nothing in the ruling on commodity tax spreads that would lead the IRS to challenge the tax-timing aspect of such transactions.

A sizable calendar spread or unmargined calendar spread need have only modest stock equivalent risk exposure. While the opportunity for gain and the risk of loss may be relatively modest, the important point is that the opportunity and risk must be there. Covered writing of calls, variable option spreads or stock hedges, and long or short straddle positions can all be used to keep the level of risk within acceptable bounds, while providing the opportunity to time the realization of gains and losses.

If one of an investor's major objectives is to defer gains, some care must be taken in timing the realization of gains and losses. Losses on long option positions are recognized for tax purposes on the trade date and gains are recognized on the settlement date. Both gains and losses from option-writing positions are recognized on the settlement date. These rules mean that if the profit is on the writing side of a spread, both sides can be closed out on the last trading day of the fiscal year. There is no need to leave one side of a position hanging to ensure that the investor's timing objectives are achieved. If the profit is on the long side of a spread and the loss is on the writing side, the loss will have to be realized before the last trading day and the gain must not be realized before the last day. While rehedging for one day is possible, leaving one side of the position unprotected for one day will reduce transaction costs and ensure that the investor is immune to charges that the transaction is a riskless sham.

The potential for timing the realization of gains and losses with options suggests how options should be integrated into the portfolio of an investor who is in a high tax bracket and prefers to realize only long-term capital gains. If this investor buys common stocks, at the end of a year, other things being equal, some stock positions will reflect gains, and others will be carried at a loss. The investor will retain the profitable positions until they qualify for long-term capital gains tax treatment. Loss positions will be closed out while they are still short-term. If this stock portfolio represents the investor's only assets, it would make relatively little difference when gains or losses were recognized for tax purposes because there is a strict limitation on the deductibility of capital losses. Any capital losses above a minimal amount would simply be carried forward and applied to long-term capital gains realized when profitable positions were sold.

On the other hand, an investor who sets up a variety of intelligently selected option positions related or unrelated to the stock positions in the portfolio should be able to realize net short-term capital gains on option transactions. To the extent that undervalued options were purchased and/or overvalued options were sold, short-term gains from options should offset short-term losses realized in the stock portfolio. Over the years, an astute investor will almost certainly realize some combination of short-term capital losses and long-term capital gains on a common stock portfolio. To the extent that this investor takes intelligent advantage of option evaluation, it should be possible to obtain net short-term capital gains in the option segment of the portfolio. These net short-term capital gains should augment the portfolio return and need not materially change the portfolio risk exposure. With options, even the investor who wants only net long-term capital gains can enjoy greater risk control, increased flexibility in timing gains and losses, and, consequently, an opportunity to minimize tax payments and to maximize aftertax return on investment.

In the real world, exact offsets of short-term capital gains from option positions against short-term losses on stocks will not be easy to obtain. The important point is that something approaching this ideal state should be possible. Even if an investor is reluctant to pay taxes on long-term capital gains, the almost inevitable occasional short-term loss can offset any short-term gains from an option portfolio.

Although taxpayers will usually prefer to delay the recognition of income for tax purposes and to offset capital gains, it may be desirable on occasion to accelerate the recognition of a short-term capital gain or to offset a short-term capital loss against a long-term gain. If a corporation has an expiring capital loss, it may be best to realize capital gains in the current year and defer losses until the next year. An individual investor who has realized a large long-term capital gain in the current year may want to realize short-term losses now and short-term gains next year. The special tax on preference income, combined with state and local income taxes, can bring this taxpayer's marginal tax rate on the long-term gain close to 50 percent. If the taxpayer is certain to have large investment interest and other deductions available in the following year, using options to "convert" the long-term gain into a short-term gain and defer it to the following year may be very desirable.

3. Investors with Capital Loss Carry-Forwards

Before the 1976 tax changes, the option market was made to order for individuals with capital loss carry-forwards and high tax rates on ordinary income. A variety of spreading strategies and the sale of straddles permitted investors to generate a combination of ordinary losses and capital gains. The ordinary losses were deductible from taxable income and the capital gains were free of tax until the investor used up the accumulated capital loss.

While using options to—in effect—convert ordinary income into capital gains is not as easy as it was under the earlier tax law, it is still possible. To make the conversion, an investor with excess capital losses begins by purchasing shares in a group of optionable stocks on margin. If high-yield stocks are avoided, interest on the debit balance in the margin account can equal or exceed total dividends from the stock position. To offset most of the risks of stock ownership, the investor can sell overpriced calls or buy underpriced puts on the stocks represented in the portfolio. On average, the combination of stock and option positions should provide the investor with net capital gains. The magnitude of any net capital gains will be a function of (1) the risk structure of the portfolio, (2) the correctness of option evaluations, and (3) the level of short-term interest rates.

The principal disadvantages relative to strategies available under the old tax law are that this technique will rarely provide large deductible losses, it requires a sizable capital commitment, and it can be difficult for the average investor to use. Only experienced option managers who are thoroughly familiar with the nuances of option evaluation should be given responsibility for managing a portfolio by using this strategy. In the hands of a skilled manager, the aftertax return from such a portfolio can be favorable and the level of risk relatively modest.

4. Nonresidents and the Withholding Problem

Nonresident alien shareholders are generally subject to a 30 percent withholding tax on interest and dividends from sources in the United States. While the tax is sometimes reduced by a tax treaty between the United States and the individual's country of residence, this withholding tax and the reporting requirements associated with it can be a substantial drawback to investment in U.S. securities.

The options market can help citizens of another country enjoy all the advantages of investment in American stocks and bonds without the penalty of a withholding tax. Income from certain securities and securities transactions is exempt from the withholding tax and, hence, from government reporting regulations. Specifically, capital gains on securities transactions are not taxed unless a foreign citizen resides in the United States for more than half of the year in which the gain is realized. Because they are the result of capital transactions, gains or losses on option trades are exempt from the 30 percent withholding tax. Interest on Eurodollar bonds is not subject to withholding, and interest earned on Treasury bills can avoid the withholding tax if the Treasury bill is sold rather than redeemed at maturity. Deposits in banks are also exempt from the withholding tax.

It is easy to understand how options can help a foreign investor avoid the 30 percent tax if we assume that the investor's ideal portfolio consists of dividend-paying common stocks with listed options. The obvious way to construct such a portfolio would be to buy the stocks. Unfortunately, any dividends on the stocks would be subject to the withholding tax. In addition, the nonresident would find it difficult to obtain a tax deduction for any margin interest charges if a leveraged position is desired.

Using options, a foreign investor can establish a portfolio with equivalent risk and with a similar or superior pretax return to that available on the ideal portfolio. Because the withholding tax is avoided, the aftertax results will almost certainly be significantly improved. The foreign investor buys Treasury bills or Eurodollar securities or deposits cash in banks, depending on interest rate patterns and collateral requirements. A small fraction of the investor's assets are then committed to the purchase and/or sale of put and call options to obtain a risk position equivalent to the desired stock position. To the extent that underpriced options can be purchased and overpriced options can be sold, the investor will enjoy a superior pretax rate of return and avoid the withholding tax as well. Readers should review discussions of options as stock equivalents in Chapter 4 to be certain they understand how the risk characteristics of the option and debt portfolio could be virtually identical to the risk characteristics of a portfolio of dividend-paying stocks.

Given the peculiarities of the U.S. tax law pertaining to nonresident aliens, it makes no sense for these investors to own common stock in any company that pays a dividend and is listed on an options exchange. As more options exchanges are organized in financial centers around the world, nonresident aliens who desire to invest in U.S. securities will learn the advantages of creating synthetic American stock positions with Treasury bills, bank deposits, Eurodollar bonds, and options.

This section has described a few unusual investment strategies designed to minimize an investor's tax payments. Obviously, not every investor can benefit from the techniques described here, but an astute investor will examine the principles behind these suggestions. The chances are good that options can help reduce most tax bills that are based on investment income.

E. TAX CONSIDERATIONS AFFECTING THE LIQUIDITY OF LISTED OPTION MARKETS

An interesting subject for a short article in one of the academic journals or for a student of finance in need of a topic for a paper would be the effect of taxation on trading activity in listed call options. A glance at option trading summaries in

The Wall Street Journal indicates that activity is concentrated in short-term options with relatively little interest apparent in options with more than 6 months remaining before expiration.

The fact that trading activity is low in long-term options does not mean that these contracts have been totally neglected. The ratio of trading volume to open interest (number of contracts outstanding) is generally lower for the longer contracts. Short-term arbitrage and in-and-out trading activity account for much of the high trading volume relative to open interest for the shorter option maturities.

Prior to the beginning of 1977 this pattern of option trading activity could be ascribed partly to the interaction of the tax laws and the weak, erratic stock market of the early 1970s. The markets of 1973 and 1974, in particular, provided many investors with sizable capital loss carry-forwards. Some of these victims may not pay taxes on any capital gain, short-term or long-term, for many years. Because of accumulated capital losses, a very sizable group of market participants was indifferent between short-term and long-term capital gains. The better market environment of 1975 and 1976 reduced the ranks of investors with capital loss carry-forwards. A systematic study might show a greater tendency for investors to use longer-term options in 1976 than in the first few years of listed option trading. The fact that it is no longer possible to obtain a long-term capital gain on a listed option purchase might be expected to reverse any trend toward the use of longer-term options. On the other hand, any tendency to abandon longer-term options may be offset by expanded interest in integrating option strategies with an investor's overall portfolio. Investment-oriented users of options tend to prefer longer-term contracts than a speculator might select.

As noted earlier, the demise, or at least the emasculation, of the commodity tax spread may expand the role of stock options in helping investors time the realization of capital gains and losses. The most obvious consequence of this development will probably be an unusual concentration of option activity in the last few trading days of the calendar year. The interaction of various efforts to influence the timing of gain and loss realization with margin requirements which favor purchase of longer-term options when a spread is constructed may have the effect of distorting option values near year-end. To the extent that tax considerations require closing transactions to take place on December 31, the astute arbitrageur may be able to take advantage of some substantial valuation discrepancies on that day. Because option positions are frequently integrated with positions in the underlying stock, the tendency for the last day of the year to be an active day for trading may be accentuated by the interaction of stock and option activity.

There is a subtle interaction of taxation with option evaluation. Fischer Black, in an article in the *Financial Analysts Journal* (see Bibliography), has pointed out that selling a given option contract will always be more attractive to a high-tax-bracket investor than to a low-tax-bracket investor. Part of this tax effect on the value of an option is a function of the lower tax rate on long-term capital gains; however, the fact that a writer can defer gains on an underlying stock position is also important. The difference in the value of an option to investors with different tax rates is usually quite small. Nonetheless, this feature of option evaluation does suggest that *tax-exempt institutional investors should be buyers* rather than sellers of options, other things being equal. Because the tax-related value differential is small and because the legal status of a call option purchase is certainly not equal to the legal status of an option sale, it is doubtful that pension funds will soon replace individuals as the principal buyers of options.

A frequently voiced doubt about the viability of large-scale option trading is concern over a potential shortage of option buyers. The implied premise behind this argument is that all rational, risk-averse investors will write options, but only the unsophisticated public will be gullible buyers. At first glance, this appears to be a cause for real concern. Many individual and institutional investors are willing to write options, but historically the "small" investor has been the primary buyer of options. The weak markets of the early 1970s have dampened the enthusiasm and decimated the portfolios of many traditional call option buyers. As more institutions, until recently foreclosed from any activity in options, obtain the necessary regulatory and legislative approvals to enter the option market as writers, there is reason to suspect that option premiums which were high in the early years of listed option trading may be chronically low.

Fortunately, as one of the leading figures in the option business once said, "Markets work." Premiums on individual contracts or on all options may be temporarily too high or too low, but arbitrageurs will detect and correct these inappropriate valuations. The correction will not be instantaneous, however, and overvaluations and undervaluations may persist for some time as writers adjust slowly to the mercurial moods of buyers. The greatest opportunities will be available to the flexible investor who can *either* write *or* buy to take advantage of a supply-demand imbalance.

6

REGULATION AND THE ROLES PLAYED BY VARIOUS MARKET PARTICIPANTS

A. THE ECONOMIC FUNCTION OF OPTIONS AND PROBLEMS IN REGULATING THEIR USE

Critics of option trading occasionally argue that the securities options market serves no economically useful purpose. In Chapter 4 we saw evidence that options permit investors to modify the risk-reward posture of their portfolios in practically any way they choose. Risk modification alone is more than ample justification for option trading. Unfortunately, this rationale for options does not satisfy critics who argue that option buyers are either innocent victims being fleeced of their hard-earned savings or gamblers who see calls as an alternative to the numbers or the ponies. This argument imposes a moral tone on the discussion that defies rational response. In spite of the hazards of trying to answer such an argument, it is at least possible to provide an alternate interpretation of the option buyer's motives.

Apart from moral issues, some observers argue that option trading disrupts the market in the underlying stock and that options somehow increase stock price volatility. Another potentially damaging criticism is that speculation in options reduces investors' interest in American Stock Exchange and over-the-counter stocks, making capital more costly and more difficult for smaller companies to raise. Excellent answers to each of these criticisms emerge as soon as the critic understands the role of options in the investment universe.

Understanding the motivations of option buyers is central to dealing with most of the emotional criticism of options. Granted, there are undoubtedly a few option buyers who consider buying a Xerox January $50 as an alternative to a $100 win ticket on Seattle Slew. If the option buyer *is* a gambler, he is a smart one. Option commissions and trading spreads consume a smaller fraction of his "bet" than the track or an underworld syndicate takes out. In most cases, however, option traders do not see themselves as gamblers.

Options are nothing more than investment tools for the acceptance or elimination of risk. Most buyers have considered the risk-reward features of call options and have concluded that calls are appropriate to their risk preferences. Consider, for example, the case of a young woman in an executive position who has very little capital but who is reasonably certain to earn a substantial and rising income. Calls offer her the opportunity to amass enough wealth to start her own business without giving up her chance for a more modest, yet still satisfactory, future. She knows she can never lose more than the call premium, and the possible profit is theoretically unlimited.

The high interest rates and erratic securities markets of the early 1970s have increased the population of another type of option buyer. This buyer has invested most of his assets in high-yielding debt instruments because the risk of equity investment appears too great in an uncertain environment. To provide some exposure to equities if the outlook improves, the buyer invests a small portion of his assets in calls.

While there are always some speculators who go overboard for any investment medium that becomes popular, most of the current crop of call buyers appear to have a fair grasp of the risks as well as the rewards associated with options. The exchanges and their member firms have done an outstanding job of increasing public awareness and understanding of call options. Broader knowledge of options should attract more sophisticated participants to both sides of the option contract, making the "horse players" a small factor in the total market.

It is widely believed that option buyers are suckers and that only writers make money on options. While Chapter 10 will explore this issue in greater depth, there is evidence that writers have enjoyed a very modest advantage in the past but that this advantage is disappearing. Regardless of past experience, the existence of an active secondary market for options should cause most listed options to sell close to their fair value, giving buyers and writers approximately equal expected profits after adjustment for risk. In fact, as more institutional investors begin to write options, it would not surprise some observers if options are consistently underpriced in the future.

There is nothing inherent in option trading that harms either buyer or writer. Existing rules for option trading suitability do an adequate job of protecting most investors. A broker who encourages inappropriate trading can be disciplined. On the other hand, an investor who is determined to find a way to increase leverage can easily find a more dangerous technique than buying options or writing "naked" call options.

Turning to the effect of options on the market in the underlying common stock, an important benefit of listed option trading can be an improvement in the liquidity of the stock market. Liquidity is defined as a measure of the average amount by which a buy or sell order pushes the price of a stock up or down. To the extent that increased option volume leads to arbitrage activity between the option and the stock, an efficient option market should have the effect of moderating stock price fluctuations. Definitive evidence of the impact of option trading and option-stock arbitrage on stock price action is not yet available, but most trading professionals believe that options *reduce* the volatility of the underlying stock.

One mechanism by which the option market improves the liquidity of the stock market merits at least a brief discussion. Assume for a moment that a block positioning house or an institution permitted to write options is asked to bid on a block of stock. To the extent that the buyer can write call options on part or all of the block, his risk is reduced and the price he can offer the seller may increase. Regardless of the size of the trade or the direction of the buying or selling pressure, the ability to lay off some of the risk is important. Any financial instrument that permits investors to reallocate risk among themselves to suit their diverse risk preferences should have the effect of improving overall market liquidity and efficiency.

One of the major criticisms that has been leveled at secondary trading of options is that this activity tends to reduce the level of stock trading activity on the Amex and in the OTC market. The concern behind this argument is that option trading may restrict the ability of smaller companies to obtain financing through public offerings of equity securities. This criticism is based on the hypothesis that many buyers of options would alternatively buy $2 stocks on the Amex or be prime candidates for an offering of a speculative new issue.

Most option buyers are not candidates for Amex or OTC issues in the recent market environment, and many will never be prospective buyers of such securities. Conservative option buyers have most of their assets in saving accounts or fixed income securities. With some care, they are investing small amounts in conservative stocks or options to provide what they feel is an appropriate degree of exposure to the equity markets. The fact that the companies with listed options are among the major names in American industry is important to these investors. They have no interest now and may never have any interest in the secondary and tertiary companies whose ability to obtain financing concerns the critics.

More aggressive option buyers are interested in maximizing the leverage their small capital base can give them. They might be candidates for Amex and OTC issues in a favorable market environment. In recent years, their alternative to options would probably have been commodities. An uncertain business environment is probably the most important reason for the aggressive option buyer's lack of interest in smaller companies. When the environment improves, this investor can be attracted to equity issues from smaller companies. The superior performance of secondary stocks in 1977 and early 1978 is evidence that smaller companies can appeal to investors even when options are a competing attraction.

In measuring the impact of option trading on the market for securities of smaller companies, it is important to keep in mind that none of the money spent on options leaves the market. For every option buyer there is a writer, and every dollar the buyer spends on options goes to a writer after a minor deduction for commission charges. The writer who receives the premium is free to invest it in securities of smaller companies *if they promise attractive returns.*

The commission revenues which are the only drain on the transfer of funds between buyer and writer are a major source of profit for many brokerage firms. If small- and medium-sized companies are to obtain financing when market conditions improve, options may turn out to have played a role in the survival of the firms that will be called upon to underwrite these offerings. In short, the argument that the option market may detract from the ability of smaller companies to obtain financing simply does not hold up. The fact of the matter is that the prices of shares in these companies would be no higher if options did not exist.

There is one real regulatory problem created by trading in listed option contracts. Some of the people who are buying and writing these contracts do not thoroughly understand the risks they are taking. Time and experience with options will help resolve this problem. In the extreme, option investors might be required to pass a simple written examination based, perhaps, on The Options Clearing Corporation prospectus. If an investor demonstrates that he knows what he is doing, he should be permitted to accept whatever risks he deems appropriate. To the extent that participation by investors mentally incapable of understanding or financially incapable of accepting the risks of option trading is the result of a zealous securities salesman overselling a product, the traditional regulatory mechanisms can deal with the problem. If the Securities and Exchange Commission and the National Association of Securities Dealers can police the scattered OTC market, they can easily regulate the relatively centralized option market.

B. OPTION TRADING BY INSTITUTIONAL INVESTORS

1. Restrictions on Institutional Participation

Before we turn to a discussion of the potential role of options in the management of institutional portfolios, a brief review of some of the obstacles to institutional participation in option trading seems in order. Legal and tax counsel should be consulted by any institutional-type investor who is considering buying or writing options. This summary is intended to provide general information, not to serve as a definitive guide to institutions interested in options.

One of the principal deterrents to institutional participation in the option market is the speculative taint associated with options. Thanks to such diverse undercurrents as the Dutch tulip bulb mania, the SEC moratorium on option trading expansion, and the focus of much written material on the investment leverage that options can provide, option trading of any sort is frequently viewed as a highly speculative pursuit. Even institutions which are not bound by strict fiduciary restrictions such as legal lists or a statutory prudent man rule must consider the lawsuits that option trading might encourage before they decide to participate. To the extent that the prudent man rule in a modified form applies to every fiduciary, nuisance lawsuits are a universal possibility.

Another serious deterrent to many large institutions is a rule adopted at the insistence of the SEC which limits the number of listed options on a single underlying stock that one investor or a group of investors acting in concert can write or buy. The present limits on each underlying stock are 1,000 contracts on the same side of the market (i.e., the number of calls *purchased* and the number of puts *sold* on any stock would be combined to determine the position size for purposes of this rule). While the precise meaning of acting in concert has not been spelled out, it is relatively clear that options will never have much of an impact on the total portfolios managed by Morgan Guaranty or Manufacturers Hanover if this rule remains in effect.

When institutions do move into options, they are far more likely to come as writers than as buyers. There are many reasons for this bias toward writing, including these:

1. It is the popular view that option writing is conservative and that option buying is speculative.

2. Fiduciary guidelines can be more readily extended to covered call option writing than to option buying.

3. Covered call writing typically reduces exposure to market fluctuations; buying call options typically increases it. Most institutions want to reduce their market risk exposure.

4. An option buyer pays for a privilege that may expire totally worthless. Its value declines inexorably over time unless the stock moves up or, in the case of a put, down.

Initially, the only significant purchases of options by institutions have been made by aggressive corporations, investment partnerships, and mutual funds and by a few conservative trustees who have been willing to buy in-the-money options selling at little or no premium over intrinsic value. Buying these in-the-money options can limit downside risk if the stock drops sharply before the option expires. The net acquisition cost of stock acquired by exercising an in-the-money option might be about the same as the cost of an outright purchase.

Before we embark upon a discussion of the current legal status of the use of options by financial institutions, a brief discussion of the prudent man rule seems in order. Since 1830 and the Massachusetts case *Harvard v. Amory*, the standard of investment selection by which fiduciaries are judged has come to be "how men of prudence, discretion and intelligence manage their own affairs."

While tracing the evolution and interpretation of the prudent man rule over 150 years is beyond the scope of these brief comments, the general principles are clear and relatively straightforward. First, a fiduciary is rarely, if ever, called to task if every investment made is profitable. Second, developments which take place after the investment is made and which could not have been reasonably foreseen may lead to litigation, but adverse judgments are rare. Third, and perhaps most important from the point of view of the fiduciary interested in using options in a portfolio, it is well established that individual investment decisions must meet the standards of prudence. Good results from the rest of the portfolio may help, but they will not completely erase the blot left by a single unsuitable investment.

Several law journal articles have argued persuasively that, on the basis of modern portfolio theory, taking more risk on individual positions can result in lower total risk and a higher expected return for the total portfolio. This viewpoint is based on faultless economics, but it does not have the force of law. Any trustee or other investment manager bound by the prudent man rule would be ill-advised to assume that any concept of aggregate prudence in the management of a portfolio can excuse a loss on an individual investment.

The item-by-item standard of prudence has important implications for option purchases in a prudent man account. To understand these implications, assume that a trustee invests $100,000 in a diversified list of options. At the end of a 6-month period the options are sold, and a total of $200,000 is realized on the sale. One would not expect to be criticized for a 100 percent profit on the original investment in 6 months. However, the fact that the total option position has been profitable does not make up for the fact that a few of the options will expire worthless or be sold at a small fraction of their original purchase price. Losses on these option purchases could be the basis of successful litigation against a trustee, even if the $100,000 was a small fraction of the total funds available for investment; in such cases, each position is judged separately.

Injecting a personal viewpoint, it seems that too many fiduciaries bemoan the rigidity of the prudent man rule and abandon the idea of buying options too readily. If delegation of investment authority is permitted and direct investment is deemed inappropriate, there are few obstacles to option purchases through secondary vehicles such as mutual funds and certain types of pooled accounts. The investment in the secondary vehicle would be a single investment for purposes of evaluating prudence. The individual investments made in the secondary fund would *not* be evaluated separately. Readers to whom this apparent "double standard" makes little sense are in good company. Nonetheless, it appears to reflect the current status of the prudent man rule as it applies to primary investments and investments through intermediaries.

Under the prudent man rule, it is a relatively simple matter to justify covered writing of call options or the sale of puts. It is more difficult (but not impossible) to justify other option positions. The rationalization of covered call writing is based on the interaction of the call and the underlying stock position. Presumably, buying the underlying stock is a prudent investment in its own right. If the stock purchase does not conform with prudent man guidelines, the fiduciary's problems are beyond the scope of this discussion. If the prudently selected stock declines, the portfolio may have a loss, but the fiduciary does not have a legal problem. If a call has been written against the stock, the price decline would permit the call to expire or to be repurchased at a profit. As long as a profit is obtained on the call position, potential critics will find nothing to attack.

If, instead of falling after the call is sold, the price of the stock rises, any "loss" on the call can be eliminated by permitting exercise. As long as there was a premium over intrinsic value at the time the call was sold, the portfolio will realize a higher effective sale price for the stock than if it had been sold on the date the call was written. It does not seem to matter that sale of the call reduced the profit that otherwise would have been received on the stock position. The law apparently does not recognize the concept of opportunity loss in this context.

Most lawyers would agree that it is not really necessary to permit the call to be exercised. A call can generally be repurchased at a loss without fear of litigation. The basis for this flexibility in closing out the option is that it might be more economical to repurchase the call than to permit exercise and then repurchase the same stock.

Apart from justification by the specific principles underlying the prudent man rule, there is a consensus among conservative investors and regulators that covered call option writing per se is a prudent strategy. The Comptroller of the Currency and numerous state insurance commissioners have authorized covered call writing as appropriate for institutions under their jurisdiction.

Although the sale of puts by fiduciaries has not received formal approval from any regulatory authorities, selling puts seems to meet the standards of the prudent man rule. If the fiduciary's records establish that the put was overpriced *relative to the corresponding call option* at the time the put was sold, the analysis of Chapter 4, Section D, establishes that the relatively overpriced put collateralized by a Treasury bill will provide a superior return to covered call writing at every possible stock price. Obviously, careful record keeping will be necessary to establish the superiority of the put.

An Internal Revenue Service ruling that predates the passage of the Employee Retirement Income Security Act (ERISA) holds that no security may be purchased by a pension or profit-sharing plan at a price that exceeds the market price at the time of the purchase. This ruling implies that the seller of a put should avoid exercise of the option because the exercise price of the put will be greater than the market price of the stock when the put is exercised. It is not clear that exercise of a put will be unacceptable under the broad provisions of ERISA, but until a ruling or a test case provides some guidance, common sense dictates that extra care be taken to close out puts if there is any danger of exercise.

Purchase of any option, uncovered writing of calls, variable hedges, and spreads are more difficult to justify in a portfolio bound by the prudent man rule. In a classic article in the *Financial Analysts Journal* (see Bibliography) Robert C. Pozen makes a compelling case that the purchase of a "protective put" to reduce the risk of a long stock position is consistent with ERISA, the prudent man rule, and the basic law on trust investments. In time Pozen's thesis may provide the basis for broader use of options by fiduciaries.

In addition to the general standard of prudence that affects the option trading policies of most institutional investors, there are a number of specific barriers peculiar to certain institutions. This listing is by no means all-inclusive.

Nonfinancial corporations The only possible obstacles to option trading by a nonfinancial corporation would be an obscure statute in its state of incorporation or a restrictive clause in the corporate bylaws. Ordinarily these restrictions can be removed by the directors or the stockholders of the corporation. Virtually any option strategy can be authorized by corporate directors.

Mutual funds The principal obstacles to mutual fund participation in the option market are restrictive provisions in most fund prospectuses. With the exception of a few extremely aggressive funds, most investment companies are prohibited by a statement in the prospectus from buying or writing puts and calls. In most cases, these provisions could be changed at the next annual meeting or at a special shareholders' meeting called for that purpose and an amended prospectus could be published. The prohibition against any trading in puts and calls has historically been inserted in mutual fund prospectuses to give them a solid, conservative sound and to avoid a registration delay while the SEC and state securities commissions look more closely than usual at the fund and its management. Some state securities laws may also restrict the use of options in mutual funds.

Several new funds specialize in trading options and related underlying stocks. Most of these funds specialize in covered call writing.

Pension and profit-sharing plans While there is a certain amount of controversy over the investment restrictions imposed on pension and profit-sharing plans by the ERISA legislation, there is a clear consensus that covered writing of call options is permissible. The sale of put options as an alternative to covered call writing is probably acceptable. Other strategies are more questionable.

Foundations Chapter 5 mentioned a possible tax problem that might be raised by the purchase of options in a foundation portfolio. As long as the foundation's investment strategy is appropriate to its charitable objectives, integration of an option program into the portfolio should present no tax or regulatory problems with the federal government. Some state statutes might restrict the use of options.

Endowments There appear to be few impediments to the extensive use of options in the management of an endowment portfolio. As long as the overall portfolio structure is appropriate and options are not used speculatively, endowments can enjoy a distinct advantage over most institutions because they can be buyers as well as writers.

Commercial and savings banks Unless forbidden to do so by state law, appropriately documented individual and commingled trust accounts managed by banks may write covered call options. A preliminary ruling by the Comptroller of the Currency prohibited national banks from any option activity for a number of months before the ruling was reversed to permit covered call writing. A growing number of state banking commissioners have adopted regulations permitting commercial and savings banks to write call options against their stock portfolios.

Insurance companies Some insurance companies were active option writers for years before listed option trading began. The major obstacles to covered call option writing by most insurance companies are inertia and a few insurance commissioners who consider options inherently speculative. Most state insurance commissions have at least tacitly accepted covered call writing, and a few, notably those in Missouri, Tennessee, and Illinois, have ruled that insurance companies may purchase calls as long as such investments are not made for speculative purposes. This recognition by a few insurance commissions that the purchase of calls can be prudent may form the basis for gradual liberalization of standards of prudence. These state rulings approving option purchases are important because they focus on the overall investment program, not on a specific position.

Most of the restrictions which prevent institutional investors from participating in the options market will be lifted in time. As these restrictions disappear, there will probably be a gradual increase in institutional participation in options. Options provide something which the institutional investor has consistently sought but rarely found: a method of structuring the risks and rewards of an equity portfolio to give it a measure of independence from market fluctuations.

One of the most frequent criticisms that institutional portfolio managers hear is that they have shown no ability to provide the ultimate owners of the portfolio with either consistent or superior returns on equity investments. As we saw in the diagrams of possible option strategies, options permit the institutional investor to be free from lockstep dependence on the vagaries of market trends. While using options does not guarantee that a portfolio will never have a down year, options can smooth out the fluctuations. Furthermore, if only overvalued options are written and/or only undervalued options are purchased, the portfolio should enjoy superior as well as more consistent performance.

Options can enable an institution to modify its risk exposure without making massive changes in the portfolio. If an institutional portfolio manager feels that the stock market will be flat or that it may decline, he usually sells the more volatile stocks in his portfolio and invests a modest fraction of the equity portfolio in short-term debt securities until he is more sanguine about the outlook for the market. If he writes calls or buys puts, he can reduce the volatility of the portfolio without selling his volatile stock positions or shifting the portfolio into short-term debt.

If options are actively traded by institutions, not only will their clients enjoy more consistent investment results, the destabilizing effect of some institutional trading decisions on stock prices might be reduced. A portfolio manager who was uncertain about the outlook for a company but not strongly negative on the stock could temper his risk by writing calls or buying puts. He would not have to disrupt the market in the stock by dumping his entire block.

The goal of many institutional portfolios can be roughly defined as protection of portfolio capital against erosion by inflation while the portfolio assets are earning a sufficient current return to meet certain fixed obligations such as pension payments or insurance claims. If this statement of purpose is even approximately correct for a large number of institutions, excessive exposure to volatile stock prices is not an appropriate investment strategy.

As the legal barriers to institutional participation in the option market begin to crumble, the pressure on all regulatory agencies to relax the remaining barriers will increase. Whether institutional portfolio managers like it or not, the existence of an active option market and its use by their competitors will force them to include options in their investment thinking. There will be growing competition to attain a consistency of performance that cannot be achieved without options.

The beneficiaries of greater use of options will be the ultimate owners of institutional portfolios. Their pensions and the payments from their trust accounts will be more stable and more certain as a result of the institutional portfolio manager's ability to restructure risks and rewards in a manner appropriate to the needs of the ultimate clients. If the portfolio manager uses option evaluation carefully, the clients should also enjoy higher average returns.

At the end of 1977, the market value of the stock necessary to cover every open listed call contract was less than $12 billion. If institutions with their multibillion-dollar portfolios become active users of options, the market should expand dramatically.

2. Implementing an Institutional Option Program

a. *Why Institutions Are Interested in Options.* Few institutional portfolio managers have a strong conviction that every client should participate in the options market. Many institutions initiate an options program because an outside director or a marketing-oriented executive has suggested an examination of options. Others react to requests from clients who have asked about selling options against a portion of their portfolios or who have suggested the purchase of a few option contracts.

Investment management groups that do not respond appropriately to questions and suggestions from clients interested in options may lose present and prospective business. A few managers, particularly those in small and medium-sized investment counseling firms and an occasional bank trust department, see development of capability in options as an important part of a new business effort. Other managers doubt that they can charge a high enough fee to earn a profit on options portfolio management. If the latter group of managers offers options at all, options will be viewed as a "loss leader." These diverse considerations will affect the business economics of an options program differently at various institutions.

If a decision is made to offer options services to clients, the most common reason given is that selling options can reduce the market risk exposure of a common stock portfolio and simultaneously enhance the rate of return. While both risk reduction and return enhancement are *possible* results of a properly structured and carefully executed options program, obtaining these results is by no means automatic, nor is the combination of risk reduction *and* return enhancement *probable*.

A casual reading of the serious literature on options should persuade skeptics that sale of a call option contract against a common stock position will *always* reduce the market risk exposure of that position but will *not always* enhance the expected rate of return. In fact, risk reduction without a corresponding reduction in the expected rate of return is possible only if the option contract is *overpriced* relative to its *fair value*. If option premiums are low, portfolio managers will find a shift from equities to debt securities preferable to the sale of options as a way to reduce portfolio risk levels.

Almost regardless of option premium levels (or of actual investment results), the mistaken belief that covered option writing provides automatic risk reduction *and return enhancement* persists as the single most important motivating factor behind the entrance of new covered writers into the options market. If this belief dominates institutional option strategies, there will be some extraordinary opportunities available to individuals and to institutions able to buy option contracts.

Institutions limited to one side of the option contract for legal reasons may find selective participation in options to be profitable. Investors whose range of strategies is restricted will be best advised to adjust portfolio risk exposure in other ways when option premium levels are too low for covered writing or too high for option buying.

b. *Organizing for Options.* Once the decision to use options is made, institutional investors follow divergent paths to implement the decision. Setting aside the legal, clerical, tax, and accounting questions that have delayed and even scuttled a number of prospective options programs, the focus here is on the portfolio management function. Although the variations are numerous, institutions have adopted three basic approaches to the options portfolio management function.

First, institutions planning large-scale involvement in options occasionally develop costly in-house options management organizations. Full-time or part-time participation by assorted members of the portfolio management, trading, and computer staffs can easily lead to an annual budget of several hundred thousand dollars. Further, as in most business organizations, an options management group tends to expand as the desirability of additional manpower and computer capability becomes apparent.

A second approach popular with many institutions is to retain responsibility for basic investment decisions (i.e., stock selection and overall equity market exposure) and to "buy" options expertise with commission dollars. Obviously, using outside options expertise is far less costly than supporting the expense of an internal group. It also provides continuous exposure to the industry's best thinking, whereas an internal group can slip into a rut. For most institutional users of options, buying some outside expertise is necessary until the level of participation in the options market justifies a major commitment.

The third basic approach, used by some smaller organizations that have few accounts which are interested in options, is to farm out the management of options portfolios. The institution monitors investment decisions and results, but it restricts its activities to a peripheral role in portfolio management.

c. *The Options Manager in the Portfolio Management Organization.* Regardless of the degree of organizational commitment to options, at least one portfolio manager or trader at an institution should be well versed in options. The precise role of the options program manager in the investment organization is less important than his or her overall capability. An intelligent manager with sound investment judgment will soon adapt to any but the most restrictive organizational framework. In most instances, the person charged with responsibility for the options program will have to recognize any deficiencies in the organizational structure and either take or recommend the steps necessary to correct them. The options operation has the greatest chance of success and can contribute most to the overall money management program when it is treated as an integral part of the portfolio management effort.

By far the most common approach to options used by large money management organizations is to assign a relatively junior portfolio manager or, less frequently, a stock or convertible bond trader the task of overseeing the options program. The results of such assignments can range from abysmal to outstanding. Frequently, a bright young portfolio manager or trader recently out of business school, and with only limited securities experience, will quickly master the mechanical aspects of options. By selectively picking the brains of older and more experienced colleagues in making stock selections and carefully adjusting the portfolio's risk orientation, the young options manager will turn in an outstanding performance.

The fact that a particular portfolio manager has been recently immersed in the academic theory of option evaluation and portfolio management does not guarantee favorable results. In all likelihood, the manager who does an outstanding job with an option-oriented portfolio would have done an outstanding job with a conventional stock portfolio. Using options makes the job more difficult in some respects and easier in others. Many options portfolio managers, including some who have compiled enviable records with options, would do better to avoid options entirely and should instead focus their obvious talents on more conventional portfolio management. In some cases, good performance has resulted more from accidental or intentional variations in the market exposure of the portfolio and from sound stock selection than from the appropriate use of options.

Whether an institution assigns options to a capable portfolio manager or trader, emphasizes the use of sophisticated option evaluation programs, or (preferably) both, the organizational structure of most institutions calls for separation of the options effort from the mainstream of the portfolio management function. This separation is usually a mistake. The more an options portfolio is integrated with the overall money management effort, the more satisfactory the performance of both is likely to be. To provide just one example, careful analysis of option premium levels can sometimes tell an investor more about the possibility of an earnings surprise, a management change, or a merger announcement than more conventional analytical techniques.

Turning responsibility for the options effort over to a computer expert rather than to a portfolio manager or trader is not a common approach to options portfolio management. This allocation of responsibilities usually occurs because an institution's management has been led to believe that successful use of options requires the skillful use of a computer and nothing more. Although few principles are universally accepted in the investment community, it is now widely agreed that a computer is important, perhaps essential, to an effective options program. Unfortunately, it is too small a step from acceptance of the computer as essential to the erroneous view that the computer provides the final answer to every problem encountered in the use of options.

d. *Options Portfolio Risk Exposure.* Relatively few individual or institutional users of options are yet measuring the degree of risk modification and/or expected return enhancement associated with a particular option strategy. The usefulness of option evaluation to measure the likely effect of an option trade on portfolio return is obvious. Less obvious is a straightforward technique for measuring the effect of an option on portfolio risk exposure. This technique, outlined in Chapter 4, requires the portfolio manager to view *each long or short option position as the equivalent of a long or short position in some fraction of a round lot of the underlying stock.*

If the price of a particular option contract is expected to rise or fall by one-half point for each one-point rise or fall in the stock, then that option is the *risk equivalent* of 50 shares of the stock. The value of the option will change roughly as much as the value of 50 shares of stock over a range of stock prices, and this relationship will hold for a reasonable period of time. Obviously, if the stock rises dramatically, the value of a call option will soon rise by more than one-half point for each one-point move in the stock. If the stock drops sharply, the call will soon fall less than one-half point for each one-point drop in the stock. Because risk equivalent relationships change, the risk analysis should be performed at least weekly and even more frequently in turbulent markets.

Translating every option position into stock equivalents permits a portfolio manager to measure diversification and stock market risk exposure, just as they would be measured in any conventional equity or equity and debt portfolio. The sale of a call option decreases the stock equivalent market risk exposure of a portfolio. Purchase of a call increases exposure. Translation of option positions into stock equivalents is important as a measure of the changes that an options program makes in portfolio risk exposure. If the impact of options on overall portfolio risk levels is not carefully and continuously appraised, the actual degree of bullishness or bearishness of the total portfolio may be quite different from what the portfolio manager, investment committee, or portfolio strategy group wants it to be.

When a portfolio manager is selling options against part or all of the equity portion of a portfolio, a consistent pattern of equity equivalent exposure can be maintained only by shifting some assets out of fixed income securities and into common stocks. On the other hand, if call option contracts are purchased, maintenance of a fixed debt-equity risk orientation will require liquidation of a risk equivalent amount of common stock and reinvestment of the proceeds in lower-risk fixed income securities. Integration of an options program with the total money management effort of an institution provides a unique opportunity to examine the rationale behind the debt-equity mix and the overall risk structure of a portfolio.

A major problem with some institutional option efforts is that no attempt is made to integrate options with risk management of the stock and bond portfolio. The options manager is frequently charged with responsibility for managing the options program in a vacuum. An option-writing program may produce quite unexpected results *unless the impact on portfolio risk is taken into account* and given adequate weight in the decision-making process. Only if options are integrated with equity and debt portfolio management policies will the overall level of market risk exposure be consciously determined and maintained.

Options are frequently part of the most *efficient* way to take a position in a stock. If options are *overpriced,* covered writing against a larger stock position than might otherwise be appropriate will usually be the most attractive way to participate in the stock. To the extent that an institution may do so, buying *underpriced* call options will be the most attractive way to purchase stock. After enough options are purchased to give desired exposure to the stock, the remaining cash would be invested in low-risk fixed income securities. Adopting any policy on option purchases or sales without attention to *both* option evaluation *and* position-by-position changes in risk exposure is likely to produce unanticipated results.

The principal focus of most institutional option participation has been, and will undoubtedly continue to be, covered call option writing. The widespread perception of covered writing as a conservative and sensible strategy is a factor in this phenomenon. Popular views of the option buyer as a speculator and of the option writer as enjoying a superior average return are pervasive. With time, the stereotypes will fade, and a wide variety of investors who are now barred (or believe they are barred) from buying options will be on both sides of the option contract. In the meantime, institutional option writers will find it advantageous to expand their underlying common stock positions during periods of relatively high option premiums, when writing against stock positions is attractive. If option premiums are low, the institution should shift funds from equity back into debt and should avoid call writing. Shifting money into and out of underlying stocks as opportunities for option writing come and go is necessary to maintain a consistent degree of overall risk exposure.

C. WHAT EVERY CORPORATE FINANCIAL OFFICER SHOULD KNOW ABOUT OPTIONS

Until recently, the only stock options that concerned most corporate financial officers were the qualified or nonqualified stock options that corporations issued to executives and other key employees. The Tax Reform Act of 1976 made employee stock option plans a much less attractive form of executive compensation than they had been prior to its passage. In contrast, trading in listed stock options promises to have a broader impact on the corporation than executive stock options ever had.

This section examines the ways in which listed option contracts and option theory affect the job of a corporate financial officer. Topics covered include

1. The merits of an option exchange listing for a corporation's stock

2. The use of options in the management of corporate cash

3. The effect of options and option theory on such diverse corporate financing decisions as setting the terms of a new security issue, weighing the impact of option trading on common stock underwritings, and analyzing debt refunding decisions

1. The Merits of an Option Listing

A few corporations have taken steps to discourage the listing of their stocks for option trading. A far greater number of corporate managements have launched campaigns to interest the listing committees of the options exchanges in their stocks. Although the evidence is not definitive, an active option market appears to reduce the tendency for the underlying stock price to fluctuate. This stock price volatility reduction results from the risk transfer characteristics of options. A brokerage firm asked to bid on a block of stock or an institutional investor offered part of the block can offset some of the risk of the stock position in the option market. Because volume in the option market is a proxy for volume in the underlying stock, each option trade increases the depth and the liquidity of the market in the stock, with a consequent reduction in stock price fluctuations.

The significance of lower stock price volatility to the financial officer is that lower volatility helps reduce the corporation's cost of capital. Other things being equal, a less volatile stock is a more desirable investment. Lower volatility means lower risk. Investors will accept a lower return on a lower-risk investment. A lower future return means a higher current stock price and a lower cost of equity capital. Even a slight reduction in stock price volatility should tend to improve the average price-earnings multiple or reduce the dividend yield that investors will demand from a common stock.

In addition to the generally favorable effect of an option listing on liquidity and stock price volatility, an option listing can reduce the corporation's cost of capital in another way. A growing number of individual investors and institutional portfolio managers work extensively or even exclusively with options and their related stocks. For these investors it is frequently a case of "no options, no interest." A growing number of advisory services and brokerage firm research departments are influenced by the combined trading volume in stocks and options when they select stocks for statistical and analytical coverage. Obviously, if a corporation has problems, more attention is not always desirable. After weighing positive and negative factors, however, managements of most large corporations have concluded that they want increased interest on the part of the investment community.

A corporation can do relatively little to encourage one or more of the option exchanges to list its stock. While an investment banker can help with a presentation to the exchange's listing committee, these committees are usually controlled by floor members. Consequently, listing decisions will be based on the floor members' expectations for option trading volume. With few exceptions (e.g., Bally Industries) most companies listed for option trading after 1975 have experienced only modest option trading volume. If a company has not already been selected for option trading, management should not expect too much from an option listing.

It is a relatively simple matter for a corporation to *discourage* an option listing if the preceding paragraphs have not been persuasive. Because option terms must be modified in the event of a noncash dividend or a stock split, any corporation that declares small quarterly stock dividends will soon have an unmanageable number of option series with irregular striking prices and unusual numbers of shares underlying each option. Traders will shy away from the issue, volume will dry up, and the option exchange will rue the day the stock was admitted to trading.

2. Management of Corporate Investments

A number of corporations have begun using options in the management of corporate funds. The most common corporate options strategy is to purchase high-yield common or convertible preferred stocks and to sell call options. This strategy can limit exposure to stock price fluctuations while the corporation takes advantage of the 85 percent intercorporate dividend deduction. This option strategy can work very well if two basic rules are observed. First, the option sold should be overpriced. Any investor, corporate or individual, who consistently sells underpriced call options will probably experience a substandard return on investment in the long run.

A second basic rule may be of even greater significance to the corporate seller of call options. Section 246(c) of the Internal Revenue Code requires a corporate taxpayer to hold shares on which the 85 percent dividend deduction is claimed for a period of more than 15 days. The holding period will be reduced by any period in which the taxpayer has an option to sell, is under a contractual obligation to sell, or has made (and not closed) a short sale of substantially identical stock or securities. The key provision for the covered call option writer is whether or not the corporation is under an obligation to sell the underlying stock. The IRS has issued a private ruling that selling a covered call does not create a contractual obligation to sell within the meaning of this statute. If this private ruling is used as a basis for aggressive conversion of short-term capital gains into qualified dividends, it may be modified.

A more sophisticated corporate option strategy uses put and call options on interest-sensitive common stocks to hedge the interest rate risk of a preferred stock or municipal bond portfolio. Because most preferred stock dividends qualify for the 85 percent intercorporate dividend deduction and because municipal bond interest is totally tax-exempt, a hedged portfolio of this nature should provide a 3 percent *aftertax* yield advantage over commercial paper or certificates of deposit. The basis of this technique is the use of options to remove a substantial element of risk from an investment vehicle that has unique tax advantages for the corporate investor. The risks and rewards are spelled out in more detail in Chapter 5.

3. The Impact of Options on Corporate Finance

One of the most obvious effects of option trading on corporate financial activity is the impact of option trading on the stock price during an equity or convertible security offering. To prevent an assault on the underwriting syndicate, no uncovered call can be sold for less than its intrinsic value during the period of price stabilization by the underwriters. The purpose of this rule is to prevent selling pressure from breaking the syndicate bid.

Listed options may not be involved in corporate financing decisions very often, but the use of put and call provisions on debt securities is common. Several recent bond and note issues received considerable publicity because buyers had the right to put the bonds to the issuing corporation at par prior to maturity. The put provision helped enable the companies to sell their debt at a lower interest rate.

The absence of a call provision on a bond can reduce the interest cost of debt financing by even more than the presence of a put. An interesting article by Jonathan Ingersoll of the University of Chicago (see Bibliography) analyzes the effect of call provisions on convertible securities. One of the key implications of Ingersoll's work is that a corporation which does not plan to call a convertible issue at 110 or 120 percent of parity will probably be able to pay a materially lower interest rate if a higher call price is used. In other words, it makes no sense to demand a call provision that the corporation has no intention of using.

At least one more facet of option analysis that can play a role in corporate financing decisions has been scarcely touched by option theorists. If long-term interest rates remain below the high levels of 1973 and 1974, many corporations will be refunding long-term debt with lower coupon issues. A corporate financial officer faced with a refunding opportunity must decide whether to refund in the current year or to wait a year in the expectation that long-term interest rates will decline even further. Extensive analysis of the debt refunding decision was published before recent developments in option theory. Renewed interest in debt refunding will lead to some interesting applications of option theory to the refunding decision.

D. THE ROLE OF THE INDIVIDUAL INVESTOR

Historically, individual investors have accounted for most of the option contracts written and nearly all of the contracts purchased. Typically, writers have been wealthy individuals who see option writing as a way to stabilize and perhaps improve the rate of return from their equity portfolios. Option buyers have been small investors or executives with high incomes and little capital. The buyer typically sees options as a way to increase investment leverage and to limit possible loss when the risk-reward characteristics of an option contract fit his expectations for the price action of a particular stock better than owning the stock outright. There are obviously exceptions to these generalizations, but they are approximately correct descriptions of the majority of conventional option market participants.

The success of listed options promises to increase institutional participation and profoundly change many historic relationships between option market participants. Institutional investors are beginning to participate actively on the writing side of the option market, but less frequently on the buying side. Their presence as writers may tend, over the long run, to depress option premiums slightly. In the past a burst of speculative option purchases has generally caused option premiums to rise sharply because buyers have tried to expand their participation more rapidly than new writers could be found. With wider institutional participation, option premiums will probably fluctuate less dramatically. In fact, option buyers may have a consistent advantage over option writers unless institutional investors are flexible in their use of options.

If premiums do become chronically low, there is a very

conservative option-buying strategy designed to take advantage of low option premiums. This strategy is suitable for investors who ordinarily would not consider purchasing an option.

When option premiums are too low, it means that the premium the buyer is called upon to pay is lower than the premium justified by the risk-adjusted expected value of the reward that might be gained from appreciation in the price of the stock. If premiums are low, conservative investors can enjoy most of the protection of a debt portfolio combined with some of the reward potential of equities. The investor simply puts most of his assets in fixed income securities and purchases underpriced options with a small portion of his capital or with part of his interest income. This investor is protecting himself from the risk of losing his capital. Should the stock on which he has bought options go up, he will participate in the rise. Though the risk-reward characteristics of this strategy are very similar to those of a high-quality convertible bond, it is doubtful that many institutions will adopt this strategy until they have had a few years' experience writing options.

Though institutional purchases of options will develop slowly, investing most assets in short-term debt and buying a few options to give equity market exposure will become increasingly common among conservative individual investors over the next several years. Because of the magnitude of the individual and institutional money involved, conservative option purchases of this type will ultimately be larger than the strictly speculative purchase of options by the small investor. These uses of options are part of a longer-term trend, however, not an overnight development.

E. REGULATING THE OPTIONS MARKETS

There are at least four levels of regulation which, by accident and by design, keep listed options markets in the United States operating smoothly and in the public interest.

The most pervasive regulatory controls are those imposed by the SEC. When listed options trading on the Chicago Board Options Exchange began in 1973, some SEC commissioners and a significant fraction of the SEC staff had serious reservations about the SEC's ability to police this new market. Fortunately, the SEC and the exchanges have produced a regulatory framework that provides a remarkably fair and orderly market.

One can argue persuasively that certain SEC-imposed regulations (such as the 1,000-contract rule limiting the size of an investor's position or the trading limitations imposed on deep-out-of-the-money options) are not necessaary. However, the fact that the options market is subsidiary to the basic market in underlying stocks suggests that it is better to err on the side of conservatism, even if that means living with a few unnecessary restrictions. In general, the SEC and its staff seem a little more comfortable with options today than when the CBOE pilot project was approved.

The SEC's decision in late 1977 to impose a moratorium on the expansion of option trading has been the subject of considerable speculation in legal and investment circles. Any speculation here would appear quite ill informed by the time the reader sees these comments. On the basis of the allegations of wrongdoing revealed to date, it is possible to anticipate some significant rule changes. Most of these changes will probably affect trading by option exchange members for their own accounts and floor procedures. The SEC's inquiry is unlikely to have significant impact on public customers.

The second level of regulation is provided by the exchanges on which options are traded. Actually, most of the SEC's influence is embodied in exchange rules or in the rules of The Options Clearing Corporation. Within an SEC-imposed framework, each exchange is responsible for policing its members and maintaining an orderly market. The exchanges also publish some excellent educational material on options for member-firm personnel and customers to ensure that ignorance is not an excuse for a rule violation.

The third level of regulation of the options market occurs in the courtroom. The courts are not, strictly speaking, an adjunct of the options market, but they are called upon to deal with allegations of serious abuse. Financial penalties imposed by the courts or by exchange-sponsored arbitration programs and legal fees associated with litigation can be effective deterrents to misbehavior.

The fourth, and in most respects the key, regulator of options trading is the market itself. It is often amusing to listen to complaints about market manipulation or to hear accusations hurled at market makers or specialists by frustrated traders. Most of this anger is misdirected. As long as the basic rules regulating the conduct of trading in a market are enforced (and in the United States they are enforced vigorously), the opportunities for gross manipulation are extremely limited. If manipulation does occur, one or more very specific rules have almost certainly been broken. The SEC, the exchanges, or the courts can force appropriate restitution and pile penalties on top of any financial settlement awarded the victims.

Even if human regulators are not equal to the occasion, the market itself is a stern disciplinarian. Pushing the price of a stock or option up or down artificially or maintaining an unfairly wide spread between bid and asked prices on the floor of the exchange will frequently penalize the offender more than the general public. Any manipulative purchases or sales are likely to encourage other market participants to trade against the manipulator in order to take advantage of the distorted prices. More often than not, countervailing market pressures will bring stock and/or options prices back in line at the expense of the manipulator. It is interesting to note that the case of alleged manipulation that has been most thoroughly described in connection with the SEC moratorium appears to have resulted in a loss of several hundred thousand dollars by a would-be manipulator.

An attempt on the part of a market maker or specialist to maintain an artificially wide gap between bid and asked prices will have the effect of discouraging investors from trading that option. The specialist or market maker who attempts to exploit investors with a wide spread will find investors avoiding the market in that security. Alternatively, competing floor traders will improve the market if active trading is possible.

Just as there are four levels of market regulation, there are four areas in which most of the impact of regulation is concentrated. By far the most important area of regulation is customer suitability. Suitability rules relate the propriety of an option or option-related transaction to the sophistication and financial resources of the investor. To choose extreme examples, it would clearly be suitable for the chief executive of a major corporation whose financial sophistication has been affirmed by a board of directors, as well as by a brokerage firm compliance committee, to undertake almost any option strategy. Conversely, a 70-year-old retired individual, with income from a net worth of $5,000 to supplement a monthly social security check, should not be in the options market at all. There are more debatable cases between these extremes.

Many of the lawsuits initiated against brokerage firms and investment advisors during the first 5 years of listed option trading focused on the customer's lack of suitability for options trading. In spite of efforts to reduce the risk of litigation, there is no formal list of characteristics that assure customer suitability. Among the key factors evaluated are financial sophistication, net worth, source and size of annual income, type of option strategy to be employed, previous experience in option trading, and length of time the firm has been dealing with the customer. If the investor is an institution rather than an individual, specific documents authorizing option trading are an important factor determining suitability.

A second area of regulation, related in some respects to suitability, covers industry sales practices. Sales-practice regulations restrict what salespeople can say or write to customers to solicit business. Telephone and face-to-face conversations are difficult for a salesperson's superiors to monitor, but written material given or sent to customers must be approved by a Registered Options Principal who has taken an examination covering the mechanics and the regulatory aspects of options. If sound sales practices are combined with careful screening of customers for suitability, the number of customer complaints and the potential for litigation will be reduced.

One aspect of the sales-practice regulations that has been liberalized recently is the use of annualized rates of return in communications with clients. Until they were relaxed, the guidelines for sales literature forbade use of an annualized rate of return for any option investment position. Among the reasons for this rule was that no position involving a listed option is held for a full year. It is not appropriate to annualize a possible return on the assumption that a similar position could be taken when the first option expires or is exercised. An even more important reason for this rule is that many salespeople and advisory letters use the annualized return if exercised or the annualized return if the stock price is unchanged on the expiration date as a measure of the relative attractiveness of a call-option-writing position. A short-term, slightly out-of-the-money call option will show a very large (and very meaningless) annualized return if exercised. The possibility of a high annualized return under the combined assumptions that the stock will rise to the option striking price or higher *and* that an identical position can be instituted at the time the first option expires is not a measure of the *probable* return. The annualized return if exercised fails to take into account the probability that the stock will be selling below the striking price on the date of expiration. While these annualized returns may be possible, they are not probable.

The only meaningful annualized return figure used in the analysis of an option position is the expected annualized return from a neutral hedge position. The expected annualized return from a neutral hedge evaluates the relative probabilities of all possible stock prices on the date of exercise. While there are obvious differences between a neutral hedge position and a covered writing position, the expected annualized return from a neutral hedge can, with modest analytical effort, be extended to project an expected annualized return from a covered writing position. This projection uses a diagram similar to the risk-return trade-off diagram of Figure 4-23. The expected annualized return from a neutral hedge also provides a way of standardizing the attractiveness of various option contracts and strategies, something that is not possible with an annualized return if exercised. Because the concept of an expected annualized return from a neutral hedge is probably beyond the understanding of the average individual investor, the best policy on annualized returns is the old policy: Annualized returns should be forbidden in sales literature.

Most of the sales-practice rules applicable to options are

similar to the rules that govern all securities transactions. In addition to standard prohibitions against promising a particular rate of return or guaranteeing a profit, a presentation to a present or prospective options customer must be balanced in its portrayal of risks and rewards.

Once an order has been placed, the investor benefits from regulation of trading practices, the third major area of option regulation. Trading rules affect the way the order is handled from the time it is received by the registered representative until the trade is settled. Trading rules govern when and under what circumstances the registered representative can accept full or partial discretion over the execution of the order. They govern the method by which the order is transmitted to the floor of the appropriate exchange and the method by which exercise notices are allocated among a firm's customers.

The final area of regulatory protection for the investor is a requirement that each registered representative have a general knowledge of option strategies and of the rules for executing option transactions. The examination given all new registered representatives contains a few questions on put and call option transactions. Representatives who were registered prior to the introduction of calls or puts are required to take special examinations which test their understanding of options.

Most professional participants in the options market have definite opinions on the necessity for various rules and regulations. These comments have already implied a personal lack of enthusiasm for restrictions on trading low-priced, out-of-the-money options and for the 1,000-contract position limit. Apart from these relatively minor points, regulation may also have gone too far in 1976–1977 episodes involving a number of Amex specialists and CBOE market makers who were found guilty of printing phantom trades. Apparently, the primary purpose of these phantom trades was to forestall an influx of public orders with unrealistic price limits. If there was no motivation behind these transactions other than the maintenance of an orderly market, this episode should be noted as one of the extremely rare instances when the extraordinarily well-drafted exchange rules did not cover a problem. To the extent that these phantom trades were the result of attempts by market makers to reduce their margin requirements, the penalties meted out were appropriate. To the extent, however, that they were a misguided response to a problem for which no effective rule existed, the penalties seem harsh.

Except for a normal antibureaucratic reaction that the amount of paperwork often seems excessive, most thinking observers would be more inclined to tighten certain regulations governing transactions with individual investors than to recommend dismantling the system. In spite of the best efforts of the exchanges and most member firms, many registered representatives are not competent to handle option business. Tests administered by the firms have weeded out a few incompetents, but a more effective system would require comprehensive exchange- or SEC-administered tests which every existing registered representative would be required to pass within 12 months after the requirement is effective. A formal examination is more likely to be taken seriously than an informal test administered by the salesman's branch manager or someone from the compliance department.

Another problem that needs regulatory attention is the enforcement of good sales practices. An investor need only answer a few advertisements to get on a large number of option mailing lists. Not all the mailings conform strictly to SEC and exchange rules. If they do not already do so, enforcement personnel might catch a surprising number of rule violators by sending for some free literature.

7 EVALUATION OF AN OPTION CONTRACT

A. THE SIGNIFICANCE OF OPTION EVALUATION

Throughout this book, the importance of careful evaluation of the specific option contract has been stressed. Rational evaluation of an option relative to the risk-reward characteristics of the underlying stock is the single most important step an investor must take to achieve superior investment performance using options.

Many option services and option users stress calculations based on (1) the leverage inherent in a particular option contract, (2) the option premium as a percent of the stock price or the striking price, or (3) the stock price parameters within which an option writing strategy is profitable. While it can occasionally be helpful to know the leverage potential of an option relative to a possible price change in the underlying stock, the option premium as a percent of the stock price, or the range of prices over which a given strategy will be profitable, a far more useful approach is to try to arrive at a single figure for the *fair value of an option*. Not only will that figure tell the investor whether, other things being equal, he should buy or write that option, but, on the basis of that single figure, he also can make any other appropriate calculations easily.

1. Fair Value

Whether the fair value of an option is expressed in dollars and cents or the desirability of the option to a buyer or writer is appraised by calculating the ratio of the market price of the option to the fair value of the contract, the important thing is to arrive at a single figure which provides meaningful guidance to the use of that option in a possible investment strategy. The purpose of this and subsequent evaluation sections is to describe and analyze the various methods of option evaluation in widespread use by arbitrageurs and advisory services. While many option and warrant advisory letters base their recommendations exclusively on an opinion on the underlying stock, some services attempt to evaluate the option contract or warrant in its own right. Although it is not possible to determine the accuracy of a stock recommendation in advance of the period for which the recommendation is made, it *is* possible to determine the *relative* attractiveness of the stock and an option on that stock. Any advisory service which does not attempt to *evaluate* the option relative to an investment in the stock will be less useful.

An appropriate standard against which to judge the usefulness of the assorted option valuation techniques, which will be examined in subsequent sections, is a simplified version of what most academic economists agree is the theoretical value of an option. Although this theoretical formulation was outlined briefly in the Introduction and in Chapter 4, it is now appropriate to expand upon those abbreviated remarks.

In Figure 7-1 and in the discussion to follow, an attempt is made to avoid visual clutter and confusion by dealing with the value of an option from the viewpoint of the buyer. Evaluation of the writer's position is essentially similar. This discussion deliberately omits several points which bear importantly on any practical application of this approach or on any advanced discussion of the theoretical value of an option.

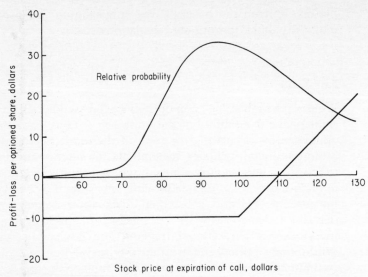

Figure 7-1. Call buyer's profit-loss line and stock price probability distribution.

The sole purpose of these omissions is to improve the clarity of the explanation.

The buyer's profit-loss line begins in the lower left-hand corner of Figure 7-1, runs parallel to the horizontal axis until it reaches the striking price (in this case $100 per share), and then rises toward the upper right-hand corner of the page. The approximately bell-shaped curve superimposed on the graph is a hypothetical probability distribution of the stock price on the day the option expires. The shape and location of the stock price distribution curve are a function of the price of the stock at the time the option is purchased, interest rates, the volatility of stock price changes, and the time remaining before the option expires. In the present instance, the price of the stock is assumed to be $95 on the day the buyer purchases the 6-month call at an option price of $10. The interest rate is the intermediate-term, low-risk interest rate. For simplicity, the volatility of the stock is assumed to be the average volatility over some past period.

While it is not possible to determine the exact price of the stock on the date 6 months in the future when the option will expire, it is possible to estimate the *probability* that it will sell at any particular price. This probability estimate is based largely on the way common stock prices have behaved in the past. The probability estimate should not be confused with technical analysis of stock price behavior. Derivation of the probability curve neither requires nor provides a forecast of the *direction* of any change in the stock price. It is concerned only with the likely *magnitude* of stock price changes.

Certain characteristics of this probability distribution are intuitively obvious if given even a little thought. For example, most observers, whether they are avid chart readers or exponents of the random walk hypothesis, would agree that the price of a typical stock is more likely to be close to the present price 6 months from today than it is to be selling for either twice or half the present price. As the time period is extended from 6 months to, say, 2 years, the probability distribution will tend to spread out. Over the longer period, doubling or halving the stock price will become more likely events.

Some stocks are more likely to double or collapse than others. Both Teledyne and American Telephone and Telegraph were selling near $60 per share in late 1977. Regardless of their opinions on the merits of the two issues, most market participants would expect Teledyne stock to trade over a broader price range than AT&T over the next several years. Beyond these areas of agreement, there is considerable controversy over the exact shape of the probability distribution of future stock prices. The curve shown here is for illustrative purposes only, though it does approximate the shape of observed probability distributions.

Once the difficult task of estimating the characteristics of the probability distribution has been completed and the shape and location of the probability curve is determined, it is a relatively simple matter to calculate the expected profitability of a call option. Using the example in Figure 7-1, we divide the probability curve into small segments. The area under the curve in each segment, say in the stock price range between $70 and $71 per share, is divided by the total area under the curve. The resulting fraction is multiplied by the profit or loss to the buyer ($10 loss) if the stock sells in the range of $70 to $71 per share on the day the option expires. When the results of these calculations over the range of all possible stock prices are added up, the total is the profit or loss the buyer of that call can expect.

This explanation of the calculation of the expected profit or loss from buying a call will seem quite straightforward once the reader understands the basic principle of multiplying the fraction of the total area under the probability curve times the profit or loss associated with the price range under that part of the curve. In practice, the calculation is very time-consuming unless the probability distribution curve is similar to one of a family of curves which can be defined by a simple equation. Readers will appreciate the complexities of option evaluation when they consider that calculation of the expected profit or loss occurs only after an analyst has carefully estimated the shape and location of the probability distribution and has made a myriad of adjustments to the probability distribution and/or the profit-loss line for the effect of commissions, dividends, and interest rates.

Before we can compare an option evaluation method with this theoretical model, we must convert the expected profit or loss figure into an estimate of the value of the call. This is simply a matter of adding the buyer's expected profit *to* or subtracting his expected loss *from* the market price of the call and subtracting an additional amount as an adjustment for risk (see pages 75–78).

The fair value or risk-adjusted break-even price of the call is the single figure most rational option evaluation techniques attempt to derive. The following appraisal of these techniques will be largely an assessment of how closely they approximate the value that the theoretical model would generate. Most of the option evaluation techniques in widespread use are the result of attempts to short-cut the process by simplifying the calculations or, less commonly, by finding the value of the option indirectly through a formula that does not explicitly incorporate the probability distribution of stock prices.

The importance of the fair value or break-even value of an option contract is hard to overestimate. Once this value has been determined, it can serve as the foundation for any further work the investor might wish to do. It can also serve as part of a simple decision rule such as

A call option is never written unless the premium received by the writer exceeds the fair value of the call, and a call option is never purchased unless the premium falls below the fair value of the option.

The fair value of a call or the ratio of the call price to fair value can serve as the basis of a whole series of calculations which permit the investor to structure the risk and return parameters of his investment position in virtually any desired way. Some of these calculations will be illustrated in Section F of this chapter.

If we use an expected value calculation, such as the fair value of a call, as the sole criterion for a decision, we implicitly assume that the investor is neutral toward risk. Stated another way, relying solely on the expected value of an option implies that an individual is indifferent to the choice between, say, a 100 percent chance of gaining $1 and a 10 percent chance of gaining $10 combined with a 90 percent chance of no gain. While there is considerable evidence that this assumption is not valid when the amounts of money involved are quite large, the calculation of expected value provides a useful starting point. An individual's risk preferences can be reflected in the development of an investment strategy once the expected value has been calculated.

From the explanation in Chapter 4, Section A, of the graphic representation technique, it should be clear that it is possible to calculate the profit or loss from any investment if we know the stock price at the end of the period. A profit-loss calculation at a particular stock price can be made in a few seconds. If the investor is willing to spend a bit more time, he can construct one of the simple graphs that was used to illustrate profit or loss at various stock price levels. When the data on the graph are processed to reflect the probability distribution of future stock prices, the investor can rationally evaluate the investment from the viewpoint of expected rate of return in addition to building a portfolio that reflects risk preferences and subjective stock price expectations.

Few investors will rely strictly on an expected value calculation in devising a portfolio strategy. It is important, however, that the rational investor understand the nature of the probability distribution of stock price changes and the possible cost of each deviation from a strategy based on expected value. Graphic representation of risks and rewards combined with an expected rate-of-return calculation permits the most intelligent evaluation of the possible results. The graphs need not be fancy to help the investor judge the appropriateness of a strategy to his expectations and risk preferences.

2. Non-Evaluation Approaches

Before turning our attention to the variety of evaluation techniques that have been devised to deal with the problem of determining the appropriate price to pay or receive for a call option, we will examine some other approaches to option selection which are in widespread use but which do not attempt to compute or estimate the fair value of the option contract as a prelude to an investment decision. These approaches are espoused by a number of advisory services and are used by some experienced investors. While each of these approaches provides some useful information, none of them is adequate when used without an appraisal of the fair value of an option contract.

Leverage calculations generally attempt to estimate the effect of a given change in the stock price on the option price. For example, a 20 percent rise in the price of a stock by the time an option expires may lead to a 100 percent profit on the option; or a 10 percent rise in the stock price may be necessary to give the call buyer a 10 percent return on investment. Such calculations are prepared by a variety of option services and are frequently used to justify the speculative purchase of options by investors with limited resources.

The problem with leverage calculations is that they tend to be misleading. In any given 6-month period the probability of a 20 percent advance in AT&T is far lower than the probability of a 20 percent advance in the price of Brunswick. As obvious as this statement may be and as unlikely as it may seem that any reasonably intelligent investor would be misled, the fact that leverage calculations ordinarily fail to discriminate among stocks with different degrees of volatility is, at best, confusing. At worst, the naïve investor could be led to make an erroneous decision. Unless the investor is deliberately seeking risk, the fact that a given option provides unusually high leverage will not be useful information. The rational investor is much more likely to be interested in expected profit or rate of return. To get these numbers the investor must try to put a value on the option itself, not on its leverage.

A large number of covered option writers base their writing decisions on a calculation of the option premium as a percent of the stock price or, alternatively, on the rate of return if the stock they own is called away from them. Using our standard example of a $95 stock and its related option, the $10 option premium for a 6-month option at $100 is 10.5 percent of the $95 stock price. If the stock is called away, the writer gets a return of

$$\frac{\$100 - \$95 + \$10}{\$95}$$

or 15.8 percent over 6 months. The annualized return would be about 31.6 percent *if the call is exercised.*

In spite of its *apparent* attractiveness, writing this option may not be a sound strategy. This call writer is giving up any incremental profit he might earn if the stock rises above $110 per share by the end of the option period. The call writer can *never* earn more than an annualized return of 31.6 percent. If the stock is extremely volatile, there is a high probability that the stock will sell for more than $110 and, *conversely, a high probability that it will sell below $85 per share, giving him a loss even after he receives the option premium.* The option premium is the covered writer's compensation for giving up the chance to participate in any appreciation of the stock beyond $110 per share on the up side and his insurance protection if the stock declines. If he sells the option too cheaply, he may be giving up too much potential appreciation relative to the risk he is accepting in the event the stock declines. The tricky feature of the single-point rate-of-return approach to option writing is that the writer *always* gets a good return if the stock rises and is *always* better off having written the call if the stock declines. If the stock is sufficiently volatile, however, the overall return will be inadequate in the long run because the writer will not make enough when the stock advances to recover losses from periods when the stock declines. It is impossible to overemphasize the importance of this point.

Many arbitrageurs and option writers use another "non-evaluation" approach to options that has a little more to recommend it than the simple leverage calculation, or dividing the option premium by the stock price. This is the so-called "parameter" approach; it involves calculation of the range of prices over which a strategy is profitable. For example, if an investor buys 100 shares of stock at $95 and writes two options with a striking price of $100 and an option premium of $10, this strategy will be profitable if the stock sells between $75 and $125 per share on the day the options expire. The range—$75 to $125—defines the profitability parameters of this strategy.

To the extent that the investor tries to evaluate the risk that the stock price will rise above or fall below this range, the parameter approach can be sensible. Unfortunately, we are all familiar with remarks such as: "The absolute maximum downside risk on this stock is 10 points." As most investors who have made such statements are painfully aware, stocks do drop or rise further than one might think possible. Unless the assessment of the risk that the stock will violate the profit parameters is done conscientiously and quantitatively, it is useless.

The principal danger of the parameter approach is that option writers who are addicted to it have a tendency to try to write their way out of any problem. Suppose that the stock in our example dropped to $65 per share, putting it outside the profit parameters the investor originally set up. The devotee of parametric analysis will often yield to the irresistible temptation to write additional options, frequently with only minimal consideration for the adequacy of the premium, to extend the lower parameter below the $65 price level. This reduction of the lower parameter can be accomplished *only by reducing the upper parameter as well*. If the stock price recovers after the upper parameter is lowered, the investor can easily be whipsawed. Furthermore, as the investor writes more options on this stock, he ties up more of his capital in a situation which his machinations prove he does not understand. Unless the underlying stock goes to zero, fluctuates violently, or moves up rapidly and steadily for a long enough period of time to bankrupt him, this investor should *eventually* earn at least a small profit. He could have a substantial fraction of his assets committed to a low-return investment by the time that happens, however.

Another problem with the use of parameters is that two strategies with similar parameters may vary greatly in attractiveness. If, in the example cited earlier, the investor purchased the stock at $120 instead of $95 and wrote two options with striking prices of $100 for premiums of $22.50 per share, the profit parameters would still be $75 to $125. Unless the investor expects the stock price to decline, this strategy is probably less attractive than the earlier example. The point of maximum profitability ($100) is well below the $120 stock price, and even a modest advance in the stock price will make the strategy unprofitable.

A more serious flaw in the parametric approach is that it provides no way except "gut feel" to compare strategies involving options with different striking prices or positions involving different stocks. Only if a fair value is calculated for each option can the investor rationally compare two strategies involving different options on the same stock or strategies involving different stocks.

The sophisticated reader may feel that we have attacked straw men in criticizing the devotees of leverage calculations, premium percentages, and parametric analysis. Nothing could be further from the truth. There are numerous investors who consider one or another of these techniques to be a sound method of managing an option portfolio. Many option buyers look primarily at leverage calculations to determine where they can get the most return on their dollar. Numerous experienced option writers are convinced that as long as the option premium is a large enough percentage of the stock price, or as long as they readjust their profit-loss line to bracket the current stock price with their profit parameters, they are bound to make money in the long run. The fact that these writers may tie up a disproportionate amount of their equity in a single situation or that the ultimate return on investment may be very small does not seem to bother them.

On the assumption that the reader is convinced of the importance of evaluating the option contract itself as a first step in the analysis of any option strategy, we turn to the consideration of the wide variety of techniques various authors have devised to compute the fair value of an option. The reader who is not persuaded of the overwhelming importance of option valuation should reread the Introduction and Chapter 4.

B. GRAPHIC EVALUATION TECHNIQUES

Graphic techniques for the analysis of option investment strategies vary greatly in usefulness and sophistication. Some investors accept the market's appraisal of the value of options and use graphs of the type examined in Chapter 4, Section A, to estimate the profitability of a strategy at specific stock prices. These investors see graphs as tools to restructure the risk characteristics of a portfolio rather than as part of an evaluation technique. If the investor is a disciple of the parameter school, he can use graphs to determine the stock price range over which a strategy will be profitable. Regardless of the approach, drawing a graph can help the investor crystallize his views on the probable course of the stock price and integrate these views with his attitude toward risk.

To take things one step further, an investor might superimpose on a graph (see Chapter 4, Section A) his personal estimate of the probability curve of the distribution of stock prices on the day the option expires. This graph might look very roughly like Figure 7-1. If, on the basis of the investor's visual assessment of such a diagram, there is a high probability that the expected return on investment will be satisfactory and if the risk characteristics of the investment are acceptable, the investor will take the position. Most graphic analysis techniques used for option evaluation are simpler than the diagrams used in this book and require less input data from the user. These graphic techniques spring from efforts to simplify the decision-making process.

One of the most widely used sets of graphs for the evaluation of conventional options was prepared by Zaven A. Dadekian for his book, *The Strategy of Puts and Calls*. The charts actually published in the book are obsolete because interest rates and commission charges have changed significantly since 1968 and, even with new charts, the results are only approximate. Nonetheless, Dadekian's graphs can be the foundation for one of the few rational option analysis techniques which the average investor can apply to the appraisal of conventional options. There is no intent to suggest that Dadekian's charts are the answer to the public's option evaluation needs. In fact, certain features of Dadekian's technique are misleading. For example, he calculates an annualized return on investment which is really a return on equity *if* the option is exercised. In spite of such weaknesses, the thinking behind Dadekian's charts can be more useful than most of the material available to the small investor.

Dadekian's contribution lies in his analysis of conventional option premiums (bids to writers) for stocks at various price levels. He collected data on a large number of conventional option transactions and divided the data into quartile rankings at 10-point stock price intervals. He found, for example, that about 25 percent of the option premiums paid to writers for a 6-months-and-10-day call on a $40 stock fell below $417 or $4.17 per share, 50 percent fell below $455 or $4.55 per share, and 75 percent fell below $492 or $4.92 per share. Figure 7-2 is Dadekian's graph for premiums on 6-months-and-10-day call options. It is easy to be overly critical of Dadekian's study from a theoretical viewpoint, but the approach can be helpful. From Dadekian's charts the would-be option writer can conclude that a $450 premium offered him on a $40 stock with average volatility is probably a fair bid, but a $475 bid on an extremely volatile stock is probably too low.

One of the problems with Dadekian's charts is that they must be updated frequently and the user must subjectively evaluate such factors as volatility and dividend payments in

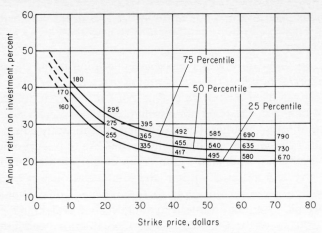

Figure 7-2. Percentile ranking of bids to writers for 6-month-and-10-day call options. Reprinted by permission of Charles Scribner's Sons from *The Strategy of Puts and Calls* by Zaven A. Dadekian. Copyright © 1968 Zaven A. Dadekian.

his examination of each proposed transaction. Another problem is that the charts are only useful for conventional options for which the market price and striking price are identical. They are almost useless for listed options or "special" options for which the two prices are different.

Because the Dadekian charts assume that, on the average, option bids to writers are fair, it is possible for a writer using the charts to accept a bid that was relatively better than most bids available, but still too low, or to reject a bid that did not appear attractive on the charts, but was actually higher than the fair value of the call. The charts are most likely to give inappropriate indications when a major change is occurring in the economy or a particular company. The intelligent option writer can probably incorporate such a change into his thinking and compensate accordingly in reaching a decision. If he is using conventional options on a small scale and does not have access to better information, an investor can do far worse than rely on this kind of chart.

The buyer or writer of listed options, where the market

price of the stock and the striking price of the option can be quite different, needs more information than can be obtained from the Dadekian charts. He needs a graph which relates the value of a particular option contract at one stock price to the value of that same contract at any other price on the underlying stock. The rest of the diagrams in this section illustrate attempts to construct this type of graph.

To use a graph which relates the value of a listed call to the market price of the underlying stock, the investor must know or estimate the value of the call at one stock price, usually the striking price. Determining this key value requires a non-graphic valuation approach or a Dadekian-type chart. Many investors claim to have a good "feel" for option values, with or without a Dadekian chart, when the stock price and striking price are equal. Investors who are more at home with the identical striking and market prices of the conventional option market than with the divergent market and striking prices of listed options will be comfortable using a graph that permits them to locate a curve based on a single valuation point where the striking and market prices are equal.

Although both models were designed for the analysis of long-term warrants, the Shelton and Kassouf econometric models, which will be examined in detail in Section D of this chapter, have occasionally been adapted to graphic evaluation of warrants and options. Neither author would approve of this adaptation of his work; however, these models were chosen to illustrate some of the problems of evaluating options with graphs, primarily because the popularity of the Shelton and Kassouf models might lead investors to misuse them. While our discussion of the graphic adaptation may point to some weaknesses in the related econometric model, failure of the graphic adaptation does not condemn the econometric model.

The series of graphic models begins with an adaptation of the Shelton model. Figure 7-3 depicts an option value line derived from the Shelton model for warrant evaluation. The reader who wishes to experiment with the Shelton line as a graphic technique for option evaluation should first draw a graph similar to Figure 7-3 for some stock and option of

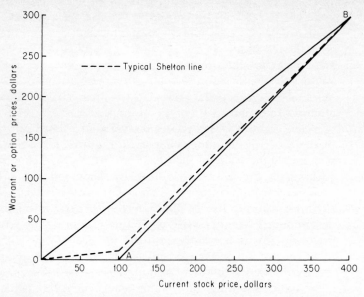

Figure 7-3. An evaluation "curve" derived from the Shelton econometric model.

interest. The triangle *OAB* in Figure 7-3 is drawn by connecting the three points in this table:

Point	Stock Price	Option or Warrant Price
O	0	0
A	Exercise price	0
B	4 × exercise price	3 × exercise price

The reasons Shelton chose these particular points will be discussed in the detailed analysis of his model. The focus of interest here is strictly on how well the model works as a graphic valuation method for options.

Once the points have been located and the lines drawn, the investor must determine the fair value of any call he wishes to evaluate at one specific stock price. As noted earlier, most active option traders claim they can assign an appropriate value to a call as long as the stock price and the striking price are identical. Evaluation techniques are most useful (and most necessary for the typical investor) when these two prices differ. In the example illustrated, the investor has concluded that a 6-month option with a striking price of $100 is worth $12.50 per share when the stock is selling at $100. Plotting this point on the graph, the investor has one of the points on the Shelton line. All that remains is to calculate the values at several more points and draw in the curve. The known point is $12.50/$75, or 16.7 percent of the distance between what Shelton calls the *minimum value* of the warrant or option (line *OAB*) and what he calls the *maximum value* (line *OB*). To estimate the value of the option at any stock price other than $100, the investor merely multiplies this percentage by the distance between minimum value and the maximum value and adds the result to the minimum value. For example, if the stock is selling at $80, the calculation is as follows:

Value of option = % of range × (value at maximum
$$- \text{ value at minimum}) + \text{value at minimum}$$
$$V_c = 16.7\% \times (\$60 - 0) + 0$$
$$= \$10.02$$

This value is clearly too high. If one makes the same calculation for this option at a stock price of $120, one will get an option value of $31.69, which is also far too high. Part of the reason for this sizable discrepancy between the values computed for the Shelton line and the prices at which options actually change hands may be accounted for by the fact that the Shelton line was derived for the evaluation of long-term warrants. For short-lived options, a graph of the Shelton line has little to offer as an evaluation tool.

Just as his entire model is more complex than Shelton's, Kassouf's basic curve is slightly more difficult to derive. For mathematically inclined readers, the formula for the curve is

$$V_c = S \left[\sqrt[z]{\left(\frac{P_s}{S}\right)^Z + 1} - 1 \right]$$

where V_c = value of call or warrant
  S = striking price of call or warrant being evaluated
  P_s = price of stock at which option is being evaluated
  Z = location parameter of curve which reflects all

determinants of option or warrant value such as interest rates, dividends, stock price, time remaining to expiration, and stock volatility

The reader who fears we are about to depart on a mathematical tangent at this point can relax. The only purposes in writing out the formula are to provide interested readers with more information and to show that the formula for the curve assumes that the value of a particular call is completely determined by the stock price–striking price relationship once the value of Z, which defines the shape and location of the curve, is known. In other words, Z describes the curve for various values of the ratio P_s/S.

The formula suggests that once the user of the formula or graph knows the value of the stock price and the striking price, he can determine the value of the call. Unfortunately P_s (stock price) is one of the variables determining Z. Thus, a given Z curve might provide a better fit to the observed data over a narrow range of values for the option than any other Z curve and yet still not fit very well if the stock price and option value move out of that range. Figure 7-4 illustrates a typical, though hypothetical, relationship between observed data and Kassouf's Z curve. When we examine Kassouf's

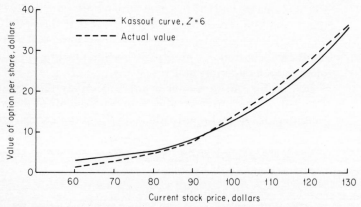

Figure 7-4. Comparison of a Kassouf Z curve with actual option values.

econometric model in detail, we will see that, unlike the graph, the model can accommodate this drift off the Z curve.

The difficulty with both the Kassouf and the Shelton lines is that they are derived from equations that do not incorporate the probability distribution of stock price changes. These figures represent their respective creators' attempts to fit a curve or a line to observed warrant price–stock price relationships. As part of the Shelton and Kassouf econometric models, these curves can give useful results, particularly in estimating the expected price of a long-term warrant. The curves themselves are of little use in option evaluation.

Figure 7-5 depicts a set of option curves based on the Gastineau-Madansky option evaluation model. Unlike the Shelton and Kassouf models, there is no simple formula for the derivation of this set of curves. The curves in Figure 7-5 have been fitted by hand to selected points calculated by a computerized model. Although the reader will understand the

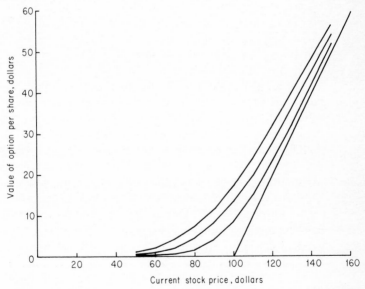

Figure 7-5. Option value curves based on the Gastineau-Madansky model for option valuation; adjusted for expected commissions, assumes no dividend paid.

lack of a simple formula better after the Gastineau-Madansky model is discussed at greater length, the principal reason no simple formula is available is that the probability distribution used in the Gastineau-Madansky model is empirically derived. As a consequence, no simple function will describe the curve with appropriate precision.

Figure 7-5 is set up in much the same way as the Shelton and Kassouf curves. The major difference is that the Gastineau-Madansky curve should fit any observed data rather well. Under normal circumstances, the market price of an option should roughly approximate the value an investor might extract from the curves, provided he has selected the proper curves. Although any departure of the option price from the value indicated by the curve *might* represent an opportunity for arbitrage profit, the user of the graph must exercise care that the option has not "jumped" to another curve.

These curves have only limited practical value to the investor because of the restrictive assumptions on which they are based. Discussion of these assumptions and limitations will aim as much at discouraging indiscriminate use of the graph as at helping the user adjust his thinking to the graph's idiosyncrasies. The most important single assumption underlying any graphic evaluation technique is that, with the exception of the stock price, the basic determinants of option value are unchanged from the moment a specific curve is selected to the moment the curve is used to derive the value of an option. This assumption is frequently invalid. Time usually passes after a particular curve is chosen, and time is one of the most important determinants of option value. If much time passed, the value of the option would lie on a different curve, not at a different location on the same curve.

The graph is most likely to be used when the stock price has changed significantly from an earlier value which was used to select an appropriate curve. Unfortunately, many of the factors that cause stock price changes also cause changes in the relative value of options. For example, gyrations in interest rates cause option values as well as stock prices to fluctuate. Other things being equal, an increase in interest rates increases the relative value of an option, and a decrease in interest rates causes the value of the option to fall. In addition, an outbreak of military activity in the Middle East could cause the price of an international oil stock to fall. Because the outlook for the oil company is now less certain and the stock is likely to be more volatile, the value of an option contract might decline *less* than the graph would predict.

Apart from these problems with the effect of external changes on the choice of an appropriate curve, graphs are difficult to adjust for commissions and dividends. A commission adjustment can be built in, but the investor will still need separate sets of curves for conventional and listed options and for high-yield stocks and low-yield stocks. This litany could continue, but it should be clear by now that a set of sophisticated valuation graphs could do as much to confuse and mislead the average investor as to help him. If Figure 7-5 helps readers appreciate the relationship between stock price and option value over a range of stock prices, it will serve its purpose. To use this graph directly in decision making is inappropriate.

C. EVALUATION RULES AND FORMULAS

To differentiate the numerous rules of thumb and simple formulas that are proposed for option evaluation from the more sophisticated econometric models of Shelton and Kassouf, a rule or formula used in option evaluation is defined as any numeric or analog relationship that does not directly incorporate an adjustment for either dividends or stock price volatility. Formulas may attempt to derive an option value from scratch or they may only describe appropriate adjustments for differences between the market price of the stock and the striking price of the option. They may be expressed as algebraic expressions, or they may be reduced either to tables designed for easy reference or to mechanical devices. In the latter category, the author has in his possession two completely different "warrant slide rules" and has seen an "option slide rule" and an option "computer."

At a very slight risk of overgeneralization, one may state that most of these rules and formulas are dangerous. While

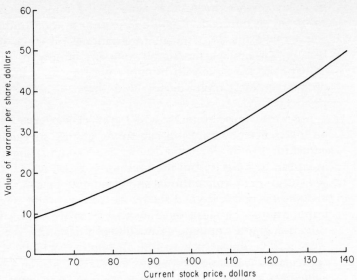

Figure 7-6. Guynemer Giguère's warrant valuation parabola for $S = \$100$.

many of the specific examples criticized come from the extensive literature on warrants, similar techniques have been applied to options now that exchange listing has focused interest on these shorter-term warrantlike instruments. Developments in the option market are proceeding so rapidly that new formulas, rules, tables, and other gimmicks will appear regularly.

One formula originally developed for the evaluation of long-term warrants was proposed by Guynemer Giguère in *The Analysts Journal* of November 1958. Modifying Giguère's symbols to conform to those used previously, his equation is $V_c = P_s^2/4S$. To state the formula in words, Giguère argues that the value of a warrant (V_c) is equal to the price of the stock (P_s) squared, divided by four times the exercise or striking price (S). The curve which this formula describes is a parabola with a value of zero when the stock price is equal to zero. The shape of the function is illustrated in Figure 7-6. The premium over intrinsic value disappears completely when the price of the stock reaches twice the exercise or striking price. Empirical studies using this formula indicate that, as a general rule, warrants with more than 3 to 5 years of life remaining will usually sell at prices higher than those predicted by the formula. Options with less than 1 year of life will usually sell at lower prices. Giguère suggests modifying the formula for shorter- or longer-term options or warrants by adding to or subtracting from the denominator of the equation. The results this modification gives are not consistently useful, however.

A more recent discussion of warrant valuation using a tabular approach was published in *Value Line Selection and Opinion*, July 1968. Though no equation is given in this article, a table suggesting the degree of positive and negative leverage in warrants at various prices is provided. An implicit fair value line for long-term warrants is obtainable from the table. Although it is not possible to say definitely, the Value Line formula appears to be a modification of either the Shelton or the Kassouf model, probably the former.

Several writers have published tables designed to show the relationship between option premiums and stock prices. Most of these tables of option values give an average or maximum premium for options of various lives. As the composite listing in Table 7-1 indicates, the appropriate premium assigned to a stock is primarily a function of the stock price. Apart from some evidence that there is an inverse relationship between stock price and volatility that makes options on lower-priced stocks more expensive than those on higher-priced stocks, the principal reason for the indicated relationship between stock prices and conventional option premiums is the extraordinarily high transaction cost of a conventional option on a low-priced

Table 7-1. Estimated Maximum Premiums* Paid by Buyers for New Conventional Calls at the Market

Stock Price	3 Months	6 Months	1 Year
10	$137.50–$150	$175–$237.50	$300–$337.50
20	$212.50–$225	$312.50–$350	$400–$450
30	$300–$325	$400–$450	$500–$550
40	$400–$425	$525–$600	$700–$750
50	$475–$525	$625–$700	$800–$875
75	$700–$775	$925–$1,100	$1,200–$1,300
100	$900–$1,025	$1,225–$1,350	$1,450–$1,700

* These premiums are composites derived from several sources. Any resemblance to actual premiums is coincidental. Most authors of such tables indicate that premiums on American Stock Exchange or over-the-counter stocks will be higher.

stock. Readers should regard these tables of option values with suspicion. Even though they may reflect option prices, they will not usually reflect option values. If an investor is careful, these tables can be used much like the Dadekian charts. Table 7-1 is based on the premiums paid by buyers in contrast to the premiums paid to writers as in the Dadekian chart in Figure 7-2. Though the data came from different sources, the principal difference is the put and call broker's spread.

With the present interest in options it was inevitable that a number of advisory services would begin to publish tables showing expected option prices at various combinations of striking price, market price, and time to maturity for listed options. Such tables could be useful to the investor if properly derived and frequently updated.

The tables published by Fischer Black in an article titled "Fact and Fantasy in the Use of Options" (see Bibliography) are probably the most useful tables readily available to the student of options who is willing to do the necessary work to use tables intelligently. The assumptions behind each of Black's tables are spelled out in detail. Although he does not simplify the user's task by pointing out which table should be used with which stock, Black does discuss how an appropriate table should be selected and how necessary adjustments for dividends and taxes can be made. Careful study of Black's article will help the reader understand the hazards of blind dependence on a set of option tables.

We turn next to the rules of thumb. It is an article of faith with many long-time traders in conventional options that if the striking price of an option and the market price of the underlying stock are close, the price of the option should change by about one-half as many points as the stock price changes. In other words, if an option with a striking price of $30 is worth $5 when the stock is selling at $30, it will be worth $2.50 with the stock at $25 and $8 with the stock at $36.

Not all rules of thumb are simple. In his book, *Stock Options,* James B. Cloonan provides a brief table of adjustment factors for in-the-money options. Briefly, he argues that if the stock is selling above its striking price and if the option has 9 months to go before expiration, the investor should expect the option price to rise by only one-half of the amount by which the option trades in the money. The reader will note that, so far, this is the same as the old rule of thumb mentioned above. Though his statement of the "new" rule is complicated, Cloonan basically argues that the percentage by which the option price will change increases as the option approaches expiration. Cloonan's estimates of the percentage of the stock price move by which the option price will move are given in Table 7-2. Though rules of thumb are frequently misleading, even a cursory examination of actual option price behavior suggests that the old rule is more accurate than Cloonan's table. In general, option prices seem to move between one-half and two-thirds as much as stock prices when the striking price and market price are roughly equal. This rule works fairly well almost regardless of the time remaining in the life of the options.

Table 7-2. Cloonan Factors for Option Price Change of In-the-Money Options

Months remaining to expiration	9	8	7	6	5	4	3	2	1	0
Percentage of any stock price move that will be reflected in an option price move	50	55	60	65	70	75	80	85	90	95

The relationship between stock price and option price is too complicated to be reduced to a simple formula or rule of thumb. Simplicity is a virtue only if a simple model or rule provides good results. One of the best simple evaluation procedures yet developed is a cross between the relatively sophisticated Black-Scholes option evaluation formula and the elementary graphic techniques described in Section B. Elroy Dimson of the London Graduate School of Business Studies has devised a set of nomograms (specialized graphs) to permit an investor to evaluate put and call options, to calculate hedge ratios, and to estimate the probability that an option will be exercised. Figure 7-7 illustrates the use of a nomogram to value a call option.

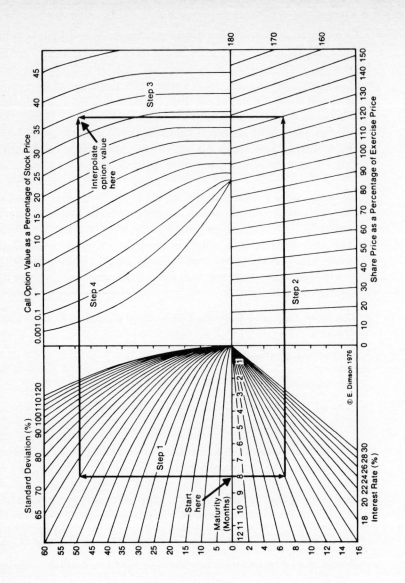

Standard Deviation (%)

Call Option Value as a Percentage of Stock Price

Share Price as a Percentage of Exercise Price

Interest Rate (%)

Maturity (Months)

Start here

Step 1

Step 2

Step 3

Step 4

Interpolate option value here

© E. Dimson 1976

Figure 7-7. Valuing a call option with a nomogram.

Step	Procedure
1. Maturity	Draw a vertical line through the maturity.
2. Interest rate	Draw a horizontal line from the point of intersection with the interest rate, through the lower right-hand quadrant of the nomogram.
3. Share price	Draw a vertical line from the point of intersection with the share price as a percentage of the exercise price, through the upper right-hand quadrant.
4. Standard deviation	Draw a horizontal line from the point of intersection with the standard deviation, through the upper right-hand quadrant.
5. Result	Interpolate the result from the intersecting lines in the upper right-hand quadrant of the nomogram.

Example: Figure 7-7 illustrates the valuation of an eight-month call option on a stock that has an annual standard deviation of 60 percent. Since the exercise price is $40.00, the current share price of $52.00 is 130 percent of the exercise price.* The annual interest rate is 10 percent. First, a vertical line has been drawn through the eight-month maturity, then a horizontal line through the 10 percent interest rate. Next a vertical line was drawn through the share price as a percentage of the exercise price (130 percent). Finally, a horizontal line was passed through the 60 percent standard deviation. The intersection of this line with the previous vertical line indicates a call option value of 34 percent of the share price, or $17.68.

---

* If cash dividends are paid during the life of the option, the present value of the dividends should be deducted from the current share price. The option is then worth the greater of the value to maturity or the value to the last cum-dividend date.

SOURCE: Elroy Dimson, "Option Valuation Nomograms," *Financial Analysts Journal,* November–December 1977, pp. 71–74.

Unlike most graphic or rule-of-thumb approaches to option evaluation, the nomogram requires an investor to use an estimate of the standard deviation (volatility) of the underlying stock. In this respect the nomogram is superior to the other graphic techniques and to the simple evaluation rules and formulas. One weakness that nomograms share with these other procedures is the need for a mental dividend adjustment. They also systematically undervalue put options.

Dimson's nomograms can be of value when a small number of options are being evaluated and when recent output from a sophisticated computerized option model is not available. Regular users of options should insist on access to a more comprehensive, fully adjusted evaluation model.

D. ECONOMETRIC MODELS

1. The Shelton Model

In a two-part article in the *Financial Analysts Journal* beginning in the issue of May–June 1967, John Shelton reviewed much of the then-existing literature on warrant evaluation and presented an econometric model which, in its most general form, permits evaluation of warrants and options with virtually any period of life remaining. Unlike the Giguère formula which is difficult to adjust for variations in remaining life, dividend yield, and other parameters, the Shelton model can be modified to handle virtually any warrant or option contract.

As was noted in the discussion of graphic techniques for option evaluation, Shelton argues that there are minimum and maximum theoretical values for any option or warrant. The minimum value is the intrinsic value. If the striking price of an option or warrant is $100 and the stock is currently selling at $110, then the intrinsic value is $10, or the difference between the current price of the stock and the striking price or exercise price of the option or warrant. If the stock is selling below the striking price, the intrinsic or minimum value of the option or warrant is zero. Largely from examination of warrant price–stock price relationships, Shelton and other observers have found that a long-term warrant rarely sells at any significant premium over intrinsic value when the price of the stock is more than four times the exercise price. Furthermore, when the stock price is below this level, the maximum value of the warrant appears to be about 75 percent of the price of the stock.

Within the range determined by the minimum of either zero or the intrinsic value of the warrant and the maximum of 75 percent of the stock price, Shelton finds that a good approximation to prices of long-term warrants is given by the following expression:

$$\sqrt[4]{\frac{M}{72}}\left(.47 - 4.25\frac{D}{P_s} + .17L\right)$$

where M = number of months remaining to expiration
  D = annual dividend payment
  P_s = current price of stock
  D/P_s = annual dividend yield
  L = 1 if warrant is listed and 0 if it is traded over the counter

Once the value of this expression has been calculated, the resulting decimal fraction is multiplied by the difference between the maximum and minimum values of the option as computed above, and the product is added to the minimum value. An example of a warrant value calculation using the Shelton model can be found in Table 7-3.

Unlike Giguère's formula and many of the rule-of-thumb warrant-stock relationships, Shelton's formula has the important advantage that it adjusts explicity for the effect of the dividend on the common stock. A further advantage of the Shelton formula is that it permits ready calculation of a warrant price by the average investor. All the information needed is in the daily newspaper.

A major drawback of the Shelton formulation, based on our earlier discussion of the theoretical valuation of an option, is that the Shelton formulation makes no adjustment for the volatility of the stock. If the dividend, stock price, and remaining life were identical, the Shelton model would give identical predicted prices for warrants on AT&T and Gulf &

Table 7-3. Sample Shelton Warrant Valuation Calculation

Issue: Fiberboard Corporation warrants

Expiration date: December 1, 1978

Exercise price: $22.50

Date of calculation: May 24, 1974

Months to expiration (M): 54

Dividend (D): $0.90

Stock price (P_s): $16.50

Dividend yield $\left(\dfrac{D}{P_s}\right)$: 5.5%

Warrant is listed on the Amex: (L) = 1

Substitute in Shelton formula:
$$\sqrt[4]{\frac{54}{72}}\,(.47 - 4.25 \times 0.055 + 0.17) = 38.1\%$$

Value of warrant (V_c) = 38.1% × ($12.38 + $0) + $0
                         = $4.72

Actual price of warrant: $5.13

Western. As strange as this result may appear, stock price volatility does seem to have less of an impact on longer-term warrant prices than on option prices. Shelton tested the effect of stock price volatility on warrant prices and found it did not materially affect the prices actually paid for long-term warrants. Volatility is absent from Shelton's formulation not because he ignored it, but because he concluded it did not matter very much in the appraisal of long-term warrants.

Besides missing a volatility factor, Shelton's model gives values for options that appear to be too high. Again, part of the problem is that the model was designed for long-term warrants. Casual observation of listed option trading suggests that any premium above intrinsic value disappears long before the stock price reaches four times the exercise price. The price at which the premium over intrinsic value disappears varies with the remaining life of the option, but it is probably between 20 and 40 percent over the striking price in most cases.

The reader has probably begun to suspect that he or she is being led to the conclusion that while the published Shelton model was not designed for use on options and gives absurd results when applied to any short-lived option or warrant, it can be reformulated to give useful results. The parameters of the valuation triangle must be changed, perhaps as implied by the line *OC* in Figure 7-8, and the multiple regression analysis which was used to devise the expression for calculating the position of the option line within the triangle must be done with option data instead of long-term warrant data. It is likely that the revised expression will contain the level of the stock price and stock volatility as important factors affecting option value in addition to dividend yield and time remaining to expiration which appear in the warrant version of the model. When these modifications are made, it would be interesting to compare the results from Shelton's model with those from the Kassouf model. Kassouf's formulation is more applicable to options than Shelton's approach and has consequently been more widely used. There is little reason to suspect that the Kassouf approach is inherently superior, however.

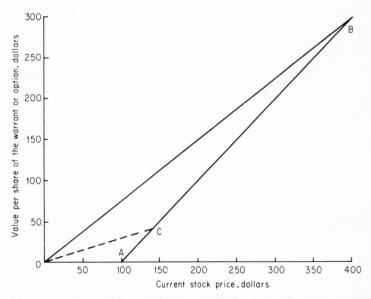

Figure 7-8. A possible modification to Shelton's econometric model to apply it to options.

Someday an ambitious doctoral candidate will undertake a study of the two approaches to determine how results from each deviate from the theoretical fair value of an option or warrant. Some deviation is inevitable in both cases because these econometric models use historic stock price–warrant price relationships as the basis for calculation of *expected* warrant or option *price*, not *fair value*. If premiums were higher than fair value during the period used to construct the model, applying the model at a later date will typically show predicted prices that are higher than fair value. This weakness is inherent in the econometric approach. It has less significance when a model is applied to warrant evaluation because overvaluation or undervaluation in warrant price may correct only very gradually. A prediction of relative warrant price may, in the short run, be as useful as a prediction of fair value. Options have a very limited life, however, and a model that predicts prices rather than values could lead to erroneous decisions. For example, if a model constructed during a period of high premiums is applied to data from a period of lower premiums, it might indicate that a particular option should be bought when in reality the option is still overpriced.

A further weakness of econometric models is that they provide no simple mechanism to adjust a coefficient if a change in the company's position occurs and is not adequately reflected in the input variables. Changing a coefficient arbitrarily could easily do more harm than good. The limitations of econometric models will be clearer after examination of the Kassouf model, which is somewhat more complex than the Shelton model and consequently somewhat more difficult for the average investor to use.

2. The Kassouf Model

The Kassouf econometric model has been widely used by professional arbitrageurs and by a few advisory services. The basic model was developed by Sheen T. Kassouf in a doctoral dissertation submitted to Columbia University in 1965. Though the model, as originally developed, was used to estimate the value of warrants, Kassouf and others have used it to evaluate virtually every kind of convertible security.

Kassouf's approach has been more widely used by professionals than Shelton's, less because of any inherent superiority in Kassouf's approach than because the rules for a doctoral dissertation require the author to reveal his methods in detail. The work behind Shelton's model may have been as sophisticated as Kassouf's work, but Shelton did not elaborate on his methods in the articles describing his model. In contrast to Kassouf, Shelton wanted a simple approach that anyone with a daily newspaper could use. Some of the material Kassouf has published is also designed for the average investor, but the backup information in his thesis has always been available. Shelton published only one simplified version of his model while Kassouf has emphasized the importance of periodic reexamination of the model to check how well an earlier formulation fits present circumstances. The detailed material he has published facilitates these checks.

For mathematically inclined readers, Table 7-4 presents the basic Kassouf equation and the coefficients Kassouf calculated for warrant evaluation for two separate time periods. Even those readers without mathematical interest or aptitude should examine the two formulas Kassouf devised to estimate warrant prices for the years 1945–1957 and 1958–1964, respectively. The formulas for the two time periods are quite different. Moreover, the warrant prices they predict are quite different when warrants with similar characteristics are evaluated. Using average values for the explanatory variables, Kassouf finds that a comparable warrant would have sold for $4.87 in the earlier period and $6.50 in the later period.

While there are several possible explanations for this difference, the most plausible is that supply and demand and other factors caused warrant premiums to be higher in the later period. Unfortunately, the Kassouf approach cannot tell us whether the buyers of the warrants or the short sellers had better chances of success *in either period.*

The Kassouf model predicts a normal or average price, not a fair value. The distinction may not be critical for a warrant that has 5 or 10 years of life remaining. An investor has little

Table 7-4. The Kassouf Warrant Evaluation Model

$$V_c = S \left[\sqrt[z]{\left(\frac{P_s}{S} \right)^z + 1} - 1 \right]$$

$$Z = k_1 + \frac{k_2}{t} + k_3 R + k_4 d + k_5 E_1 + k_6 E_2 + k_7 x + k_8 S + a$$

V_c = expected price of warrant

S = striking or exercise price

P_s = price of underlying stock

$k_1 \ldots k_8$ = coefficients derived by multiple regression analysis

t = number of months before expiration

R = dividend yield on common stock

d = number of outstanding warrants divided by number of outstanding shares (i.e., potential dilution ratio)

E_1 = slope of least squares line fitted to logarithms of monthly mean price of common stock for previous 11 months

E_2 = standard deviation of natural logarithms of monthly mean price of common stock for previous 11 months

$x = \dfrac{P_s}{S}$

a = random variable

Calculated values for Z:

1945–1957

$$Z = -1.061 + 6.922 \left(\frac{1}{t} \right) + 8.768R + 1.876x + 0.357d + 0.074S$$

1958–1964

$$Z = 1.526 + 2.717 \left(\frac{1}{t} \right) + 13.421R + 0.301x + 1.340E_2$$

reason to expect that a long period during which average values have exceeded fair value will come to an abrupt end while he owns the warrants. On the other hand, options have short lives, usually less than a year. Overvaluation or undervaluation of an option cannot last longer than the option. If an investor regularly buys options at normal or average prices that are higher than fair value or writes options at normal or average prices that are below fair value, he will earn an inferior rate of return.

The Kassouf model or any other econometric model generates a figure that is not equivalent to the fair value generated by the theoretical option value model; this fact sharply reduces the usefulness of the econometric valuation methods. If options on a particular stock are overpriced during the period used to calculate the coefficients in the Kassouf equation, the estimated normal value from the model will probably be above the fair value level until the coefficients are recalculated. Only in a very approximate way does the Kassouf model indicate when an option premium is higher or lower than the price one should rationally be willing to pay. The model assumes that past option price–stock price relationships were appropriate.

Although the result it produces is not exactly the number we are looking for, the Kassouf model has at least three important advantages over either the Giguère formula or the Shelton warrant model.

First, it explicitly considers more variables. Any factor from interest rates and stock price volatility to dividends has an opportunity to demonstrate its importance when a multiple regression analysis derives the equation for Z. If a factor drops out of the equation, it drops out because it does not appear to have affected price relationships during the period under study.

Second, the Kassouf model explicitly considers the effect of stock price volatility. Stock price fluctuations are extremely important in option evaluation. None of the other methods examined assign any significant weight to this variable, though Shelton would have used volatility if he had found it meaningful.

Finally, unlike the other two equations, the Kassouf model is not wedded to a particular curve. Although the basic price relationship curve is fixed, as was noted in the discussion of graphic techniques for option analysis, Kassouf introduced stock price as a variable affecting Z, the exponent in the equation, to permit the warrant or option value to drift from one curve to another. This considerably loosens the tie to a particular price relationship equation and improves the predictive value of the model.

The Kassouf model, from the time of its publication until recently, has been the only reliable and practical method for estimating the average or normal price of a wide variety of convertible securities. Its principal weakness is that the value it generates is only an approximation, based on past price relationships, of what the price of a convertible security *might* be, not a statement, based on the behavior pattern of the underlying common stock, of what the value *should* be.

We turn next to the probability models, a group of approaches that try to determine what the price of an option or other convertible security should be, based on the probability distribution of the price of the underlying stock.

E. PROBABILITY MODELS

1. Sprenkle, Samuelson, Merton, and Others

A number of leading economists have, at one time or another in their careers, written articles on option or warrant pricing. Most of this work has used options or warrants as a tool to study some other phenomenon which interested the author. To the reader who appreciates the nuances of academic literature, few of the option value models developed by these economists are exactly identical. To the reader less concerned

Table 7-5. Sprenkle Probability Model (As restated by Black and Scholes)

$$V_c = k\ P_s\ N(b_1) - k^*\ SN\ (b_2)$$

$$b_1 = \frac{\ln\ (kP_s/S) + \tfrac{1}{2}v^2(t^* - t)}{v\sqrt{(t^* - t)}}$$

$$b_2 = \frac{\ln\ (kP_s/S) - \tfrac{1}{2}v^2(t^* - t)}{v\sqrt{(t^* - t)}}$$

V_c = fair value of option

k = ratio of expected value of stock price at time option or warrant expires to current stock price

P_s = stock price

$N(b)$ = cumulative normal density function

k^* = discount factor that depends on risk characteristics of stock

S = striking or exercise price

ln = natural logarithm

v^2 = variance rate of return on stock

t^* = maturity date of option or warrant

t = current date

---

with nuances, the similarities among these models are either comforting or boring, depending on one's mood.

Tables 7-5 and 7-6 describe two of the more important probability models. The first of these models, outlined in Table 7-5, was derived by Case M. Sprenkle in his doctoral dissertation at Yale University in 1960. Sprenkle's work was published in *Yale Economic Essays*, and reprinted in *The Random Character of Stock Market Prices*, edited by Paul Cootner. The Sprenkle model is similar in most respects to other classical option and warrant models based on the probability approach. Apart from a few practical considerations that limit its usefulness, Sprenkle's model describes fairly well the relationship between the probability distribution of stock price changes and option or warrant values. The Sprenkle model approximates the description of the probability approach already given and soon to be developed further.

The other model, outlined in Table 7-6, was developed by Paul Samuelson and Robert Merton of M.I.T. and described in an article in the Winter 1969 issue of *Industrial Management Review*. The unique feature of this model is that it is based on what the authors call a "util-prob" or combined utility and

Table 7-6. Samuelson-Merton "Util-Prob" Model

$$V_c = e^{r(t-t^\circ)} \int_{S/P_s}^{\infty} (ZP_s - S) \, dQ \, [Z; \, (t^* - t)]$$

V_c = fair value of option

r = interest rate

t = current date

t^* = maturity date of option or warrant

$\int_{S/P_s}^{\infty}$ = integral over interval from $\dfrac{S}{P_s}$ to ∞

S = striking or exercise price

P_s = stock price

Z = random variable return per dollar invested in common stock

$dQ \, [Z; \, (t^* - t)]$ = risk-adjusted probability density function of Z over a time period of length $t^* - t$

e = base of natural logarithms = 2.71828

probability distribution. Though most observers would argue that some of the complexities of the Samuelson-Merton model are rendered obsolete by the work of Fischer Black and Myron Scholes, which will be discussed in the next section, this model in its most general form is one of the most flexible approaches to warrant and option evaluation.

The purpose here is not to compare and contrast the myriad of theoretical option and warrant pricing models suggested by various economists. The material in Tables 7-5 and 7-6 is provided strictly for the benefit of readers who are mathematically inclined. For the majority of readers, the simplified version of the general probability model for warrant and option evaluation which was used in earlier chapters will be expanded on. This simplified model lacks the refinements and the complexities of the mathematical formulations favored by the authors of the works cited. The intention is not to give readers an elegant formula, but to help them understand relationships. Consistent with the goal of making option evaluation understandable to the reasonably sophisticated investor who does not necessarily have a strong grounding in mathematics, the continued emphasis will be on graphic, rather than algebraic, explanations. Some of the simplifying assumptions of the basic probability approach are deliberately glossed over to avoid entanglement in some important but nonetheless confusing refinements.

Figure 7-9 is a reproduction of Figure 7-1 which shows the profit-loss position of a call buyer with a stock price probability distribution superimposed on the diagram. This diagram will be used to review and expand upon the basic explanation of the probability model outlined in the first section of this chapter.

The reader will recall that once the characteristics of the profit-loss line and the probability curve are known, calculation of the expected profit or loss and the fair value of the call is straightforward, if perhaps a bit time-consuming. As noted earlier, the expected profit or loss to an option buyer is calculated by adding up the results obtained by multiplying the profit or loss over a particular range of stock prices by the probability that the price will fall in that range when the

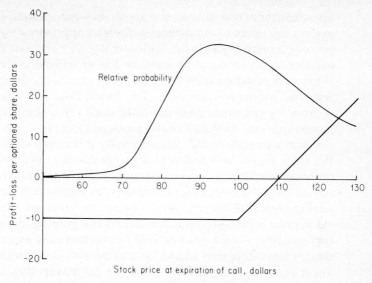

Figure 7-9. Call buyer's profit-loss line and stock price probability distribution.

option expires. To phrase it another way, the expected profit or loss is equal to the sum of all possible outcomes multiplied by their respective likelihoods of occurring. The fair value of the call before risk adjustment is simply the call price plus any expected profit or less any expected loss to the buyer.

The key to superior common stock investment performance is usually superior ability to predict the direction and magnitude of stock price changes. The investor who can accurately estimate the shape and location of the probability curve of the stock price changes should enjoy superior results using options even if he is completely unable to predict a specific stock price move. Buying options that are selling for less than fair value and writing those that are selling for more than fair value is the key to these superior results. With this in mind, it is time to examine some of the basic characteristics of the curve in Figure 7-9.

If we draw a line vertically through an expiration price of $100 per share on the graph, we see that approximately half of the area under the curve falls to the left of this price and approximately half falls to the right. In other words, if we neglect the effect of commissions, there is approximately a 50 percent probability that the option will expire without being exercised and an equal probability that it will be exercised. If the option does expire without being exercised, the buyer will lose the entire premium. The buyer does not begin to recover the premium paid until the stock price at expiration moves into the right half of the probability curve.

When we examine the curve carefully it becomes clear why the size, shape, and location of the probability distribution of future stock prices become so important. It is theoretically possible for the stock price to increase by almost any amount over the 6-month life of this call option. In actual practice, the stock price will rarely even double. As the graph is drawn in this example, even a price of $130 per share on the expiration date of the call option would have to be considered unusual. Yet it is these extreme values that the call buyer must count on to make the investment worthwhile. When large profits are weighted by low probabilities, the resulting impact on the call buyer's profit position can be material.

If there were only a 5 percent chance that the stock price would exceed $130 and the mean of expected prices over $130 was $140, this sector of the curve would add 0.05 × $40, or $2, to the call buyer's expected profit. If this segment of the curve accounted for 6 percent of all possible stock prices, the expected profit contribution would be $2.40. The additional $0.40 is 4 percent of the option price. If the curve in this example moved a single percentage point to the right, the expected profit to the call buyer would increase by about $0.25, or $2\frac{1}{2}$ percent of the option price. Clearly, the shape and location of the curve are important.

Since the first paper on the modern theory of options was published by Louis Bachelier in France in 1900, economists have debated the shape and location of the curve representing the probability distribution of future stock prices. A thorough discussion of this controversy would involve mathematical relationships beyond the scope of a book which is designed for practitioners. Nevertheless, any student of options should have a basic understanding of what the argument is about.

Most arguments over the shape of the probability distribution of stock prices have resulted from attempts to simplify calculations by postulating a particular mathematical function as an approximation of the empirical relationship. The purpose here is to help the reader understand certain generalizations about the shape and location of the probability curve. After an intuitive discussion of the stock price distribution, we will examine the mathematical functions that have been suggested as approximations to the actual stock price distribution.

One important characteristic of the probability distribution curve drawn in Figure 7-9 is that its arithmetic mean or average lies at least slightly above the current stock price. This characteristic of the curve reflects the fact that, in spite of the experience of recent years, there is a definite secular uptrend in stock prices. It also reflects the fact that this stock must compete with other possible investments. No investor would hold the stock if he did not expect it to appreciate. Over the 6-month period depicted in this example, the expected increase is not very great, but the present price of the stock will discount an expected increase related to such factors as the size of the dividend, the level of interest rates, and the likely volatility of the stock price.

A second characteristic of this curve is that it reflects the tendency for a stock price 6 months from today to be close to today's stock price. The tails of the curve suggest that there is a significant probability that the stock price will diverge materially from the current level, but the stock price 6 months from today will more likely be close to today's price than far away from it.

A third characteristic of the curve is that it is slightly skewed in a positive direction. That is, if we pick a price $10 higher and another price $10 lower than today's price, the probability of reaching the higher price is somewhat greater than the probability of reaching the lower price. There is nothing esoteric about this characteristic of the stock price probability distribution. It simply reflects the nature of stock price changes. While it would not be common for the price of a stock selling today at $95 a share to rise by $100 over the next 6 months, a price change of this magnitude is possible. It is not possible for the stock price to decline by $100 because the price cannot drop below zero.

Most techniques that attempt to estimate the fair value (as opposed to the average or normal price) of an option approximate the shape of the stock price probability curve with one of two mathematical functions used as the probability distribution. The simplest of these distributions is the normal distribution, which is the basis of most statistical analysis. The other widely used probability distribution is the lognormal distribution. The lognormal distribution is simply the normal distribution applied to the logarithms of the data, in this case, stock prices.

Although the lognormal distribution is slightly more difficult to use than the simple normal curve, most economists have used it in their option models because it more closely approximates the process by which stock prices change. The normal distribution assigns equal probabilities of occurrence to a $100 increase in stock price and a $100 decrease. With the lognormal distribution a 100 percent price rise is as probable as a 50 percent decline. The lognormal distribution appropriately reflects the skewness in the actual distribution of stock prices.

While economists are satisfied that the lognormal distribution provides a better approximation to the actual probability distribution of stock prices than the standard normal distribution, the lognormal distribution does not fit observed data on stock prices well enough to permit its use for all purposes. Empirical studies have shown that the probability distribution of stock prices differs from the lognormal approximation in several ways. First, there is a slight tendency for future stock prices to cluster more around the current stock price than might be expected on the basis of the lognormal distribution. Second, and even more significant when options are involved, there is a pronounced tendency for stock prices to be more concentrated in the tails of the distribution than predicted by the lognormal curve.

Figure 7-10 illustrates for comparative purposes the difference between the lognormal distribution (dashed line) and the observed distribution with its higher peak and fatter tails

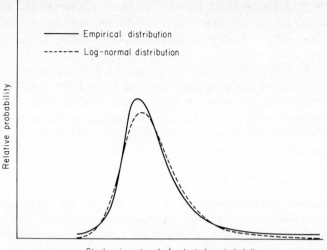

Figure 7-10. Comparison of empirical distribution of stock prices with lognormal distribution.

(solid line). If the reader will compare these distributions and consider the earlier discussion of the theoretical evaluation of an option, it will be clear that if the striking price of the option and the market price of the stock differ materially, these two distributions will give considerably different values for an option.

Option evaluation techniques based on the lognormal distribution give reasonably satisfactory results as long as the market price and the exercise price are identical. When these prices differ materially, however, an option evaluation based on a lognormal distribution of expected stock prices is subject to substantial error. For example, a call option selling well out of the money might appear, from the lognormal distribution, to have little value. The "skinny" tails of the lognormal distribution suggest a low probability of a large price advance. Using the empirical distribution, with its fatter tails, the value of the out-of-the-money call would be much higher.

Although very little has been said about the problems of estimating the precise characteristics of the probability distribution applicable to a particular stock at a particular time, the reader should appreciate that practical use of a probability model for option evaluation is difficult and time-consuming even with the help of a computer. Adjustments for dividends and commissions present a further complication. It is small wonder that most models designed for practical use in the appraisal of stock options and warrants have bypassed the probability approach for econometric models. Publication of the Black-Scholes model, to be discussed in the next section, has been instrumental in focusing renewed attention on the probability models.

2. The Black-Scholes Model

Almost as if it were timed to coincide with the opening of the Chicago Board Options Exchange, a theoretical valuation formula for options, derived by Fischer Black and Myron Scholes, was published in *The Journal of Political Economy* for May–June 1973. The principal difference between the Black-Scholes formulation and the techniques proposed by other economists over the years is that Black and Scholes focus on the neutral option hedge as the key to the determination of option value. The Black-Scholes formula and its major assumptions are outlined in Table 7-7. While the mathematical derivation of the formula is an important feature of the Black-Scholes article, the focus here will be on the principle behind the Black-Scholes approach and its usefulness as a practical method of evaluating options.

The Black-Scholes model is based on the fact that it is possible, subject to a number of assumptions, to set up a perfectly hedged position consisting of a long position in an underlying stock and a short position in options on that stock, or a long position in the options and a short position in the stock. By perfectly hedged, they mean that over a stock price interval close to the current price, any profit resulting from an instantaneous increase in the price of the stock would be exactly offset by a loss on the option position, or vice versa. The Black-Scholes formula, then, is developed from the principle that *options can completely eliminate market risk from a stock portfolio*. Black and Scholes postulate that the ratio of options to stock in this hedged position is constantly modified

Table 7-7. The Black-Scholes Model

$$V_c = P_s \, N \, (d_1) - S e^{r(t-t^*)} \, N(d_2)$$

$$d_1 = \frac{\ln \, (P_s/S) + (r + \frac{1}{2}v^2)(t^* - t)}{v \sqrt{(t^* - t)}}$$

$$d_2 = \frac{\ln \, (P_s/S) + (r - \frac{1}{2}v^2)(t^* - t)}{v \sqrt{(t^* - t)}}$$

V_c = fair value of option

P_s = stock price

S = striking or exercise price

$N(d)$ = cumulative normal density function

r = "risk-free" interest rate

t = current date

t^* = maturity date of option or warrant

v^2 = variance rate of return on stock

e = base of natural logarithms = 2.71828

$\ln$ = natural logarithm

Key Assumptions of the Black-Scholes Model

1. The short-term interest rate is known and is constant through time.
2. The stock price follows a random walk in continuous time with a variance rate proportional to the square of the stock price.
3. The distribution of possible stock prices at the end of any finite interval is lognormal.
4. The variance rate of return on the stock is constant.
5. The stock pays no dividends and makes no other distributions.
6. The option can only be exercised at maturity.
7. There are no commissions or other transaction costs in buying or selling the stock or the option.
8. It is possible to borrow any fraction of the price of a security to buy it or to hold it, at the short-term interest rate.
9. A seller who does not own a security (a short seller) will simply accept the price of the security from the buyer and will agree to settle with the buyer on some future date by paying him an amount equal to the price of the security on that date. While this short sale is outstanding, the short seller will have the use of, or interest on, the proceeds of the sale.
10. The tax rate, if any, is identical for all transactions and all market participants.

SOURCE: Fischer Black and Myron Scholes, "The Pricing of Options and Corporate Liabilities," *The Journal of Political Economy*, May–June 1973, pp. 637–654. Copyright © 1973 by the University of Chicago. All rights reserved.

at no commission cost to offset gains or losses on the stock by losses or gains on the options. Because the position is theoretically riskless, the option premium at which the hedge yields a pretax return equal to the risk-free short-term interest rate is the fair value of the option. If the price of the option is greater or less than fair value, then the return from a risk-free hedged position could be different from the risk-free interest rate. The reader may wish to compare the Black-Scholes derivation of fair value from the neutral hedge position with the diagram in Figure 4-23, which formed the basis of our discussion of the effect of option transactions on the risk-reward characteristics of a portfolio. Readers familiar with modern capital market theory should recognize the Black-Scholes valuation of options with a neutral hedge and the risk-reward analysis in Chapter 4 as extensions of capital market theory. Establishing the relationship of options to other securities was one of the more important contributions of the Black-Scholes papers. The Black-Scholes articles are an appropriate starting point for anyone wishing to explore option theory in greater depth.

This brief chapter is not intended to provide a detailed critique of the Black-Scholes model. Readers can examine the accompanying table and list of assumptions (Table 7-7) and judge the realism of the model for themselves. Some of the Black-Scholes assumptions can easily be relaxed to make the model more realistic. For example, the assumption that the option can only be exercised at maturity is not critical. Likewise, it is not overly difficult to adjust for commissions and other transaction costs or even taxes. Conversely, a number of the Black-Scholes assumptions are both difficult to accept and difficult or impossible to modify within the framework of their model. Unless these assumptions are relaxed, however, the model is likely to encourage misleading option evaluations.

Some of the same features of the Black-Scholes model which contribute to its computational efficiency detract materially from its practical usefulness. While some of the weaknesses of the Black-Scholes formulation are too technical for a clear nonmathematical explanation, most of the problems are easy enough to understand. First, in its basic form, the model assumes that the stock pays no dividend. On the assumption that we are dealing with listed options, it would appear at first glance to be a simple matter to adjust the formula for dividends by subtracting the dividend yield from the interest rate used in the computation. Unfortunately, while interest usually accrues steadily over time, dividend payments are discrete sums, usually paid once a quarter. Timing of the dividend payment can have an important effect on the value of a short-term option when the market price of the stock is above the striking price of the option. As if the *timing* of dividends were not enough of a problem, many companies pay irregular quarterly dividends. The dividend in the final quarter or two quarters of the year may be materially larger than the dividend paid in the first half. Correctly adjusting the Black-Scholes formula or any probability model for dividends is complicated but critically important for some of the higher-dividend-paying stocks with listed options.

A second weakness of the Black-Scholes model is its use of a single "risk-free" interest rate as the discount factor in the formula. The risk-free rate causes several problems which are beyond the scope of this book. However, there are a few simple reasons why the strictly risk-free rate is inappropriate.

While it is theoretically possible to iron out all fluctuations in the value of the investor's equity in a hedged position by continuously changing the ratio of options short to shares long, or vice versa, few investors will actually modify their option hedges so frequently. Frequent minor adjustments of the hedge ratio would lead to an intolerable level of commission cost. The fact that the actual rate of return will fluctuate as a result of the fact that frequent adjustments in the hedge ratio are impractical suggests that a rate slightly higher than the risk-free interest rate should be used. Black and Scholes argue that any deviations from the risk-free rate will be unsystematic (unrelated to the market trend) and that they can be eliminated through diversification. Empirical studies suggest that even unsystematic risk requires a higher rate of return than the so-called "risk-free" rate.

Another problem with the Black-Scholes single interest rate is that an investor cannot really borrow and lend at the same rate. If the rate an investor receives on short-term debt instruments is 7 percent, he may find that he is paying 9 percent or more for money borrowed in his margin account. A related problem is that the short-sale assumption adopted by Black and Scholes is unrealistic. The short seller will not usually have access to the proceeds of his sale. Interest on the proceeds of the short sale technically belongs to the owner of the shares the short seller borrowed to deliver to the buyer.

Probably the most important shortcoming of the Black-Scholes model is that it relies heavily on the assumption that the probability distribution of future stock prices is a lognormal distribution. As we saw earlier (page 244), the lognormal distribution is simply the conventional normal distribution applied to the logarithms of stock prices. Unfortunately, for the usefulness of the Black-Scholes model, virtually every significant empirical study ever made of the distribution of stock price changes indicates that the actual probability distribution of stock prices deviates materially from the lognormal curve.

Under some circumstances the lognormal assumption can give satisfactory results. For example, the assumption of lognormality provides fairly good results as long as the market price of the stock and the striking price of the option are identical. If, however, the market price and the striking price are materially different, the lognormal assumption can lead to a very poor estimate of the fair value of the call.

Unless it is used with care, the Black-Scholes model will give option values that are, on average, too low; moreover, these values differ significantly from the actual fair value of the option if the striking price and the market price of the stock differ. Widespread use of the Black-Scholes model by institutional investors may have the effect of both depressing and distorting actual option premiums. It is unlikely that all the option traders using the Black-Scholes model have made appropriate corrections for the inherent biases of the Black-Scholes model and for commissions and dividends.

Probably the most important contribution Black and Scholes have made to the literature of options is not their formula but the fact that their equation is based on the construction of an option hedge. They highlight the fact that the investor can completely eliminate systematic or market risk. As any student of portfolio management theory learns early in the course, portfolio diversification permits an investor to reduce exposure to the fortunes or misfortunes of a particular company and its securities. Prior to publication of the two Black-Scholes papers and the creation of listed options, most portfolio management texts argued that it was impossible to eliminate market risk through diversification. These texts argued that, while it might be possible to reduce a stockholder's total risk by buying Polaroid and IBM as well as U.S. Steel and General Motors, the only way to reduce exposure to market risk is to put some of the assets in short-term debt or to invest in less volatile stocks. As long as the portfolio retains any significant exposure to common stocks, its value will probably fluctuate with the trend of the overall market.

Black and Scholes have highlighted the fact that it is possible to reduce or even eliminate market risk by constructing a hedged position with options. The significance of this point will be easy to understand if the reader will put himself or herself in the place of an individual investor or institutional portfolio manager who has been looking frantically for a way to insulate investment results from the vagaries of the market. Options may be an answer to this problem.

3. Merton, Cox and Ross, Geske, and the Distribution Problem

Most of the sophisticated option articles published since the two Black-Scholes papers appeared have extended option analysis to various corporate finance and market evaluation problems or have attempted to cope with the fact that stock prices are not lognormally distributed. Several articles by Jonathan Ingersoll are outstanding examples of the extension of option evaluation theory to other economic and financial problems. The Ingersoll articles are reviewed in the Bibliography. The papers of primary concern here are attempts to modify or adapt the work of Black and Scholes to reflect the actual shape of the stock price probability distribution.

Even before the Black-Scholes articles were published, a number of writers focused on the analytical complexities caused by the fact that the actual distribution of stock price changes is not lognormal. The work of Mandelbrot, Fama, and Press preceded the Black-Scholes articles and focused primarily on finding a standard function that fit the observed data better than the lognormal curve. More recent articles have explored the *whys* of nonlognormality with the analytical tools provided by Black and Scholes. Because most readers of this book have not taken graduate courses in capital market theory, a highly technical discussion of this post-Black-Scholes analysis is not appropriate. Although the authors referred to in subsequent paragraphs have much more to say, we will focus on their analysis of why the distribution of stock price changes is not lognormal.

Robert Merton has probably done more to extend and improve the realism of the theoretical framework developed by Black and Scholes than any other individual. Though their work differs in some respects from Merton's, Cox and Ross have also attempted to reconcile the Black-Scholes model with empirical data. One of the major contributions of Merton, Cox, and Ross has been to develop a model that combines the lognormal Black-Scholes equations with a "jump" process. Their explanation for nonlognormality is that the lognormal movement of stock prices in the absence of new developments is combined with jumps caused by major events that significantly change the mean value around which lognormally distributed fluctuations take place. In essence, they argue that the observed stock price distribution is really a combination of several interacting distributions. Merton points out that this dual distribution approach helps explain not only the observed stock price distribution but also the tendency for certain options to sell for relatively more or less than the Black-Scholes model predicts.

Robert Geske has proposed another explanation for the observed distribution of stock price changes that is consistent with the work of Merton and of Cox and Ross. His approach also helps tie option theory more closely to capital market theory, a process initiated by Black and Scholes. Geske argues that a call option is really an option on an option if the firm's capitalization consists of debt as well as common stock. Because common shareholders cannot be assessed if a firm is bankrupt and because they have an "option" to purchase the balance of a firm's assets and cash flows from bondholders by redeeming the bonds, *common stock can be evaluated as an option to purchase the entire firm.* A call option on common stock is therefore best analyzed as an option on an option. Like the Merton-Cox-Ross dual distribution analysis, Geske's compound option approach improves on some of the empirical weaknesses of the simple Black-Scholes model. In addition to explaining the Black-Scholes undervaluation of deep-out-of-the-money options, Geske's model explains the tendency of stock price volatility to increase as the stock price declines.

The problem with these extensions of the Black-Scholes model is that the user of these complex models is called upon to deal with more unknowns than the average human mind can handle. It is almost certain that several probability distributions do interact to determine the observed pattern of stock price changes. Likewise, the leverage characteristics of the firm do affect the volatility of the stock and the shape of the stock price distribution. These models may be intuitively more satisfying, but they require a user to deal with too many variables. Whereas the Black-Scholes model has five variables, four of which are known, Geske's model has seven variables, and four of them require complex estimation techniques. The practitioner needs a model which is as easy to use as the Black-Scholes formulations but which gives results closer to the more sophisticated extensions that attempt to deal with the nonlognormality of the distribution of stock prices.

The author of this book and Professor Albert Madansky of the University of Chicago have developed a model which uses an empirical stock price distribution rather than the lognormal distribution. As an article prepared by Professor Madansky (reprinted here as Appendix C, pages 324 to 331) indicates, the empirical distribution used in this model fits stock price data much better than the lognormal distribution does. The Gastineau-Madansky model is used in much the same manner as the Black-Scholes model; it requires similar input data and provides essentially similar output. The major difference is that it provides a better fit with observed stock price and option price data.

F. THE GASTINEAU-MADANSKY MODEL

1. General Characteristics of the Model

The development of the Gastineau-Madansky model has drawn heavily on the work of the authors whose formulations were discussed in the preceding sections. In general form, the Gastineau-Madansky model is a probability model. By modifying an assumption here and dropping an equation there, it is possible to reduce the Gastineau-Madansky formulation to the format of any of the probability models, including the Black-Scholes model. In terms of its mathematical relationships, the Gastineau-Madansky model probably is closest to the Samuelson-Merton model.

The fact that there is a family relationship to these other models can be misleading, however. Because it is designed to be used for practical calculation of option values, the Gastineau-Madansky model is substantially more complex than most models discussed in the academic literature. This is not meant as an indictment of any of these formulations. Their creators were not trying to demonstrate a practical technique applicable under all circumstances. They were primarily concerned with the advancement of the theory of options.

The fair value of an option determined by the Gastineau-Madansky model can be adjusted for dividends, interest rates, and option commission charges. The model can also be adjusted for tax rates. One feature, but by no means the only unique feature, of the Gastineau-Madansky model is that it does not use a simple mathematical function to represent the stock price probability distribution. The complex empirical probability distribution gives more useful results than the commonly used lognormal distribution.

One of the most important features of the model is that it is almost completely modular. In most cases an adjustment can be added or removed without affecting the rest of the model. Modularity is important for theoretical as well as for practical reasons. Modularity permits the model to be used to test new ideas and to be improved if the new idea is useful. Furthermore, should any option trading entity adopt an option contract format different from the standard listed or conven-

Table 7-8. The Gastineau-Madansky Model

$$V_c = a_1\, e^{a_2 r(t-t^*)} \int_{a_3 S/P_s}^{\infty} a_4(ZP_s - S)\, dQ\ [Z;\ (t^* - t);\ a_5]$$

V_c = fair value of option

$a_1 \ldots a_5$ = adjustment factors designed to reflect commission charges, dividends, interest rates, taxes, and other variables. Each adjustment factor in this formulation may incorporate part or all of the adjustment for more than one variable. The adjustment factors are frequently complex functions in their own right

r = basic interest rate

t = current date

t^* = maturity date of option or warrant

$\int_{a_3 S/P_s}^{\infty}$ = integral over interval from $\dfrac{a_3 S}{P_s}$ to ∞

∞ = infinity

S = striking or exercise price

P_s = stock price

Z = random variable return per dollar invested in common stock

$dQ\ [Z;\ (t^* - t);\ a_5]$ = an empirical probability density function of Z over a time period of length $t^* - t$

e = base of natural logarithms = 2.71828

Key Assumptions of the Gastineau-Madansky Model

1. The interest rates at which an investor can borrow and lend money are known and constant through time.
2. Stock price fluctuations conform to the efficient markets model which states that the stock price at any moment reflects all information available to the market participants. The variance is proportional to the square of the stock price.
3. The distribution of possible stock prices at the end of any finite interval conforms to an empirical probability function.
4. The variance of the stock price distribution is the same for each period.
5. The effect of dividends and other distributions is reflected in the adjustment factors.
6. The option can be exercised at any time prior to expiration.
7. Commissions and other option transaction costs are reflected in the adjustment factors.
8. The investor is subject to standard margin requirements and borrows at a higher rate than he lends.
9. The short seller can, through option conversion, effectively have the use of the proceeds of a short sale, provided exchange-listed put options are available.
10. The tax rate, if any, is the actual rate paid by each market participant. The tax rate is symmetric in that the tax credit for a loss is computed at the same rate as the tax payment on a gain. Tax rates may differ on each of three types of income: (a) ordinary income, (b) short-term capital gains, (c) long-term capital gains.

tional option contract, the Gastineau-Madansky model can be readily adapted to the new format. In contrast, many of the classic probability models and, most particularly, the Black-Scholes model, are limited in their flexibility. They are wedded to a particular concept or probability distribution and cannot be readily adapted to a different perception of reality.

Table 7-8 provides an outline of the general form of the Gastineau-Madansky model as it is used to evaluate listed options. The equation in the table is highly simplified, but it should give the reader a feeling for the complexities of adapting a theoretical model for practical application. The formula can be compared with the Samuelson-Merton formulation which, in this simplified version, it most closely resembles. The assumptions should be compared with the Black-Scholes assumptions. If the user is willing to rerun the computer program a few times, several more of these assumptions can be relaxed.

2. What the Gastineau-Madansky Model Tells the Investor

Table 7-9 lists some of the data generated by the Gastineau-Madansky computerized option model for listed options on McDonald's Corporation and Polaroid. Even a casual examination of these data suggests, under the assumptions incorporated in the model, that the McDonald's option was slightly underpriced and that the Polaroid option was substantially overpriced. At the risk of repeating a point, it should be emphasized that the terms "overpriced" and "underpriced" do not imply *anything* about the likely direction of stock price movement; they suggest *only* how an option should be used. If an investor is bearish on McDonald's, he might not be interested in buying a call just because it is cheap. Instead, an underpriced call might be reversed to create a put, or the call might be purchased to hedge a short sale. Likewise, a bull on Polaroid might want to write uncovered puts, write straddles against a long position, or set up a bullish hedge. The option evaluation model is a tool to help the investor choose a strategy that is appropriate to his attitude on the stock, the value of the option contract, and his personal risk preferences.

Table 7-9. Partial Listing of the Output of the Gastineau-Madansky Computerized Option Model (Date of analysis: August 12, 1974)

Data	Stock McDonald's	Stock Polaroid
Symbol	MCD	PRD
Expiration month	January	January
Striking price	$50.00	$30.00
Stock price	$41.125	$26.375
Call price	$ 2.75	$ 3.75
Stock price variance assumption	0.8	1.0
Gastineau-Madansky fair value	$ 3.00	$ 2.79
Call price ÷ fair value	0.92	1.34
Black-Scholes fair value fully adjusted	$ 2.82	$ 2.72
Neutral hedge ratio (pretax)	0.37	0.47
Net margin required for uncovered writer (30% rate) per share	$ 0.71	$ 0.53
Probability option will be exercised	31%	39%
Probability uncovered writer will lose money or buyer will make money	25%	26%
Probability writer of pretax neutral hedge will lose money	36%	24%
Profit parameters pretax neutral hedge	$33.72–$59.62	$18.47–$40.40
Expected annualized return on equity from a neutral hedge	5.8%	34.9%
Implied stock price variance	0.7	1.6

NOTES:

1. Stock and option prices are closing prices for the previous Friday.
2. Margin requirements are based on an assumed 30 percent margin rate for uncovered writers and expressed net of any credit for the premium received by the writer.
3. The profit parameters are simply the prices which bracket the stock price range over which a neutral hedge is profitable.
4. The expected annualized return on equity from a neutral hedge is the annualized probability weighted profit or loss from a neutral hedge divided by the net equity of the investor in the hedge after option premiums received are credited.
5. Implied stock price variance is the level of stock price volatility that is consistent with the market price of the option. This concept is discussed at length in Chapters 9 and 10.

If Table 7-9 is examined carefully, the reader will observe that some of the calculations are based on the fair value of a call option. Others, such as the probability that an option will be exercised or the probability that an uncovered writer will lose money, require direct reference to the probability curve of the stock price distribution. Still others, such as the required margin calculation, are easy enough to obtain without reference to a particular model and are included on the computer run for convenience.

While the amount of data that a computerized model generates can be truly staggering (most of the computations that can be furnished by the computer are not listed on this table), very few data need be understood or evaluated to reach an intelligent decision on a *particular* option strategy. In fact, the most important lessons that a portfolio manager who uses options must learn are to analyze assumptions about the underlying stock carefully and to organize the computer output in a format that is relevant to a decision. Usually, organizing the output means disregarding all but a few pertinent numbers.

The variety of possible option strategies is too great to permit one or two examples to be representative of all possible uses of this or any other computerized option model. To illustrate the need to focus on limited data, however, we will study several simple examples in some detail.

On August 1, 1974, an investor considering a position in Monsanto might have checked the market and obtained the following data on stock and option prices:

Stock price		$60.50	
	October $60	January $60	April $60
Option price	$4.50	$6.38	$8.25

The investor decides to use the Gastineau-Madansky computer model to evaluate these options. He examines the historic volatility or stock price variance data on Monsanto. In summary form, the volatility data base looks like this:

Period	Logarithmic Daily Stock Price Variance $\times 10^3$
Lowest quarter	0.082
Low quartile	0.134
Average volatility	0.261
High quartile	0.317
Highest quarter	0.474

These volatility or variance numbers describe the shape of the probability curve of stock price changes. The higher the number, the greater the average daily stock price change during the period studied.

Although Monsanto had not been volatile immediately prior to August 1974, the overall market had been volatile and the economic outlook was highly uncertain. Because of this uncertainty, the investor tentatively decides to assume a volatility factor of .280 in his evaluation of the options. From the computer he obtains the following information:

	October $60	January $60	April $60
Actual price	$4.50	$6.38	$8.25
Fair value (variance = 0.280)	$3.81	$5.54	$6.90
Actual price ÷ fair value	1.18	1.15	1.20
Variance at which option price equals fair value (implied variance)	0.435	0.405	0.445

Several important conclusions are readily apparent. First, on the basis of the volatility figure selected, the April option is most overpriced. Second, the market is implicitly assuming, by virtue of the price it assigns to the options, that Monsanto will be almost as volatile over the next 9 months (0.445 variance on the April option) as it was during a single quarter (0.474) in the period covered by the data base. While the computer cannot promise profitability every time, the Monsanto options appear overpriced, and the April option seems to be most overpriced on the basis of both the ratio of the call price to the fair value of the option and the variance at which the option price equals fair value. Writing these options against a position in the stock appears to be an intelligent investment decision for the investor who wants to own Monsanto.

In the Monsanto example, the number of shares of stock purchased and the number of options written against the stock position depend on the investor's tax position, his attitude toward risk, the structure of the remainder of his portfolio, and his judgment on the stock. The computer helps organize the data to facilitate the decision. The computer does not manage the portfolio; it simply provides additional input and helps the investor structure his or her thinking. The computer can tell the investor what ratio of options to stock constitutes a neutral hedge at various tax rates. In the case of the Monsanto April $60 call options, the computer tells one that to set up a pretax neutral hedge one needs to sell approximately 1.46 options for each 100 shares of stock. Furthermore, the neutral hedge would be profitable if the stock sold between $48.47 and $85.14 at the end of April 1975. Based on the 0.280 volatility figure, this neutral hedge should be profitable about 79 percent of the time and the expected annualized pretax return on investment from such a hedge should be about 16 percent. Obviously, the *actual* return will be greater or less than the calculated *expected* return, which is simply a probability-weighted average of possible results.

Another example shows the versatility of the model and how it can be used to divide the decision-making process into manageable segments. In 1974 and 1975 brokerage firms generated a sizable volume of commission business by encouraging investors to buy or write options on AT&T stock and hedge or margin these positions with long or short positions in AT&T warrants. The following brief table compares the prices and the values of the options and warrants as of the close of trading on August 9, 1974. Value figures are calculated by both a modified Black-Scholes formulation (adjusted for dividends) and the Gastineau-Madansky method (also adjusted for dividends).

Option or Warrant	Actual Price	Gastineau-Madansky	Black-Scholes
Oct. $45	$ 1.125	$1.23	$1.32
Jan. $45	2.125	2.10	2.22
Apr. $45	2.75	2.65	2.91
Oct. $50	0.25	0.23	0.21
Jan. $50	0.6875	0.67	0.74
Warrant	1.75	0.91	0.97
Stock price	43.875		

The most obvious conclusion to be drawn from this table is that, *under a consistent set of assumptions,* the warrant is conspicuously overvalued relative to the options. This apparent overvaluation may or may not represent an arbitrage opportunity for the small investor. A pricing discrepancy of this magnitude rarely occurs without one or more good reasons. In this case, the short interest in the warrants was fairly high and the price of each warrant was low. This combination made the warrants difficult for a short seller to borrow. Furthermore, many investors felt that if these warrants were about to expire unexercised, the company would extend them or offer new warrants in exchange, in spite of the expressed determination of management to let the warrants die. The would-be arbitrageur must estimate the probability and possible cost of a short squeeze or a warrant extension for himself; the computer merely tells how the market has valued these possibilities. The computer quantifies the risk which the market implicitly assumes the warrant short sale involves. The investor can then decide to agree or disagree with "the market's" assumptions.

A further note of caution seems appropriate: The figures in this table are *not* adjusted for commissions. Because the commissions on low-priced securities are quite high, an investor should check commissions carefully. The approximate round-trip commission cost on a hedge transaction involving 5,000 warrants and 50 option contracts would have been $0.20 to $0.25 per underlying share. These commissions would have consumed about one-fourth of the expected profit even though the warrants expired on schedule.

The figures in this brief table also suggest that valuations computed using the Gastineau-Madansky model might approximate actual prices more closely than values derived by the Black-Scholes method. As a very broad generalization the Gastineau-Madansky model, because of its more realistic formulation, does give values closer to and more consistent with actual prices when the same variance data are used in both models. We do not wish to imply that this relationship will hold true in every case, however. In fact, the purpose of the model is to uncover instances in which the value of the option is different from its price.

Readers who wish to compare the Gastineau-Madansky and Black-Scholes models more closely may find Table 7-10 useful.

Table 7-10. Comparison of the Gastineau-Madansky and Black-Scholes Models

Assumptions:

Daily stock price variance (log)	0.632×10^{-3}
Interest rate	10% per annum
Remaining life of option	3 months
Exercise price	$40
Dividends, commission, and taxes	No adjustment

(1) Stock Price	(2) Gastineau- Madansky Option Value	(3) Black-Scholes Option Value*	(4) Ratio (Col. 2 ÷ Col. 3)
$28	$ 0.22	$ 0.13	1.69
32	0.70	0.60	1.17
36	1.76	1.72	1.02
40	3.72	3.67	1.01
44	6.59	6.38	1.03
48	10.12	9.66	1.05
52	13.99	13.29	1.05

* From Fischer Black, "Fact and Fantasy in the Use of Options," *Financial Analysts Journal,* July–August 1975, pp. 36–72.

The Gastineau-Madansky model usually gives higher relative valuations, particularly when options are significantly out of the money, than the Black-Scholes model. Both models suggest that in-the-money options are worth more than the values assigned them by the market.

The data that an investor needs in order to make a decision or evaluate an option opportunity will change with the occasion. Though no list would cover every possibility, the following list includes some of the more frequently asked questions:

1. What is the fair value of every available option on a given underlying stock?

2. Which, if any, of these contracts is attractive to a would-be writer? A would-be buyer? Is there an attractive spread possibility?

3. What is the expected profit in dollars or as a return on investment from a particular strategy?

4. What ratio of options short to shares of stock long constitutes a neutral hedge, or, in other words, how many shares of common stock is each option equivalent to?

5. What will the probable price of each of these calls be if the stock price rises or falls by a specific amount over the next few weeks? Over the next few months?

6. What is the option market implicitly assuming about the volatility of the underlying stock? Is this assumption consistent with the investor's own expectations? Is this implicit volatility assumption higher or lower than the historical volatility of the stock?

7. How do taxes affect a position?

8. What are other computer models telling their users?

The two tests of any option evaluation system are the realism of the underlying model and the speed and ease with which the investor can get valid answers to questions like these.

G. EVALUATING PUTS

With appropriate caveats, the material on puts in Chapter 4 focused on the evaluation of a put in terms of its conversion to and from a call with the same striking price and expiration date. The major caveat related to the tendency of in-the-money puts to be exercised early. The reader who does not understand why a put would be exercised early should reread the discussion of early exercise beginning on page 107.

Unless a stock is about to pay a significant dividend, exercising a *call* prior to the expiration date of the option will rarely be appropriate. On the other hand, if a *put* is substantially in the money, it may be worth more dead than alive. Because early exercise of puts often makes sense, particularly if there is no dividend payment due before the expiration of the option, the appropriate value of a put is greater than would be predicted by the conversion equation in Chapter 4 (page 96).

The definitive work on the evaluation of puts subject to early exercise was done by Michael Parkinson. A paper describing his work is listed in the Bibliography. Mathematically inclined readers with a serious interest in put evaluation will find Parkinson's work fascinating, but they will soon despair of incorporating it directly into a working option evaluation model complete with dividend adjustments. Fortunately, values approximating those given by the Parkinson formula can be obtained without reworking the formula for each option.

Most users of option evaluation models will find it difficult to determine whether Parkinson's analysis is reflected in their model's evaluation of put options. As a preliminary check, the value of a put might be calculated from the value of the corresponding call using the conversion equation. This value of the converted put should be compared with the put evaluation provided by the computer model. The fair value of the put provided by the evaluation model should *exceed* the value from the conversion equation. The difference will be most obvious on longer-term contracts and on low-volatility stocks.

H. EVALUATING COMPUTERIZED OPTION MODELS

A number of readers of the first edition of *The Stock Options Manual* have requested some guidelines on how to distinguish a good option advisory service from a bad one. This edition complies with this request in two ways. First, the Bibliography lists the major option advisory services and describes the option evaluation and other information they provide. Second, this section provides a framework for evaluating option computer runs that is equally applicable to independent advisory services and to brokerage firm reports.

Readers should understand at the outset that any stock information or recommendations provided by an option service must be evaluated separately from option evaluation data. One service may have excellent option evaluation tables but give terrible recommendations. Another service may not have worthwhile option evaluation data but may provide excellent stock and market advice. The focus here is strictly on option evaluation. Readers are urged to make their own judgments concerning the value of a service's other features.

No single option service will have all the features suggested here. Most of the weaknesses of a service will be due to the fact that developing and updating an option evaluation computer program is an expensive undertaking if it is done properly. Because relatively few investors appreciate the nuances of a good program, many advisory services and brokerage firms conclude that they can get by with low-quality service. It is hoped that these paragraphs will encourage a change in this attitude.

Even the best of the widely distributed option services will provide calculations of the covered call writer's return on investment if the stock price is unchanged or if the price of the stock equals or exceeds the exercise price of the option on the expiration date. As indicated earlier, these calculations are of virtually no value in developing a rational option strategy because they do not take into account the probability that the stock will sell at a particular price on the date of expiration. The fact that a service bows to public demand by providing these figures should not be held against it.

1. The Evaluation Model

The only information that requires sophisticated computer programming is related to the evaluation of the option contract or to the probability that the stock price will be above or below a certain level on the expiration date. Option evaluation data can be quite abbreviated and still be useful. Some services bury their subscribers in meaningless numbers rather than investing in the programming necessary to provide sound, fully adjusted values. If a service's evaluation technique is sound, the more information it provides, the more thoroughly an investor can analyze the underlying assumptions and the validity of the model on which the service is based. If the evaluation data are limited, the investor should ask some key questions before relying on these data. The investor has a right to know the type of option evaluation model used and, assuming it is a probability model, the basis for the adviser's volatility estimates. The method of adjusting for dividends should also be explored because correct dividend adjustments require some fairly expensive computer programming and data-base maintenance.

The evaluation model should be a probability model. While

there may be a major breakthrough in the development of econometric models, such a breakthrough seems highly unlikely. Most of the better option services use the Black-Scholes option evaluation model or a variant of it, adjusted for dividends. If a service does not explicitly acknowledge its debt to Black and Scholes, the term "fair value" or "theoretical value," as opposed to "normal value," suggests a probability model.

If the list of factors taken into account in developing option values includes interest rates, dividend payment patterns, striking price–stock price relationships, time remaining to expiration, and stock price volatility, the model is almost certainly a probability model. A good probability model will use *only* the input data listed. If a service lists a stock's relative strength, earnings projections, or other factors as determinants of option value, skepticism is in order. These factors may help determine the stock's likely behavior or even help develop a volatility estimate, but they are *not* directly involved in evaluation of the option. If the literature provided with the first issue of an option service does not describe the option evaluation technique, a direct inquiry should elicit the necessary information. While the computer program itself may be proprietary, any subscriber is entitled to a clear explanation of the basic techniques used by an advisory service.

Most option evaluation programs claim to have dividend adjustments built in. One way to test the validity of the dividend adjustment is to compare the relative evaluations of options on stocks with sizable dividends shortly before and shortly after an ex-dividend date. If the calculated fair value of an at- or out-of-the-money option changes materially *relative* to the market price of the option on the ex-dividend date, the dividend adjustment may not be appropriate.

To get the greatest value from an option service, the investor must extend the life of the valuation data it provides. Just as the neutral hedge ratio can be used to translate options into stock equivalents, it can also be used to extend the useful life of an option evaluation calculation. To illustrate how this extension works, suppose a call option is attractive for purchase at a price of $4, with the underlying stock at $58 a share and the neutral hedge ratio as 0.5. If the price of the stock moves to $59 the next day, the option would be approximately as attractive for purchase at a price of $4.50. The stock price has moved by a full point, and the neutral hedge ratio suggests that the option price should change by one-half point.

2. Volatility Estimates

The text which accompanies an option evaluation service will rarely describe the method used to develop the stock price volatility estimates used in the evaluation formula. Here again, a direct inquiry will usually provide the answer.

Volatility estimates are as important as earnings estimates, and they should be developed just as conscientiously. Few investors would accept earnings estimates made by fitting a line through the past 5 years' reported earnings and extrapolating to next year. Likewise, there is no reason to base estimates of future stock price volatility on a mechanical extrapolation or weighting of historic stock price volatilities. The historic volatility pattern of a stock does provide the best single clue to future volatility; however, an increase or decrease in the uncertainty of the economic outlook, changing levels of competition in an industry, and the announcement of a possible acquisition are a few of the factors that can change stock price volatility. In general, these factors will change stock price volatility by more than they will change the earnings outlook.

Most option advisory publications use historic measures of stock price volatility as the basis for their option evaluation calculations. A subscriber should ask whether a service uses a long-term average volatility figure, a figure based on volatility for the latest 3- or 6-month period, or a weighted average of recent and long-term volatilities. The possible variations are endless, but as long as the method is known, the investor can make some mental adjustments to reflect his personal expectations for volatility.

Ideally, an option evaluation model should permit the user to compare results on the basis of the following:

1. Historic volatility data for various periods

2. A personal estimate of likely future volatility

3. The volatility that the option market is implicitly assuming for the underlying stock in its pricing of the option contract

Only the most sophisticated probability models will provide opportunities for in-depth volatility analysis. Most evaluation models provide a historic volatility figure as a point of departure. From that point, the user is on his or her own. A few option services do attempt to modify historic volatility figures to reflect a judgment on future volatility. In principle, this approach is highly desirable. In practice, it means that the investor relying on the service will have no fixed frame of reference unless the assumed departure from past volatility patterns is described in detail. The complex statistical derivation of a volatility estimate is both the greatest strength and the greatest weakness of the valuation services based on Fischer Black's volatility calculations.

Though it should not be necessary to mention this point, the measure of volatility used in any option evaluation model must be a variance or standard deviation of the logarithm of the stock price or stock return, *not* the stock's beta factor. The ubiquitousness of beta figures and their use as a proxy for stock price volatility in portfolio risk analysis have led many analysts to adopt beta as a proxy for the stock price variance or standard deviation. Using the beta factor in option evaluation leads to a multitude of distortions. The stock price variance or standard deviation is an *absolute* measure of the volatility of the stock itself. The beta factor is a measure of stock price volatility *relative* to a broad market index.

Apart from the fact that the volatility of the market index may change dramatically from one period to another, different groups of stocks fluctuate with, or counter to, the market in different degrees. Gold stocks, perhaps the most obvious example, frequently move counter to broad market trends. As a consequence, gold stocks may have low beta factors despite relatively high absolute volatility. Though the disparity between variance or standard deviation and the beta factor is significantly less dramatic for most stocks than for the gold shares, distortions are present throughout the stock list. If the only volatility measurement provided by an option evaluation service is a stock price beta, the investor should beware.

3. Rating the Services

The author is not affiliated with any published option service. The Gastineau-Madansky model, described in the previous section, is used solely for the benefit of certain individual and institutional clients. The absence of an ax to grind should permit an objective appraisal of advisory services and their offerings. On the other hand, a reader looking for concise ratings of option services will be disappointed. Because the choice of an advisory service is a highly personal matter, it seems inappropriate to downgrade a publication unless the option evaluation technique it uses is seriously misleading. Likewise, it seems inappropriate to single out any service for praise unless it stands out from the other services in terms of price, convenience, and soundness of evaluation.

The now defunct Standard & Poor's *Option Guide* seemed clearly superior to most other evaluation-oriented services. Its option values were those developed personally by Fischer Black using a fully adjusted Black-Scholes option evaluation model. Because Black incorporated an approximation of Parkinson's put formula into his evaluations, the values for puts were satisfactory. Until another weekly service incorporates Black's service, his tables (see page 363) are the best evaluation data available to the average investor.

At the other end of the quality spectrum, the *Value Line Options and Convertibles* service seems to be based on a Kassouf-type model. The option values that this service provides seem seriously distorted in some cases. While other features of the Value Line service are generally satisfactory, the option values should not be used.

Programmable hand calculators have been promoted aggressively as a quick way to calculate option values. Making an adjustment for dividends on a hand calculator is difficult and time-consuming. Even without a dividend adjustment, the calculator will slow the evaluation process. Few owners of programmable calculators use them regularly for option evaluation after the initial novelty wears off. Using the neutral hedge ratio to update a weekly (or daily) computer printout is usually much faster.

8 OPTIONS ON BONDS AND COMMODITIES

For the reasonably foreseeable future, stock options will be much more important than bond and commodity options. However, if necessary regulatory approvals are obtained, bond and commodity option activity will enjoy a more rapid rate of growth over the next few years.

Apart from negligible over-the-counter activity, the option market in bonds was virtually nonexistent at the beginning of 1979. Several of the option exchanges would like to begin trading options on short-, intermediate-, and long-term U.S. government obligations. If regulatory approval is received, the bond option market should eventually be more important than existing interest rate futures markets. Options will probably be more attractive than futures contracts for the type of interest rate hedging described in Chapter 5 (pages 144 to 161).

The major obstacles to development of an options market for debt securities are regulatory. Some concern has been expressed about the impact of Treasury bill futures trading on the maintenance of orderly money markets. Most of the evidence indicates that an active option or futures market has a stabilizing rather than a destabilizing influence on the market for the underlying security. Because the standard of proof for this stabilizing influence is appropriately high, the market for options on fixed income securities may develop slowly.

It is no overstatement to say that the regulatory status of commodity options is extremely unsettled. After investors lost large sums in unregulated, inadequately margined, and even fraudulent commodity option schemes, securities and commodities regulators imposed tight restrictions on the commodity options market.

In a July 1977 speech, William T. Bagley, Chairman of the Commodity Futures Trading Commission, stated that the Commission needed more resources to oversee the futures markets and to "try to structure and regulate the wild and wooly world of commodity option sales." While the principal purpose of Bagley's speech was to exert pressure on Congress to increase his organization's budget, his description of the market was not hyperbole. As Bagley said at another point in that speech, the commodity options business is "occupied by an inordinate number of fly-by-night hustlers."

Ironically, a well-enforced set of rules similar to those which govern the stock options market would encourage more competition in commodity options and force the "hustlers" out of business. The commodity options market will not begin to achieve its potential until a structured regulatory environment is imposed.

The ultimate structure of the bond and commodity options markets is far from clear. When the rules are established, the analytical techniques discussed in Chapters 4 and 7 will be applicable with only minor modifications. On the other hand, the tax and regulatory aspects of those markets may be significantly different from the stock options market.

9 AN INDEX OF LISTED OPTION PREMIUMS

Since 1973, when listed call option trading began, investors have been intrigued by the idea of a continuously updated index of the average level of option premiums. While it is easy to dismiss such an index as irrelevant to a specific option-buying or option-writing decision, an index of option premium levels could be useful in other ways. For example, a properly constructed index could

1. Demonstrate the relative importance of the various factors affecting the value of an option contract

2. Show whether current option premiums are high or low by historical standards

3. Settle, at least in retrospect, whether option premiums were too high or too low during a given period

A. REQUIREMENTS FOR AN OPTION INDEX

Options obtain their value from the underlying common stock. Any index of option premiums based directly on the *price* of a specific option or group of option contracts would be extraordinarily sensitive to the level of stock prices and would, as a result, be useless as an indicator of *relative* premium levels.

Furthermore, listed options are standardized; that is, the striking price rounds to the nearest $5 or $10. Consequently, the market price of the stock may differ quite materially from the striking price of an option. No simple relationship between the actual option premium and current stock price can give a meaningful indication of premium levels.

Finally, options are wasting assets; their value declines as time passes if the price of the underlying stock remains approximately unchanged. An index must take this inevitable decline in premium over intrinsic value into account and avoid confounding the time relationship with the measurement of premium levels.

An index which measures option premium levels must therefore be constructed differently from the way other indexes commonly used in the securities industry are constructed. The index must measure not the absolute price of option contracts but the relative magnitude of the premium over the option's intrinsic value adjusted for such variables as dividends, interest rates, time to expiration, and the option striking price–current stock price relationship. This brief review of some of the unique characteristics of options suggests that the index should be an *indirect* measure of the relative level of option premiums and that very-short-term and very-long-term options should be excluded from the index to avoid distortions.

An index containing very-short-term options would be quite sensitive to changes in sentiment and would tend to be a highly volatile reflection of the mood of the underlying market. While some sensitivity is desirable, too much can create problems. The most serious problem with very-short-term options is that many of them sell at very low prices or at nominal premiums over intrinsic value. Consequently, a small change in the price of the option or in the price of the underlying stock can have a pronounced effect on the value of that option's representation in the index. This effect can be out of proportion to the significance of the stock or option price change. To minimize this problem, the index described here uses options with lives of from 3 to just less than 6 months. In addition to eliminating distortions from very-short-term option contracts, this also eliminates the option contracts with a life of more than 6 months, where inactive markets can distort the relationship between stock and option prices. (Also, prior to the end of 1976, long-term capital gains tax considerations affected the premiums on options with more than 6 months of life remaining.)

Because options do not expire every month, the value of the index on a given day will sometimes be based on options that have almost 6 months of life remaining and at other times on options that have slightly less than 3 months of life remaining. While this procedure leads to its own set of distortions, it appears to eliminate as many problems as possible while providing an index that can be calculated at the end of any trading day. There does not seem to be any systematic price or premium level distortion associated with options that have more than approximately 2 months and less than 6 months of life remaining. The technique used in constructing the index will permit a systematic study of any such distortions, how-ever, once data on enough option cycles are available.

B. THE VALUE LINE INDEX

It is possible to construct an index in the form of an average percentage premium with the striking price and market price set equal and the expiration period standardized, interpolating from actual data wherever striking prices, market prices, and expiration periods vary. Two such indexes, for 3- and 6-month options, are published weekly in *The Value Line Options and Convertibles*. While interesting, the Value Line indexes have a few drawbacks. The 3-month index seems to be based on some options with much less than 3 months of life remaining; consequently, it is unstable during those periods when many options are expiring. At times, the 6-month index has appeared to be overly affected by changes in the value that option buyers attached to the possibility of getting a long-term capital gain. Lengthening the required holding period should elim-inate this source of distortions. Finally, the method used in constructing the two Value Line indexes does not seem to compensate properly for changes in interest rates. A 10 percent premium on a 6-month option in the high interest rate environment of 1973 and 1974 was relatively lower in every meaningful way than a 10 percent premium in late 1976.

Apart from these drawbacks, Value Line's reliance on the percentage premium approach does give the investor a number he can relate to his own investment decisions. As long as the investor recognizes that a 10 percent premium for a 6-month option is unheard of for American Telephone and Telegraph and inadequate for Polaroid, he will find the Value Line 6-month index a fair indicator of broad movements in premium levels.

C. IMPLIED VOLATILITY: A BETTER WAY

The index presented here is intended as a more precise index of option premiums that can be related to changes in specific assumptions for the variables affecting option values and to changes in the volatility of the underlying stocks. Although it looks roughly similar to one of the Value Line indexes when charted, it is based on the option market's implied volatility for the underlying stock. Though slightly more abstract than percentage premiums, the concept of implied volatility has important implications for both researchers and option market participants.

With only minor oversimplification, the major factors affecting option value can be reduced to five: (1) time, (2) interest rates, (3) the relationship between the striking price of the option and the market price of the underlying stock, (4) dividends, and (5) stock price volatility. An investor who has access to a probability-type option evaluation model will enter known values for the first four of these variables. Ordinarily, the investor will also enter an estimate of the stock's future volatility and then solve for the fair value of the option. If, instead of solving for fair value, he uses the actual price of the option in the model equation, he can solve for the implied volatility of the underlying stock. *Implied volatility is the value for the stock price volatility variable that equates option price and fair value.* To phrase it another way, implied volatility is the value for the volatility variable that buyers and sellers are accepting when they determine the market price for the option on the trading floor of the exchange.

The index itself is a measure of the relationship between the volatility of underlying stocks *implied* by the current level of option premiums and the *historical* volatility of the same underlying stocks. The formula for the index is given by the equation

$$I = \frac{\sum_1^n \sqrt{V_i}}{\sum_1^n \sqrt{V_h}}$$

where I = value of the index on a particular date

V_i = implied variance of the logarithm of stock price changes calculated by applying a rational option evaluation model to observed values of the stock price and option premium

V_h = historical base-period variance of the change in the logarithm of the underlying stock price

n = number of options used in the construction of the index

Figure 9-1 illustrates the value of the index calculated from this formula for month-end prices of 14 stocks and appropriate options from June 1973 through May 1978. Figure 9-2 plots daily values for the index from September 1, 1975 through May 31, 1978.

To minimize the impact of the difference between the market price of the stock and the striking price of the option, the option used is the one with the appropriate expiration date that has a striking price closest to the market price of the stock. Like the choice of a 3- to just less than 6-month option, this choice of striking price–market price relationship serves to focus the index on that sector of the option market of greatest interest to most investors and of greatest market efficiency.

Large changes in interest rates can have a material impact on results if they are not dealt with properly. An interest rate equal to $1\frac{1}{2}$ percent above the 3-month Treasury bill rate on the date the index is calculated has been used.

The base period for construction of the index is the 4-year

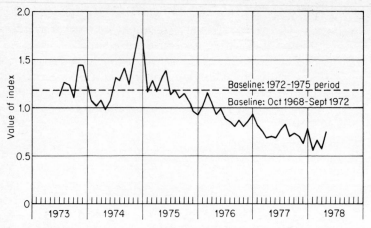

Figure 9-1. Index of month-end option premium levels. (Base period stock price volatility: October 1968–September 1972 = 1.0)

period from October 1968 to September 1972. The reader may protest that listed stock options were not traded during this period. Actually, the choice of a particular base period has no bearing on the usefulness of the index. The index relates option premium levels to the historical volatility of the underlying stocks. A change in the base period would change the *level* of the index but not the *relative values* of the index over the period for which it has been calculated.

What the index shows is that the actual level of listed option premiums has usually been above the level that might have been predicted on the basis of the October 1968–September 1972 volatility of the underlying stocks. This does not necessarily mean that listed options were overpriced during most of the period since trading began or that option writers could count on superior returns with a high degree of reliability. The apparently high option premiums during much of the period, particularly late 1974, reflected the high concurrent volatility of the underlying stocks and an uncertain outlook for the economy and the stock market.

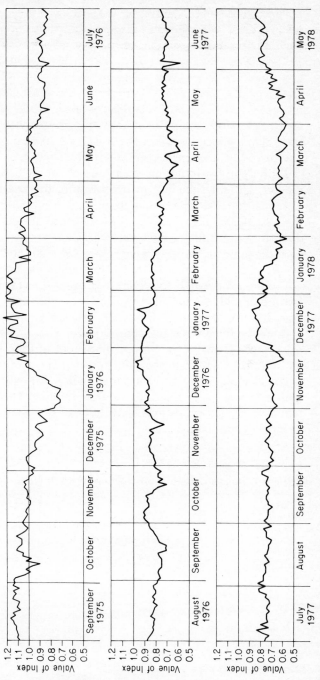

Figure 9-2. Index of daily option premium levels. (Base period stock price volatility: October 1968–September 1972 = 1.0)

279

The actual volatility of most underlying stocks was somewhat greater over the period covered by the index than it was during the base period. If we used calendar years 1972–1975 for the base period, the baseline would intersect the index line at 1.18 (the dashed line in Figure 9-1), and the scales would have to be appropriately adjusted. Explicitly recognizing the higher volatility of most stocks during the 1972–1975 period helps eliminate any unwarranted implications that a specific level of the index means that options are overpriced or underpriced in an absolute sense.

Though professionals generally agree that the listed options market is highly efficient in determining the relative values of the various options available on a given underlying stock, the approach taken here can be used to measure market distortions caused by such factors as the long-term capital gains tax, the commission structure, and differences in liquidity (such as those related to the remaining term of the option and the extent to which it is in or out of the money). No one should be greatly surprised if measurements of implied volatility over a number of market cycles cast a modest degree of doubt on the universal assumption that volatility and option prices are proportional to the square root of time remaining to expiration. In all probability most of the systematic discrepancies that appear in the time relationship will be attributable to taxes, commissions, and the market structure and will be confined to options with lives of less than 2 months or more than 6 months.

Table 9-1. Stocks Used in Construction of the Index

AT&T	K-Mart
Atlantic Richfield	McDonald's
Bethlehem Steel	Polaroid
Eastman Kodak	Texas Instruments
Exxon	Upjohn
Ford Motor	Weyerhaeuser
INA	Xerox

An index of the implied volatility type is probably one of the simplest ways of determining *after the fact* whether a particular level of premiums was too high or too low, given the subsequent volatility of the underlying stocks. When the *implied* volatility measured by the index is compared with the *actual* volatility of the underlying stocks *over the remaining life of an option*, we have an excellent measure of overpricing or underpricing. In the next chapter we apply this measure to one of the option market's classic questions: Who makes money and who loses money in options?

10 WHO MAKES MONEY IN THE OPTIONS MARKET?

Many people believe that determining the answer to this question should be easy. It is not. In many respects the issue of option profitability is the most controversial of all option topics. The number of erroneous or misleading claims made *for* options is only slightly greater than the number of inaccurate statements made *against* options. It is time to examine the issue objectively.

Sections A and B of this chapter provide an extensive review of studies that have addressed the question of investor profitability in the options market. Because each of these studies is flawed, Section C concludes with a new perspective on the effect of options on portfolio returns. This new approach to the question of option profitability should help settle the debate over which side of the option contract (buyer versus writer) was most advantageous during specific historic periods. For those who cannot stand suspense, the evidence suggests that anyone who advocates covered call writing, call buying, or any other option strategy based on the argument that a specific strategy is inherently or consistently superior to any other strategy is, at best, naïve.

A. EARLY STUDIES OF INVESTOR PROFITABILITY IN THE OPTIONS MARKET

Many of the books and articles listed in the Bibliography describe studies of option profitability. The academic community was fascinated with this issue even when the high transaction costs of conventional options made it difficult to believe that either option buyers or option writers could enjoy consistently superior results unless astute investment decisions overcame the cost disadvantages of dealing in options. Most of the early studies reached the conclusion that the option writer enjoyed a modest advantage over the option buyer. As one might expect, the results of each study were primarily a function of the behavior of the stock market during the period examined. None of the early surveys of option profitability covered a long enough period to assure representative market behavior.

Probably the most widely cited examination of option profitability is a study by the Securities and Exchange Commission covering option transactions for the month of June 1959. The SEC study concluded that only 43 percent of the call options included in the study were exercised and that only 18 percent were exercised at a profit to the buyer of the option. On the basis of this study of option transactions for a single month, the notion that at least four out of five option transactions will be "profitable" to a writer of call options has been accepted as gospel by many advocates of option writing.

Though many of the authors recognized the difficulty, none of the early examinations of opinion profitability succeeded in solving a basic problem. The results of a specific option purchase or sale transaction are a function not only of the magnitude of the subsequent change in the stock price but also of the direction of stock price change. Though efforts were made to select time periods that were "typical" of long-term stock market behavior, meaningful conclusions were impossible without an accurate probability-type option evaluation model and an understanding of the impact of an option transaction on the risk characteristics of a portfolio. As indicated in Chapter 7, Fischer Black and Myron Scholes contributed to the solution of this problem.

In connection with one of their two basic articles on option evaluation, Black and Scholes examined conventional option premiums in an attempt to determine whether options tended to be overpriced or underpriced relative to the values suggested by their model. On the basis of their examination of selected conventional option premiums, Black and Scholes concluded that option writers probably did better on a relative basis than option buyers but that transaction costs in the conventional option market were so high that it was hard to believe that either party to a conventional option contract enjoyed a significant advantage over an investor using nonoption investment strategies with similar risk characteristics. The tendency of the Black-Scholes model to compute a low value for options probably accounts for part of the advantage that Black and Scholes attribute to the option writer.

B. STUDIES OF LISTED OPTION PROFITABILITY

A large number of lengthy articles, brief commentaries, and unelaborated statements about the profitability of listed option trading have surfaced since 1973. The volume of this material makes a definitive survey of the "literature" on listed option profitability an interminable and, candidly, a thankless task. Because the stock market was weak in the mid-1970s, most early studies reached the conclusion that option writers enjoyed an advantage over option buyers. This verdict was certainly not unanimous, however. Managements at one of the largest bank trust departments and at one of the first mutual funds to write options concluded that the sale of options was not in the best interests of their clients.

Rather than focus on casual surveys and commentaries that are difficult to evaluate objectively, we will analyze two well-documented studies in detail. Both these surveys of option profitability were prepared by respected members of the academic community and by practicing option managers. Interestingly, one of the studies concludes that covered call writers have a distinct advantage over call buyers, and the other implies that call buyers have had the advantage over call writers in recent years.

1. Kassouf

The leading apologist of the "covered writing is best" school is probably Sheen Kassouf, whose early work in warrant evaluation was described in Chapter 7. Kassouf has published a great deal of material which purports to show that covered call option writing is an inherently superior investment strategy. We focus here on a paper he presented at a spring 1977 seminar sponsored by the Columbia University Graduate School of Business (see Bibliography). This paper is representative of Kassouf's recent work and provides a more detailed description of his assumptions than material he has prepared for more general audiences.

Using what he contends is a series of "typical" over-the-counter option premiums for stocks making up the Dow-Jones industrial average, Kassouf simulated a continuous covered call writing program over a 25-year period ending January 31, 1975. He concluded that the total return from the covered writing portfolio was superior to the return from ownership of the underlying stocks or from a portfolio that combines Treasury bills with call option purchases. Table 10-1 shows the result of Kassouf's simulation.

If one accepts Kassouf's conclusion that the covered writing portfolio would exhibit a 16.54 percent compound annual return, compared with a 9.69 percent compound annual return for the stock-only portfolio and a −5.91 percent compound annual return for the Treasury bill–call purchase portfolio, the

Table 10-1. Results of Kassouf's 25-Year Simulation of Three Strategies Using the Dow-Jones Industrials

	Buy Stock Only, %	Buy Stock, Sell Calls, %	Buy T bills, Buy Calls (91% T bills, 9% calls), %
Average quarterly return	2.74	4.20	−1.35
Standard deviation (quarterly)	6.74	3.63	5.13
Annual growth rate (compounded quarterly)	9.69	16.54	−5.91

attractiveness of covered writing seems overwhelming. Unfortunately, successful investing is rarely so simple.

One of Kassouf's errors lies in his failure to adjust conventional option premiums for dividends paid on the stock. In calculating returns, he credits the covered writing portfolio with all dividends, but he does not reduce the striking price of the option by the amount of the dividend. Striking price reduction is the established practice in the conventional option market. To avoid the necessity for a dividend adjustment, Kassouf could have reduced the premiums to make them comparable to listed option premiums. This dividend adjustment alone would reduce the assumed premium level by between 0.5 and 1.0 percent for a 3-month option.

Even after a dividend correction, Kassouf's assumed premium levels are simply too high. There are no data on listed option premium levels for most of the 25-year period Kassouf used for his simulation, but it is possible to calculate listed option premium levels as of September 30, 1977, on the same percentage basis Kassouf used. As a quick comparison of the two columns in Table 10-2 indicates, most recent listed option premium levels are far below Kassouf's estimates. For the 24 stocks on Kassouf's list which have listed options, he assumed an average premium for a 3-month call option of 6.34 percent. The September 30, 1977, premium level for those stocks was an average of 4.57 percent. Kassouf states that the covered writing portfolio would have the same growth rate as the stock-only portfolio at an average premium level of 4.77 percent. If the September 30, 1977, level of premiums is typical of the 25-year period, the alleged superiority of covered writing disappears. Recent premiums have been below the levels that characterized the first $2\frac{1}{2}$ years of listed option trading, but there is little evidence in Kassouf's work to suggest that the recent level is atypical or, more importantly, that *future* premiums will be high enough to provide an adequate return for the covered call writer.

Although Kassouf states it quite differently, the essence of his argument is that option premiums have been persistently above risk-adjusted fair values. These overpriced options have provided the covered writer with the superior returns Kassouf

Table 10-2. Comparison of Kassouf's Assumed Premiums with Actual Premium Levels on September 30, 1977 (Percentage of common stock price for 3-month call options)

Stock	Kassouf Assumptions, %	Sept. 30, 1977, Listed Option Premium Level, %
Allied Chemical	6.00	5.15
Aluminum Company of America	6.67	4.62
American Brands	5.33	
American Can	5.33	
American Telephone	4.00	2.09
Anaconda	6.67	
Bethlehem Steel	6.67	7.25
Chrysler	8.00	
Dupont	6.00	3.89
Eastman Kodak	6.67	6.62
Esmark	6.67	
Exxon	6.67	3.55
General Electric	6.00	3.91
General Foods	5.33	4.12
General Motors	6.00	3.94
Goodyear Tire	6.67	5.01
International Harvester	6.67	5.09
International Nickel	6.67	
International Paper	6.67	4.87
Johns Manville	6.67	3.29
Owens Illinois	6.00	4.89
Procter & Gamble	6.00	2.10
Sears Roebuck	6.00	5.04
Standard Oil of California	6.67	2.10
Texaco	6.67	3.71
Union Carbide	6.67	4.79
United States Steel	6.67	6.28
United Technologies	8.00	4.28
Westinghouse	6.67	7.18
Woolworth	6.00	5.90
Average percentage premium on stocks for which both Kassouf estimates and listed premium levels are available	6.34	4.57
Actual or comparable level of premium index (see Chapter 9)	1.02	0.74

calculates. Because he assumes relatively high premium levels and provides few data on how the premiums were developed, his results are difficult to verify or accept.

One more aspect of Kassouf's paper seems to require a

comment because it reflects a common misunderstanding of the causes of fluctuations in option premiums. In justifying his assumption of a constant premium, expressed as a percentage of the stock price, Kassouf notes: "If premiums tend to be high at market tops and low at market bottoms, then our results would have shown the covered call portfolio to have an even higher growth rate and lower standard deviation." Kassouf goes on to suggest that option premiums do, in fact, seem to behave this way.

The notion that option premiums expand at market tops and contract at market bottoms is pervasive but incorrect. While there is no evidence that option premiums can predict future stock price movement, they do reflect both recent stock price volatility and investor perceptions of uncertainty in the outlook for the underlying stock. Market tops are characterized by a perception of certainty—by a belief in the favorable outlook for the market and for individual stocks. Option buyers may be more optimistic at market tops, but so are covered call writers. The latter are willing to accept smaller premiums because they believe downside risk to be limited. Because option buyers include buyers of puts as well as buyers of calls and because the option buyer's risk of loss is limited to the amount of the premium, option premiums tend to be highest when uncertainty is greatest. To the extent that any generalization can be made, uncertainty characterizes weak markets, not strong ones.

Kassouf's list of stocks provides some excellent examples of the tendency of option premiums to expand when a company has problems rather than when investors are euphoric. In Table 10-2 option premiums on only two underlying stocks exceeded Kassouf's assumed levels on September 30, 1977. Bethlehem Steel was about to post the largest quarterly loss ever reported by any corporation, and Westinghouse Electric was trying to settle claims arising out of one of the largest contract abrogations in history. The three other companies with actual option premium levels close to Kassouf's assumptions—Eastman Kodak, United States Steel, and Woolworth—also had more than their share of problems. The fact that the high point of the option premium index described in Chapter

9 coincides with the market bottom of 1974 is further evidence that premiums expand when markets are troubled, not when optimism is unbounded.

2. Merton, Scholes, and Gladstein

Another series of simulations with implications for the profitability of various option strategies was conducted by Robert Merton, Myron Scholes, and Mathew Gladstein. Their work is described in the April 1978 issue of *The Journal of Business*. Earlier drafts of this article and advance publicity of the authors' findings focused on the conclusion that buying call options seemed to be a better investment strategy than either straight stock ownership or covered call writing. The focus of the final version of the article is on the pattern of returns, rather than on the frequently cited implication of the $12\frac{1}{2}$-year simulation that call buying is a superior strategy.

For a variety of commercial paper, common stock, and call option strategies, the Merton-Scholes-Gladstein article describes the pattern of semiannual returns and the sensitivity of the level of return, standard deviation of return, and skewness of return to such factors as option premium levels and the striking price–market price relationship. Inevitably, such a study will calculate average return and portfolio volatility (risk) data under assumptions that the authors feel are representative. It is these average return and portfolio volatility data that suggest call option buyers had an advantage over stock buyers and covered call writers during the period of the simulation. This conclusion has brought more nonacademic attention to the Merton-Scholes-Gladstein article than most articles in *The Journal of Business* attract.

Tables 10-3 and 10-4 summarize the return and portfolio volatility calculations for stock investments and option simulations covering the 30 stocks in the Dow-Jones industrial average (Table 10-3) and the 136 stocks on which listed options were available in December 1975 (Table 10-4). Figures 10-1 and 10-2 display the risk and return data of the two tables in a format similar to the risk-return trade-off diagram of Figure 4-23.

Table 10-3. Comparison of the Merton-Scholes-Gladstein Simulation Results—Dow-Jones Sample

Strategy	Semiannual Return (Return), %	Standard Deviation (Risk), %
1. Dow-Jones stock portfolio	4.1	13.7
2. Commercial paper	3.3	1.1
SIMULATED COVERED CALL WRITING (DOW-JONES STOCK SAMPLE):		
3. Exercise price = 0.9 × stock price	2.9	3.7
4. Exercise price = 1.0 × stock price	2.9	6.2
5. Exercise price = 1.1 × stock price	3.2	8.6
6. Exercise price = 1.2 × stock price	3.5	10.4
SIMULATED 90% COMMERCIAL PAPER–10% CALL PURCHASE (DOW-JONES STOCK SAMPLE):		
7. Exercise price = 0.9 × stock price	4.2	7.3
8. Exercise price = 1.0 × stock price	5.1	10.1
9. Exercise price = 1.1 × stock price	7.2	14.6
10. Exercise price = 1.2 × stock price	10.6	25.7

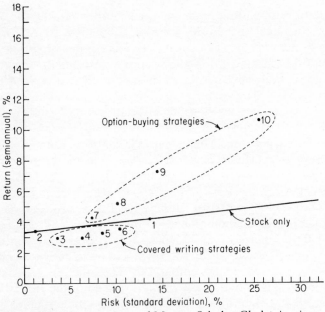

Figure 10-1. Comparison of Merton-Scholes-Gladstein simulation results—Dow Jones stock sample.

Table 10-4. Comparison of the Merton-Scholes-Gladstein Simulation Results—136-Stock Sample

Strategy	Semiannual Return (Return), %	Standard Deviation (Risk), %
1. 136-stock portfolio	7.9	16.6
2. Commercial paper	3.3	1.1
SIMULATED COVERED CALL WRITING (136-STOCK SAMPLE):		
3. Exercise price = 0.9 × stock price	3.3	4.9
4. Exercise price = 1.0 × stock price	3.7	7.1
5. Exercise price = 1.1 × stock price	4.5	9.3
6. Exercise price = 1.2 × stock price	5.3	11.2
SIMULATED 90% COMMERCIAL PAPER–10% CALL PURCHASE (136-STOCK SAMPLE):		
7. Exercise price = 0.9 × stock price	6.3	7.8
8. Exercise price = 1.0 × stock price	8.2	10.6
9. Exercise price = 1.1 × stock price	11.1	15.7
10. Exercise price = 1.2 × stock price	16.2	27.2

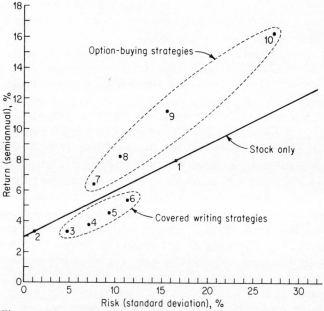

Figure 10-2. Comparison of Merton-Scholes-Gladstein simulation results—136 stock sample.

The reader will recall from the discussion in Chapter 4 that the essence of successful investment management is the construction of a portfolio that has the highest possible expected rate of return at a level of risk acceptable to the investor. Figures 10-1 and 10-2 indicate rather clearly that the simulated 90 percent commercial paper–10 percent purchased call option portfolios gave consistently higher returns at various levels of risk than either stock ownership or covered call writing. The call purchase portfolios dominated the other strategies whether the calls purchased were 10 percent in the money (Strategy 7) or 20 percent out of the money (Strategy 10). On the basis of the risk-return trade-off, the covered call writing strategies appear inferior to both stock purchase (Strategy 1) and call purchase. Covered writing ranked at the bottom of the list of strategies whether the calls sold were 10 percent in the money (Strategy 3) or 20 percent out of the money (Strategy 6). The implications of the Merton-Scholes-Gladstein simulations are clear: Either (1) the simulation has some serious flaws, or (2) investors should have bought calls to obtain any desired degree of equity market exposure during the period covered by the study.

The method used in the Merton-Scholes-Gladstein study seems reasonable upon superficial examination. The return and standard deviation calculations for the benchmark common stock investment positions were computed for equal dollar-weighted portfolios of (1) the 30 stocks in the Dow-Jones industrial average and (2) the 136 stocks for which listed call options were available in December 1975. The option simulations were based on option premiums calculated by a Black-Scholes option evaluation model adjusted for dividends. The interest rate used in the model was the 6-month prime commercial paper rate available at the beginning of each 6-month period. The variance (volatility variable) used in the model was the sample variance of the previous 6 months of daily logarithmic price changes. The idea behind these assumptions was to create simulated portfolios based on the purchase and sale of options at or very close to fair value. Using option premiums calculated in this manner, Merton, Scholes, and Gladstein computed simulated returns and standard deviations for a variety of call purchase and covered call writing strategies for twenty-five 6-month intervals ending in December 1975.

The reader has studied the risk-return trade-off argument of Chapter 4 and the option evaluation discussion in Chapter 7. On the basis of these studies, one would not hesitate to predict that, on the average, the risk-return characteristics of portfolios in which options were purchased or sold at fair value would fall along the trade-off line determined by the risk-return characteristics of commercial paper and the benchmark stock portfolio. As Figures 10-1 and 10-2 demonstrate, the Merton-Scholes-Gladstein study produced markedly different results.

The major contribution of the original Black-Scholes papers was to integrate option evaluation and modern portfolio theory. Subject to some modestly restrictive assumptions, Black and Scholes established that an investor could obtain essentially any risk-return position along the trade-off line by buying or selling fairly priced options either alone or in combination with stock positions and Treasury bills. The results of the Merton-Scholes-Gladstein simulations appear seriously inconsistent with this fundamental tenet of option evaluation theory. To put the degree of inconsistency in perspective, option premiums would have to have been more than 20 percent higher to have made the simulated option strategies for the 136-stock sample consistent with the risk-return trade-off line of Figure 10-2 and more than 28 percent higher to have made the simulations for the 30-stock Dow-Jones sample consistent with the trade-off line of Figure 10-1. Somehow, the Merton-Scholes-Gladstein study either has used option premiums that are too low or has introduced other sources of bias.

Merton, Scholes, and Gladstein are fully aware of the inconsistency between their results and the foundations of option theory. They even include a disclaimer:

The relative risk characteristics of the strategies described by the simulations are representative of the strategies. The specific *levels* of the returns generated, however, are strongly dependent on the actual experience of the underlying stocks during the simulation period. To avoid the creation of new myths about option strategies, the reader is warned not to infer from our findings that any one of these strategies is superior to the others for all investors. *Indeed, if options and their underlying stocks are correctly priced, then there is no single best strategy for all investors.*

The three authors attribute the anomalous results of their simulations not to an error in evaluating options but to unusual behavior by the underlying stocks during the test period. Part of the inconsistency is blamed on the fact that the $12\frac{1}{2}$-year period studied included some extremely sharp market rallies and declines. Another explanation offered is that the dispersion of returns on individual stocks may have been unusually large during the study period. Even if these explanations are valid (and they do help explain the results), they are red herrings that draw attention away from the central problems: The option premiums used in the Merton-Scholes-Gladstein simulations are systematically too low, and the simulation portfolios have built-in biases. An examination of these weaknesses of the Merton-Scholes-Gladstein study has important implications for the "inherent" profitability of various option strategies and for the use and misuse of option evaluation techniques.

The major reasons for the anomalous results of the Merton-Scholes-Gladstein simulations can be listed briefly or discussed at length. For most readers the brief listing will suffice:

1. The Black-Scholes model led to the use of option premiums that were too low.

2. A higher interest rate than the commercial paper rate should have been used and would have given higher option values.

3. The simulation technique in the Merton-Scholes-Gladstein study created stock equivalent portfolios biased toward the greater use of less volatile underlying stocks in the option purchase strategies. Because the study covered a period of below average stock market performance, this bias probably favored the option-purchase strategies.

4. Because underlying stock price volatilities rose in an irregular pattern over the simulation period, the Merton-Scholes-Gladstein simulation technique permitted the option buyer to purchase options at less than their fair value. If stock price volatility had declined over the period and other biases had worked in opposite directions, the implications of the study might have been quite different.

The remainder of this section will expand on these points and touch upon some other criticisms of the Merton-Scholes-Gladstein study. Readers interested in the more general question of option profitability may prefer to skip to Section C on page 306.

Low option values from the Black-Scholes model   The most obvious reason behind the low option premiums in the Merton-Scholes-Gladstein study is the study's reliance on the Black-Scholes option evaluation model. Any model based on a lognormal distribution of stock price changes will translate a variance or standard deviation calculated from actual stock price data into a systematically low option premium. The magnitude of the systematic undervaluation of the premium will depend on a combination of the level of stock price volatility and the extent to which the option is in or out of the money.

As the data in Table 7-10—comparing the Black-Scholes and Gastineau-Madansky models—indicate, the Black-Scholes model will undervalue a typical option with a striking price equal to the market price of the stock by 1 to 2 percent. If the striking price is above or below the market price of the stock, the undervaluation will be greater. It is possible that an empirical distribution developed from stock price data for the entire 12½-year period covered by the Merton-Scholes-Gladstein study would show a larger or smaller deviation, but a 1 to 2 percent systematic undervaluation (when the striking price and market price are equal) is a reasonable estimate.

The interest rate assumption   The construction of a riskless, market-neutral hedged position using stock and fairly priced options to provide an expected return on investment equal to the return on a risk-free debt instrument is the foundation of modern option evaluation theory and the major contribution of the original Black-Scholes papers. A second reason behind the low option premium levels in the Merton-Scholes-Gladstein study appears to be use of the commercial paper rate as a proxy for the "risk-free" interest rate of option theory. While many users of option models have taken the Treasury bill or commercial paper rate as a proxy for the risk-free interest rate, it is probably appropriate to use a higher interest rate.

In theory, one can construct a risk-free neutral hedge with options; in fact, no hedged portfolio could be instantaneously adjusted. The return from an actual hedged portfolio will fluctuate more than the return from a Treasury bill or commercial paper portfolio. As a consequence, the rate of interest used in an option evaluation model should be greater than the Treasury bill or commercial paper rate. This point is made in an article by Edward Thorp (see Bibliography), and most sophisticated users of option evaluation models add a percent or two to the interest rate on Treasury bills or commercial paper. In calculating the index of option premium levels described in Chapter 9, for example, $1\frac{1}{2}$ percent was added to the Treasury bill rate. While there is room for disagreement on the magnitude of the systematic premium undervaluation introduced by use of the commercial paper rate, undervaluation from this source appears to be roughly 2 percent. Thus, between the Black-Scholes model's lognormal distribution and an artificially low interest rate, it is possible to account for approximately 4 percent out of the 20 to 28 percent systematic undervaluation in the simulation.

Measurement of stock price volatility   While the magnitude of the effect is more difficult to quantify, another cause of systematic undervaluation of options in the Merton-Scholes-Gladstein simulations may have come from improperly calculated volatility (variance) measurements. The variances used in the Merton-Scholes-Gladstein study were the sample variances of daily logarithmic stock price changes for the preceding 6-month period. This method of estimating historic variances is considerably more accurate than most techniques used to estimate past stock price volatility. However, for a variety of reasons, most of which are considerably beyond the scope of this book, the variance estimates can be distorted.

Many standard statistical techniques rely on the similarity of a population distribution to the normal (or lognormal) distribution. If a distribution is not normal or lognormal, it may not be appropriate to estimate a variance for a 6-month period from a daily variance. This point is examined at length in Appendix C, and the Bibliography lists a number of articles which explore some of the problems associated with the facts that stock prices and returns are not lognormally distributed and that the variance is not constant over time.

Additional work may indicate that the Merton-Scholes-Gladstein technique for estimating variances leads to systematic distortion. Until contrary evidence is available, however, it seems appropriate to assume that any systematic error introduced by this method of estimating variances is probably small.

Creation of biased portfolios The single most important problem with the Merton-Scholes-Gladstein simulations is not undervaluation of option premiums per se but, rather, the creation of biased portfolios. Some types of portfolio bias cancel out when risk is correlated with return, as in Figures 10-1 and 10-2. Other types of bias are not so easily eliminated. The major weakness of the Merton-Scholes-Gladstein simulations is that the stock equivalent composition of the simulation portfolios is a complex function of the strategy employed, the volatility of each stock in the portfolio, and the behavior of each stock during each simulation period.

The nature of this bias in portfolio composition will be clarified by an examination of Tables 10-5 and 10-6, which illustrate the computation of stock equivalent positions for stocks with various volatility characteristics under the assumptions used in the Merton-Scholes-Gladstein simulations. Table 10-5 shows the neutral hedge ratio and percentage call premiums for typical low-, medium-, and high-volatility stocks. Using the data from Table 10-5 as input, Table 10-6 lists, by volatility class, the beginning stock equivalent weightings that the Merton-Scholes-Gladstein simulation techniques build into a portfolio. This table demonstrates rather clearly that *the stock equivalent representation of different volatility segments varies greatly, depending on the strategy employed.*

Table 10-5. Selected Black-Scholes Call Values and Neutral Hedge Ratios

Assumptions:
Interest rate, 5%; option life, 6 months; no dividend. (Neutral hedge ratio expressed as decimal fraction of round lot of stock; call value expressed as percentage of stock price.)

Exercise Price ÷ Stock Price	Low-Volatility Stock (Annualized Standard Deviation = 0.20)		Medium-Volatility Stock (Annualized Standard Deviation = 0.30)		High-Volatility Stock (Annualized Standard Deviation = 0.40)	
	Neutral Hedge Ratio	Call Value, %	Neutral Hedge Ratio	Call Value, %	Neutral Hedge Ratio	Call Value, %
0.9	0.84	13.51	0.76	15.50	0.73	17.78
1.0	0.60	6.90	0.59	9.65	0.59	12.41
1.1	0.34	2.92	0.41	5.60	0.46	8.39
1.2	0.15	1.03	0.26	3.06	0.34	5.53

Table 10-6. Relative Stock and Stock Equivalent Weightings by Volatility Class at the Beginning of Each Period in the Merton-Scholes-Gladstein Simulations

Strategy	Low-Volatility Stock (Annualized Standard Deviation = 0.20), %	Medium-Volatility Stock (Annualized Standard Deviation = 0.30), %	High-Volatility Stock (Annualized Standard Deviation = 0.40), %
1. Stock only	100	100	100
2. Commercial paper	0	0	0
SIMULATED COVERED CALL WRITING:			
3. Exercise price = 0.9 × stock price	16	24	27
4. Exercise price = 1.0 × stock price	40	41	41
5. Exercise price = 1.1 × stock price	66	59	54
6. Exercise price = 1.2 × stock price	85	74	66
SIMULATED 90% COMMERCIAL PAPER— 10% CALL PURCHASES:			
7. Exercise price = 0.9 × stock price	62	49	41
8. Exercise price = 1.0 × stock price	87	61	48
9. Exercise price = 1.1 × stock price	116	73	55
10. Exercise price = 1.2 × stock price	146	85	61

This table depicts, for the same three volatility levels and four exercise price-to-stock price ratios as Table 10-5, the resulting portfolio stock equivalents for the strategies used in the Merton-Scholes-Gladstein simulations. For example, in Strategy 5 (covered call writing, exercise price = 1.1 × stock price) in the low-volatility case, the investor buying 100 shares of stock and selling one call with a neutral hedge ratio of 0.34 (from Table 10-5) is left with a risk equivalent position of (100 − 34 = 66) shares of stock or 66 percent of the basic stock only portfolio. In Strategy 9 (90% commercial paper − 10% call purchase, exercise price = 1.1 × stock price) in the same low-volatility case, the investor committing 10 percent of resources to call purchase is in the risk equivalent position of holding (10% ÷ 2.92% × 34 shares = 116) shares of stock or 116 percent of the basic stock only portfolio.

The index of underlying stocks used in the Merton-Scholes-Gladstein simulations is an equal dollar average of the 30 or 136 stocks comprising each sample portfolio. While this equal dollar weighting technique is not the method used in the construction of popular stock market averages such as the Dow-Jones industrials or Standard & Poor's 500, it is a perfectly reasonable approach to portfolio weighting *if it is followed consistently.* In the Merton-Scholes-Gladstein simulations, however, the weighting varies with the simulation strategy employed. As the relative stock and stock equivalent weightings in Table 10-6 indicate, low-volatility stocks will be comparatively underweighted when in-the-money covered call options are written (Strategy 3) and slightly to markedly overweighted for most other option strategies. If the stock equivalent measurements in Table 10-6 were modified for dividends (which are typically higher for low-volatility stocks than for high-volatility stocks), *the bias in overweighting low-volatility stocks in the option buying strategies would be even more pronounced.*

Merton, Scholes, and Gladstein explicitly recognize the mediocre performance of the broad market averages during the simulation period. Given this indifferent market performance, a low-risk bias in portfolio construction (i.e., emphasis on low-volatility stocks) might have been a more successful strategy than an aggressive posture (emphasis on high-volatility stocks). Though quantifying the effect is difficult, the inherent bias of the Merton-Scholes-Gladstein simulation technique in *overweighting low-volatility stocks in the option purchase strategies seems to account for most of the apparent superior performance of these call-buying strategies* over the simulation period.

Dollar cost averaging and the rising trend in volatility A final perspective on the inherent biases of the Merton-Scholes-Gladstein simulations is based on an analogy to dollar cost averaging in the accumulation of a common stock position. Dollar cost averaging is not widely used by investors today. During the post-World War II expansion of the large mutual funds and the promotion of the New York Stock Exchange's now defunct Monthly Investment Plan, dollar cost averaging was very much in vogue. The idea behind dollar cost averaging is that an investor commits a periodic, fixed dollar amount to the purchase of shares in a diversified mutual fund or a specific common stock. For example, the investor might buy $100 worth of stock on the first day of each month. When the price of the stock is low, $100 buys more shares than when the price of the stock is high. Unless the stock slips into a long-term decline, the investor's average cost per share is likely to be less than the price of the stock a few years after the dollar-cost-averaging program is initiated. Something quite similar happens in the Merton-Scholes-Gladstein simulations.

Under the Merton-Scholes-Gladstein assumptions, a covered writer receives less option premium money, and an option buyer owns more option contracts, if stock price volatility was very low during the preceding 6-month period. The effect of fluctuations in volatility is most pronounced in the case of the option buyer. When volatility has dropped, stock equivalent risk exposure will be significantly greater for the option buyer committing a fixed dollar amount to option purchases because the dollars committed to option purchases will buy more options. If volatility has been high, the amount allocated to option purchases will buy fewer options. Just as in a dollar-cost-averaging stock purchase program, tying the option purchase policy to a fluctuating volatility figure will result in the purchase of *more* options than if the average volatility of the stock over the $12\frac{1}{2}$-year simulation period had been used to calculate the price to be paid for options at the beginning of each 6-month period.

An important difference between a real dollar-cost-averaging program in either stocks or options and the Merton-Scholes-Gladstein simulations is that the price at which an option purchase might be made is unlikely to fluctuate as widely as the volatility of the underlying stock. Though the brief trading history of listed options does not permit definitive conclusions on this point, option premiums will probably not fall as low as a single period of very low stock price volatility might indicate or rise as high as an extremely volatile period would suggest. When a historically volatile stock has been extremely stable for 6 months, the premium levels of its options will usually reflect a compromise between the high long-term volatility and the recent low volatility. Likewise, if a historically stable stock goes through a period of extraordinarily wide fluctuations, its option premiums will typically reflect a compromise between the high recent volatility and the more moderate longer-term volatility. As a consequence of the tendency of option premiums to iron out extreme volatility fluctuations, it may not be possible to buy options at the extremely low premiums or to sell them at the extraordinarily high premiums implied by short-term stock price volatility data.

The principal weaknesses of a dollar-cost-averaging program in stocks or mutual funds are (1) the tendency to abandon the program during periods when stock prices decline, and (2) the possibility of a secular decline in the price of the shares purchased. While the Merton-Scholes-Gladstein option purchase programs are as subject to abandonment in early years as any cost-averaging program, this does not detract from the validity of the approach. On the other hand, a long-term decline in stock prices *and stock price volatility* could lead to greater pressure for abandonment than most dollar-cost-averaging programs face.

Because stock price volatilities *rose* on the average during the 12½-year period of the simulation, the prior-period volatility measurement (used to determine the option price and the number of options purchased) tended to be *lower* than the volatility during the period over which results were calculated. If stock price volatilities had declined over the simulation period, as they did from the end of 1974 through 1977, the simulation results would have been materially different. The rise in stock price volatility over the simulation period is just one more factor biasing the results in favor of option buying strategies.

Key weaknesses in the Merton-Scholes-Gladstein technique. The combination of (1) stock equivalent portfolio weighting bias in favor of low-volatility stocks in a period of below-average market performance, (2) the tendency of fluctuating stock price volatilities to lead to the simulated purchase of an unrealistically large number of option contracts, and (3) the secular increase in stock price volatility over the simulation period probably accounts for nearly all the apparent superiority of the option buying strategies.

While many of the criticisms leveled at the Merton-Scholes-Gladstein simulation may seem relatively technical in nature, the important point for the reader to bear in mind is that these criticisms relate to distortions which bear significantly upon the levels of returns indicated for various strategies. The point of these criticisms is that the Merton-Scholes-Gladstein simulations have not demonstrated that option buying is inherently superior to option writing *or even that option buying would have been a superior strategy during the 12½-year period studied.*

Whenever the reader is tempted to conclude that *any* option strategy is inherently superior to other option strategies, appropriate therapy would include a cold shower and a rereading of this key statement from the Merton-Scholes-Gladstein article:

The relative risk characteristics of the strategies described by the simulations are representative of the strategies. The specific *levels* of the returns generated, however, are strongly dependent on the actual experience of the underlying stocks during the simulation period. To avoid the creation of new myths about option strategies, the reader is warned not to infer from our findings that any one of these strategies is superior to the others for all investors. *Indeed, if options and their underlying stocks are correctly priced, then there is no single best strategy for all investors.*

Investors who keep this point in mind will save themselves a great deal of time and, in all probability, a considerable amount of money.

The pattern of returns: rational versus irrational investment strategies Before we set their study aside, a few comments on the patterns of returns described by Merton, Scholes, and Gladstein seem in order. Their paper is organized around two sentences from the introduction: "Investors have different objectives including differences in tolerance for risk. Hence, one strategy may be preferred by one investor while a different strategy is preferred by another." That there are differences in investor risk tolerances is not controversial. That these differences in risk tolerances necessarily lead to significant differences in option *strategy* preferences is very much open to question.

The discussion in Chapter 4 of the relationship between risk and reward made the elementary point that the buyer of a put or call risks only the premium paid for the option, while the option seller's potential loss is much greater. If the option seller's position is carefully monitored and the stock equivalent exposure is appropriately controlled, the risk of large losses from option-writing strategies is readily manageable. For all practical purposes, then, translating options into stock equivalents is the appropriate way to measure the risk impact of any option position. With this point in mind, it becomes clear that *the return patterns from the Merton-Scholes-Gladstein simulations result from unplanned and uncontrolled changes in risk equivalence.*

The characteristic return patterns of the Merton-Scholes-Gladstein simulations are obtained by setting up a portfolio and not modifying it for 6 months. Avoiding all changes in investment policy for a fixed time interval might make sense if a portfolio consisted entirely of common stocks. However few economists, psychologists, or even ordinary investors would consider this a rational investment policy when options are involved.

Psychologists and economists might insist on phrasing their objections in terms of utility theory and the construction of an efficient securities portfolio. Investors would simply note that as the stock equivalent risk exposure of a portfolio changes, steps must be taken to bring the risk back into line with their desired level of stock exposure. Taking the Merton-Scholes-Gladstein simulation portfolios as a starting point, most investors examining Table 10-6 will recognize that selling in- or out-of-the money calls on American Telephone and Telegraph is a much different strategy from selling calls on Polaroid with similiar striking price–market price relationships. Likewise, the stock equivalent risk exposure associated with buying calls is a complex function of a number of factors, including the striking price–market price relationship, the volatility of the underlying stock, and the premium level. The investor who wants equal dollar equivalent participation in several stocks will have to spend more dollars buying call options on volatile stocks than he or she spends buying call options on more stable stocks. Investing equal dollar amounts in calls on every stock will leave highly volatile stocks under-represented on a stock equivalent basis.

Even an investor who finds the beginning stock equivalent structure of one of the Merton-Scholes-Gladstein strategies in agreement with personal risk preferences would not want to leave the position untouched for 6 months. The stock equivalent risk exposure of the overall portfolio and of individual positions can change dramatically over that time period. Table 10-5 indicates that at the beginning of a 6-month simulation period each 20 percent out-of-the-money call option on a stable stock (annualized standard deviation = 0.20) would give exposure equivalent to 15 shares. For a volatile stock (annualized standard deviation = 0.40) each 20 percent out-of-the-money call would give exposure equivalent to 34 shares when the position is originally established. With a 30 percent increase in the price of each stock and the passage of time, either option might provide stock equivalent exposure equal to 90 shares or more. If most stocks are rising, the stock equivalent exposure of a portfolio based on the purchase of out-of-the-money options could double or triple in response to a 25 to 30 percent rise in the broad market averages. Under such circumstances most investors would want to realize some profits and reduce their market risk exposure.

In contrast to the investor who owns out-of-the-money calls in rising market, a seller of in-the-money calls against a portfolio of underlying stock will find stock equivalent exposure reduced to a negligible level as time passes and/or as stock prices advance. While the market exposure of an owner of out-of-the-money calls will decline if stock prices fall, the in-the-money covered call writer's risk exposure will rise sharply if stock prices drop below the striking price of the options sold. A rational investor who gives any thought to the risk characteristics of a portfolio or of individual positions will usually want to make some changes before 6 months have passed.

The Merton-Scholes-Gladstein simulations are grounded on the erroneous assumption that a rational investor might seek specific patterns of returns. Investors seek the highest possible return at a level of risk they can tolerate or the lowest level of risk consistent with an investment return adequate to maintain a desired standard of living. The return patterns described in the Merton-Scholes-Gladstein paper will not be attractive to a rational investor who examines the drastic changes in intraperiod risk exposure which rebalancing the portfolio only once every 6 months imply. The Merton-Scholes-Gladstein return patterns are not inherently characteristic of call option buying or covered call writing strategies. They are simply the result of failure to adjust portfolio risk exposure in response to changing stock prices. Identical patterns of returns could be obtained with other strategies if an investor really wanted to make large and erratic changes in stock equivalent exposure. An investor shown the changing patterns of stock equivalence (rather than patterns of returns) would find the fluctuations in risk exposure unacceptable and irrational.

C. OPTION BUYERS VERSUS OPTION WRITERS: THE HISTORIC PERFORMANCE RECORD

The criticism leveled at Kassouf's work and at the Merton-Scholes-Gladstein simulations in the previous section suggest a few of the problems which confront anyone who tries to determine whether buyers or writers have had the most desirable side of the option contract. Careful study of Table 10-6 and the related discussion of changes in stock equivalence will help clarify the central problem of option performance measurement: the virtual impossibility of maintaining consistent risk equivalence between a conventional portfolio and any portfolio that contains options. Simulation techniques will not give meaningful results. What is needed is an indirect measure of performance which gauges the extent to which options are overpriced or underpriced relative to the volatility of the underlying stock. While the paragraphs which follow do not provide a definitive evaluation of option buying versus option writing for all time, they describe a technique which can be the basis for determining the relative attractiveness of various option strategies for any past period. When the technique is applied to the relatively short history of listed option trading, the results will surprise many investors.

Before describing either the methodology or the results, a few caveats seem in order:

1. This analysis of historic option profitability covers only the period during which listed call options have been traded.

2. The conclusion that options in general were overpriced or underpriced during some part of this period is perfectly consistent with the possibility that options on some stocks might be overpriced when most options were underpriced, or vice versa.

3. The fact that an option is overpriced or underpriced relative to the volatility of the underlying stock does not mean that it is impossible to make money by being on the "wrong" side of the option contract. Overpricing or underpricing means only that the buyer of an underpriced option or the seller of an overpriced option has the expectation of a (risk-adjusted) profit and that the party on the other side has the expectation of a (risk-adjusted) loss. The statement that an option is overpriced or underpriced does nothing more than describe that option's probable attractiveness relative to alternative ways of taking an equivalent stock position.

4. Call options can be as underpriced during a market decline as during an advance. The fact that the price of a stock moves sharply *in either direction* is evidence that options were probably underpriced. Even if the owner of calls will lose money in a market decline, a buyer of puts might make a large profit. More to the point, a buyer of underpriced calls will ordinarily lose less in a sharp stock price decline than the holder of a risk equivalent position taken directly in the stock. The greatest losses in a sharp decline will fall to investors who establish stock equivalent positions as sellers of underpriced puts or covered calls.

A careful reading of the earlier sections of this chapter and these caveats suggest that the problem with most examinations of option profitability is that they study the performance of a limited number of positions over a limited time period. They neglect the analysis of portfolio bias and changing stock risk equivalence. The quantity of data and the statistical refinements needed to make a realistic option profitability study using conventional performance evaluation techniques would dwarf even the relatively complex Merton-Scholes-Gladstein simulations. Fortunately, it is possible to eliminate most problems of portfolio bias and changing risk equivalence by measuring option profitability indirectly, much as an astronomer measures distance or velocity.

When Black and Scholes developed the neutral hedge technique for valuing options and laid the foundation for the integration of option evaluation and portfolio theory, they made it possible to examine the issue of option profitability without constructing a real or simulated portfolio. As demonstrated in Chapter 4, a fairly priced option will provide both a buyer and a writer with risk-adjusted expected returns that fall on the risk-return line in Figure 4-23 (page 76). If the option trades at more than its fair value, the average risk-adjusted return to the option *writer* will be above the risk-return trade-off line. If the option sells for less than its fair value, the average risk-adjusted return to the option *buyer* will be above the line. Because of the relationship between option values and returns, careful evaluation of the option contract itself will give a more meaningful answer to the question of option profitability than the most complex simulation.

The approach to the analysis of option profitability advocated here is based on comparisons of actual and implied stock price volatility. Chapter 9 provided a description of an index of option premium levels based on the stock price volatility implied by the market values of option premiums. In preparing the index, the Gastineau-Madansky option evaluation model is used to calculate the value of the stock price volatility variable which is implied by the actual price of the option. Each stock's contribution to the index is a measure of the implied (or expected) stock price volatility reflected in the premium on a representative option.

Because of the way in which it is constructed, the index is

more than a measurement of actual premium levels. It is also an excellent tool for comparing *implied* or expected stock price volatility with *actual* levels of stock price volatility over the life of the options. As with the astronomer's indirect measurements, the relationship between implied and actual volatility is analogous to the relationship between the *price* of an option on the exchange floor and the *fair value* of that option as determined by the subsequent movements of the underlying stock.

Table 10-7 and Figure 10-3 compare implied and actual volatilities for selected stocks and options since shortly after trading began on the Chicago Board Options Exchange. The solid line in Figure 10-3 represents the index of option premium levels (implied volatility), and the dashed line shows the actual level of stock price volatility. The technique and the principles behind the option premium index or implied volatility calculation were detailed in Chapter 9. The actual stock price volatility index was constructed in a similar manner from actual variance data on the same underlying stocks. The variances were calculated for each 3-month period from 5-day lagged logarithms of closing stock prices. These variances were adjusted to the single-day lag basis used in the index calculation and the resulting actual volatility numbers became input to the index formula on page 277. As a result of this calculation, the actual and implied volatilities are expressed in comparable index numbers. If the index of implied volatilities (premium levels) exceeds the index of actual volatilities (fair values), the average option is overpriced. If the actual volatilities exceed the implied volatilities, the average option is underpriced.

Because the appropriate comparison is between implied volatility *at the time an option transaction is considered* and the actual stock price volatility *over the life of the option*, Column 4 of Table 10-7 is the difference between the average implied volatility for one quarter and the actual volatility for the subsequent quarter. The actual volatility line in Figure 10-3 is also set back by 3 months to make the comparison meaningful.

This juxtaposition of implied and actual volatilities indicates that, on the average, listed options have been slightly over-

Table 10-7. Comparison of Quarterly Average Implied Volatility (Premium Levels) and Lagged Actual Volatilities (Fair Value) for Selected Stocks and Options

(1) Quarterly Period for Implied Volatility	(2) Average Implied Volatility (Index)	(3) Actual Volatility Lagged by One Quarter	(4) Magnitude of Overpricing or (Underpricing) (Col. 2 − Col. 3)
1973 Q3	1.20	1.20	—
Q4	1.38	1.30	0.08
1974 Q1	1.05	1.15	(0.10)
Q2	1.12	1.60	(0.48)
Q3	1.32	1.65	(0.33)
Q4	1.66	1.29	0.37
1975 Q1	1.21	1.06	0.15
Q2	1.27	1.01	0.26
Q3	1.15	0.92	0.23
Q4	0.98	0.87	0.11
1976 Q1	1.07	0.75	0.32
Q2	0.93	0.73	0.20
Q3	0.84	0.79	0.05
Q4	0.87	0.69	0.18
1977 Q1	0.75	0.76	(0.01)
Q2	0.72	0.77	(0.05)
Q3	0.75	0.79	(0.04)
Q4	0.70		
	Average difference		0.055

NOTE: The average implied volatility (Col. 2) is the average of the month-end values for the index of premium levels described in Chap. 9. The actual volatility lagged by one quarter (Col. 3) is derived, in a manner analogous to the computation of the index, from stock price variances based on 5-day differences of stock price logarithms for the 3-month period *following* the quarter covered by the index numbers in Col. 2. The magnitude of overpricing or underpricing (Col. 4) is the difference between these implied and lagged actual volatility measurements.

priced. The overpricing from late 1974 through the end of 1976 seems to be primarily attributable to a lag in the downward adjustment in option premium levels as stock price volatility declined over the period. A few quarters of high stock price volatility not reflected in higher premium levels would erase the modest relative advantage that option writers have enjoyed to date.

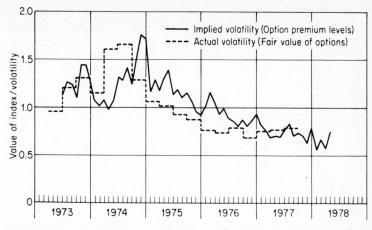

Figure 10-3. Comparison of option premium levels with fair values as measured by subsequent stock price volatility.

While most features of Figure 10-3 and Table 10-7 will be readily apparent to a careful observer, there are some important implications of this data that merit emphasis:

1. Although listed options have been very slightly overpriced (on the average), there have been periods of significant underpricing.

2. Even though the typical option has traded fairly close to its fair value most of the time, there have been occasions when most option premiums have been significantly out of line with subsequent stock price volatility. Because this analysis is based on the aggregation of a number of stock and option relationships, it conceals rather than reveals profit opportunities in specific issues.

3. Recent low premium levels and the growth of institutional covered call writing portfolios indicate that any systematic overpricing may be more of a historic than a contemporary phenomenon.

4. With more sophisticated statistical methods, a larger sample of stocks and options, and more elaborate weighting techniques, the accuracy of the results could doubtless be improved. The apparent magnitude of overpricing or underpricing at various times might change as a result of such refinements, but the overall conclusion would probably not be changed by a more complex or comprehensive analysis.

5. While commissions and tax considerations have been ignored in this analysis, these factors can have an impact on investment results. In general, commissions will penalize option strategies (particularly covered call writing) relative to many non-option strategies. On the other hand, a high tax rate will make covered call writing relatively more attractive.

Every effort has been made to avoid the implication that any option strategy is inherently better than any other strategy. This effort will have been wasted if readers interpret Table 10-7 and Figure 10-3 as evidence that the option writer will typically enjoy even a modest advantage over the option buyer in the future. Anyone who reaches this conclusion has missed the point.

An even more serious error would be the conclusion that the relatively modest average difference between option premium levels and fair values means that individual option contracts are nearly always fairly priced. While the average option tends to be fairly priced, discrepancies between market value and fair value are both substantial and frequent. An alert investor who has mastered the material in Chapters 4 and 7 will find many opportunities for profit.

The implication that the average option tends to be fairly valued is consistent with the broad provisions of the efficient market model of security prices. The existence of material deviations from efficient pricing in the option markets simply reflects what most participants in the securities markets have known all along: An astute investor whose thinking is carefully organized and whose judgment is sound can make money consistently in an efficient market environment.

APPENDIX A
MARGIN REQUIREMENTS

Margin requirements serve two purposes. First, they protect the investor from his own folly. By limiting an individual's ability to accept risk, margin requirements prevent (or at least delay) his total financial ruin. Second, and most important, they ensure the continuing viability of the market by protecting innocent bystanders from the excesses of speculators who are mindless of the effect their own downfall would have on others. Since the 1930s, the minimum margin requirements set by appropriate regulatory bodies have been adequate to protect the investing public and the brokerage firm carrying the margin account. Option margin rules have usually been stricter than the requirements for other securities.

Apart from disputes stemming from falling stock prices, margin requirements probably cause most of the misunderstandings between investor and broker. Margin requirements for option transactions were particularly troublesome in the early days of the Chicago Board Options Exchange because they depended not only on an individual firm's policies but on its stock exchange affiliations as well. Uniform minimum margin rules were adopted at the end of

1974 by the New York Stock Exchange, the CBOE and the Federal Reserve Board. Minor changes were made in 1977 in connection with the introduction of listed puts. Some firms may adopt stricter "house rules" or impose supplementary requirements for the equity in an account or a customer's net worth.

The purpose of this appendix is to help the investor understand the effect of option margin rules on his portfolio even if he never actually calculates the required margin on a specific investment. Most published discussions of margin requirements are of no help to the average investor because they do not provide a frame of reference. Few investors really understand the meaning of a 50 percent margin requirement or the statement that an account must be marked to the market. Without more information than is usually provided, it is impossible for the investor who has not worked in a margin department to calculate the margin requirement for a particular transaction. This appendix will not qualify readers for a position as margin clerk, but it should permit them to calculate the required margin for any new option position they may initiate and to determine what kind of stock price behavior would subject them to a margin call.

Rule 1: Long option positions have no loan value; therefore, the option buyer must pay 100 percent of the option premium in cash.

Example: An investor buys a call option at a price of $10.

Cost of option	$10 × 100 shares = $1,000
Required cash payment	$10 × 100 shares = $1,000

Rule 2: If he is the covered writer of a call option, the investor need post no additional margin beyond the initial or maintenance margin required to carry the stock or other security convertible into the underlying stock. Also, the investor's account is credited with the option premium received.

Example: An investor writes a covered call option for a premium of $10. The striking price of the option is $100, and the current price of the stock is $95.

Market value of stock position	$95 × 100 shares = $9,500
Regulation T initial margin requirement on the stock	50% × $9,500 = $4,750
Less: option premium received	$10 × 100 shares = 1,000
Net initial margin required	= $3,750

For margin purposes, the value of the stock underlying a covered writing position cannot exceed the striking price of the option, in this case, $100 per share.

Rule 3: If he is an uncovered writer, the investor must post margin equal to the required margin percentage times the market value of the shares under option less the option premium received, less the amount by which the option is trading out of the money or plus the amount by which the option is in the money. Notwithstanding the result of this calculation, the investor must post a minimum margin of $250 per uncovered option contract written, including the amount of any option premium received.

Example: An investor writes an uncovered listed call option at a price of $10. The striking price of the option is $100, and the current price of the stock is $95.

Market value of shares under option	$95 × 100 shares = $9,500
Basic margin requirement	30% × $9,500 = $2,850
Less: option premium received	$10 × 100 shares = $1,000
Less: amount by which option is out of the money	($100 − $95) × 100 shares = $ 500
Net initial margin required per contract	= $1,350

The margin percentage is 50 percent for conventional options.

Table A-1 illustrates the calculation of initial margin requirements on a call option with a $100 striking price at various stock prices.

Table A-1. Calculation of Initial Margin Requirements for the Writer of an Uncovered Listed Option with a $100 Striking Price

(1) Value of 100 Shares of Stock	(2) 30% of Stock Value	(3) Price of Option Contract	(4) 100 × Striking Price minus Stock Price	(5) Net Required Margin	(6) Margin Advantage over Shorting Stock
$ 6,000	$1,800	$ 100	$4,000	$ 150	$2,850
$ 7,000	$2,100	$ 200	$3,000	$ 50	$3,450
$ 8,000	$2,400	$ 400	$2,000	$ 0	$4,000
$ 9,000	$2,700	$ 800	$1,000	$ 900	$3,600
$10,000	$3,000	$1,300	$ 0	$1,700	$3,300
$11,000	$3,300	$1,800	($1,000)	$2,500	$3,000
$12,000	$3,600	$2,200	($2,000)	$3,400	$2,600
$13,000	$3,900	$3,000	($3,000)	$3,900	$2,600
$14,000	$4,200	$4,000	($4,000)	$4,200	$2,800

KEY TO COLUMNS:

(1) The market value of 100 shares of stock at the time the option is written.

(2) The basic initial margin requirement for writing an uncovered listed option is 30% of the market value of the stock when the position is taken.

(3) This column should be taken only as an indication of a price at which this option contract might sell. The price is rounded for simplicity.

(4) In applying the 30% margin rule to options, 100 times the amount by which the striking price exceeds the stock price is subtracted from the required margin. If the market price exceeds the striking price, the difference is added.

(5) Calculated: (2) − (3) − (4). If the result of this calculation is less than $250 minus the premium received per contract, the writer must still post $250 *less the premium received*.

(6) Stock margin requirements are 50%. The investor should note that *maintenance margin* rules are stricter when applied to options than to short positions.

Rule 4: Unlike the margin rules applicable to many security positions, the net maintenance margin requirement for an uncovered option writing position is calculated in essentially the same manner as the net initial margin requirement.

Example: The market price of a stock underlying the option written in the example for Rule 3 drops to $70 per share.

Market value of shares
under option $70 × 100 shares = $7,000
Basic margin requirement 30% × $7,000 = $2,100

Less: option premium received originally (*not* the current value of the option)		=	$1,000
Less: amount by which option is out of the money ($100 − $70) × 100 shares		=	3,000
Net maintenance margin required		=	($1,900)
Because this would violate the 250 per contract minimum, the net required is $250 − $1,000 premium received		=	($ 750)

The reader's attention is called to several features of this calculation. First, because the stock has declined so sharply, the option is unlikely to be exercised. As a consequence of the decline, the uncovered writer can not only withdraw any collateral he posted as margin, he can also withdraw most of the option premium he originally received. (Actually, the writer could have invested the option premium in Treasury bills or substituted other collateral for the portion of the margin contributed by the premium received.) Second, the $250 minimum margin requirement is reduced by the amount of any unwithdrawn premium received.

Example: The market price of the stock underlying the option written in the example for Rule 3 rises to $130 per share.

Market value of shares under option	$130 × 100 shares	=	$13,000
Basic margin requirement	30% × $13,000	=	$ 3,900
Less: option premium received		=	1,000
Plus: amount by which option is in the money ($130 − $100) × 100 shares		=	3,000
Net maintenance margin required		=	$ 5,900

The key point to be learned from these maintenance margin examples is that the required maintenance margin moves up and down 30 percent *faster than the value of the underlying shares.* Unless great care is exercised, the uncovered writer runs a high risk of having to meet margin calls.

Rule 5: Calculation of the required margin for puts is similar to the calculation for calls.

Rule 6: If a straddle writer owns the underlying stock, the call is covered, but he must put up additional margin to collateralize the put side of the transaction. If both a put and a call are sold uncovered, the margin requirement is that of the option requiring the highest margin plus any unrealized loss on the other option.

Rule 7: The initial or maintenance margin on a listed option spread is:

  A. When the long option position expires before the short option position, the investor must pay 100 percent of the cost of the long option and post margin on the short option according to the rules for uncovered options.

  B. When the short option position expires concurrently with or before the long option position, spread margin rules apply.

  1. If the striking price of the short call (put) is equal to, or greater (less) than, the striking price of the long call (put), the required margin is equal to the premium on the long option less the premium on the short option.

Example: An investor buys a July $100 call at $10 and sells an April $100 call at $7 on the same underlying stock. He must post ($10 − $7) × 100 shares = $300.

  2. If the striking price of the short call (put) is lower (higher) than the striking price of the long option, the required margin on the short option is the lesser of the margin required if the options are not treated as a spread, or the difference between the striking prices of the two options.

Example: An investor buys a July $100 call at $3 and sells a July $90 call at $10.

Her net margin requirement is 100 percent of the long position	$3 × 100 shares = $ 300
Plus: the difference in striking prices ($100 − $90)	$10 × 100 shares = 1,000
Less: the premium received from the option written	$10 × 100 shares = 1,000
Net margin required per pair of contracts	= $ 300

There is no further maintenance margin required. Regardless of the behavior of the underlying stock or the option contracts that make up the spread, the short option position is not marked to the market as in the examples for Rule 4.

Rule 8: When a call is covered by a position in a convertible security, the convertible security must be adequately margined and the investor must also post margin equal to the amount, if any, by which the conversion price exceeds the striking price of the call if conversion requires a cash payment.

Example: An investor buys listed warrants at a price of $15 with an exercise price of $105 and sells a July $100 call option on the same underlying common stock at $10.

Initial margin on the warrant position	100% × $15 × 100 shares = $1,500
Less: option premium received	$10 × 100 shares = 1,000
Plus: amount by which exercise price on warrant exceeds striking price of call	(105 − $100) × 100 shares = 500
Net margin required	$1,000

This summary of the margin rules pertaining specifically to options cannot possibly cover all aspects of the margin requirements. The fine points of margining options with convertible securities and the margin relationship between the rest of an investor's portfolio and his option portfolio are extremely complex subjects and are probably more suitable topics for a book on margin than a book on options. The purpose of this appendix is to provide a general explanation of the margin rules. This brief discussion should help the reader understand how margin rules and the possibility of margin calls affect the risk characteristics of a portfolio.

Using this description of option margin rules, the reader may uncover several ways to improve the efficiency and return of his or her portfolio. For example, an investor may own some marginable securities that can be substituted for the premium received on an option written, permitting investment of the premium. Alternatively, a credit balance in an option account at one brokerage firm can offset a debit balance in another account if the second account is moved to the firm where the investor trades options. An understanding of option margin requirements is one of many ways in which the effective use of options separates a well-managed, controlled-risk portfolio from the typical investor's carelessly handled collection of stocks.

APPENDIX B
CALCULATING THE RETURN
FROM OPTION WRITING

Rate of return on investment is a fuzzy concept when it is applied to uncovered option writing. Although the dollar profit or loss is simple enough to compute if the price at which a transaction will be closed out is given, the amount of capital invested (the denominator in the rate-of-return calculation) is not easy to determine.

Calculating the incremental investment required for one investment strategy versus an alternative is ordinarily straightforward. To illustrate, the incremental rate of return on investment from holding a stock for a long-term gain is equal to the incremental aftertax profit (or loss) from holding the stock until it goes long-term divided by the net proceeds the investor would have received earlier by selling for a short-term gain. This return can be annualized for comparison with other investments by multiplying it by 12 and dividing the product by the number of months until the gain goes long-term. If the transaction takes place in a margin account and the investor wants to calculate his return on equity, he subtracts aftertax interest costs from the profit (or loss) in the numerator of the fraction and the amount of his borrowings from the denominator.

Writing options complicates this kind of rate-of-return calculation in several respects. The option writer's margin account is credited with cash equal to the net premium from the option he writes. This *reduces* the net cash or equity investment for any investment strategy that involves writing options. *On a cash or equity basis the required investment for writing an option is negative.* Nevertheless, the option writer is required to post margin for the options written. In the margin sense, his incremental investment for writing the option will be the net margin requirement after adjustment for the cash premium he receives. Neither the negative cash investment figure nor the net margin requirement is entirely satisfactory as the denominator in a return-on-investment calculation. This complication is created by the unique cash-flow characteristics of option writing and the margin rules that apply to it.

The choice of whether the denominator in a rate-of-return calculation for a strategy involving option writing should be adjusted by adding the net margin required for writing the option or by subtracting the net option premium is not necessarily a choice between the right way and the wrong way of making the calculation. Either method may be appropriate or not, depending on the investor's overall margin and portfolio risk position. Investors may find the results more meaningful if they assume that the net margin for writing an option is part of the denominator in the rate-of-return computation. Any rational estimate of the fair value of an option will already have credited interest on the premium received by the writer, so only the net margin above this amount will be involved.

A possible refinement to the approach of adding the net required margin to the denominator of the return calculation would be to adjust the calculated return for any interest or profit earned by investing that margin. For example, if a margin deposit is invested in short-term debt, it could earn interest at, say, a 7 percent rate. Alternatively, if a cash deposit reduces the investor's debit balance, the interest credit might be at a 9 percent rate.

To simplify calculations and to clarify explanations, assume that securities deposited as margin would be earning interest or some other return even if they had not been used to meet the margin requirement. The rate of return on net required margin, then, is an approximation of the *incremental* return from a strategy involving option writing. The denominator is a measure of the assets "tied up" in the investment, but the rate-of-return calculation understates the true return on these assets because the margin collateral included in the denominator is *already invested.* In a sense, these assets are working twice as hard when a put or call option-writing strategy is adopted. Rather than attempt to adjust for this "double duty," the rate of return can be expressed as an *incremental return on net margin employed.*

The true expected rate of return on the assets employed in an option-writing strategy will always be higher than indicated by this kind of calculation. The difference will be the amount of interest an investor would receive from investing the net option margin requirement for that writing position. A consequence of this approach is that an uncovered option-writing strategy is attractive *if* (1) it shows a positive expected incremental return on net margin required and (2) it modifies the risk structure of the portfolio in a manner the investor deems appropriate.

The principal weakness of simplifying the explanation in this manner is that the investor might consider a transaction less attractive than it really is because the basic return on the margin deposit is not added back. This weakness is at least partly, though only approximately, offset by the fact that investors tend not to adjust their thinking for commissions.

A growing number of investors are estimating risk-adjusted returns by reference to market rates of return and diagrams like Figure 4-23. This approach overcomes most of the problems created by conventional rate-of-return calculations.

APPENDIX C
SOME COMPARISONS OF THE
USE OF EMPIRICAL AND
LOGNORMAL DISTRIBUTIONS
IN OPTION EVALUATION*

Albert Madansky
University of Chicago

A number of years ago, Gary Gastineau, who is now with Kidder, Peabody, and I got together (as most tinkerers do) in my garage, trying to develop an options analysis system. The Black-Scholes paper† had appeared and we were concerned at that time about whether in fact the distribution of the natural logarithms of the changes in daily stock prices was lognormal and whether, if indeed it was not lognormal, the deviation from lognormality made a difference in options evaluations. Our concern was more focused because we knew about all the work that had been done at the University of Chicago, summarized quite well in Fama's paper,‡ on the behavior of stock market prices, showing that the distribution of logarithms of changes in the stock market prices was not normal.

* Adapted by permission of the author, from Albert Madansky, "Some Comparisons of the Use of Empirical and Lognormal Distributions in Option Evaluation," *Proceedings of the Seminar on the Analysis of Security Prices*, University of Chicago, May 1977, pp. 155–168.
† Fischer Black and Myron Scholes, "The Pricing of Options and Corporate Liabilities," *Journal of Political Economy*, May–June 1973, pp. 637–654.
‡ Eugene Fama, "The Behavior of Stock Market Prices," *Journal of Business*, January 1965, pp. 34–105.

That was not sufficient evidence for us to say that the lognormal distribution was inappropriate because those studies were dealing with *all* stocks and we were concerned with a special class of stocks that we called "optionable stocks"— stocks that would ultimately be listed on some options exchange. Perhaps the return on that subset of stocks might have a probability distribution which was neither the kind found in the University of Chicago studies, nor would it be a lognormal distribution. We just did not know.

So we got 4 years of daily data on a small list of 40 optionable stocks and fitted a probability distribution which we thought would characterize the behavior of the logarithm of the change in optionable stock prices. Figure C-1 is a rough picture of that distribution.* That picture is really a smoothed graph of the density function. What we actually did was to fit the distribution as a step function over a 22-point interval from -5.5σ to $+5.5\sigma$ with intervals of 0.5σ.

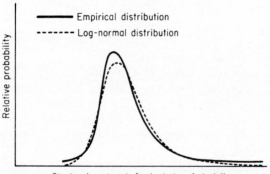

Figure C-1. Comparison of empirical distribution of stock prices with lognormal distribution.

We chose 5.5σ because everybody learns in a first course in statistics that after 3σ the normal distribution disappears. And so we added another 2.5σ to the tail area. We chose a 0.5σ

---

* Gary Gastineau, *The Stock Options Manual*, New York, McGraw-Hill Book Company, 1975.

interval only because a finer grid would have taken a lot more computer time. (Remember, we were just tinkering around at the time.) I will make some remarks about the effect of the 0.5σ later on, especially with regard to the put formulation.

We discovered that the distribution was significantly different from what the lognormal distribution would produce. And so we proceeded to develop an alternative options evaluation which, given our distribution, is a simple thing to do because, effectively, all one needs to do is calculate an expected value of some random variable, be it an expected profit or an expected return. An expected value is just the integral of the random variable times the density function. It is very nice to know that, in a lognormal distribution, the density function has a nice, simple closed form of parametric representation. And so one could, on the back of an envelope, use theorems of calculus to calculate what the value of the integral was going to be. In the case of the empirical distribution, we were not even interested in finding a mathematical functional form that fit the empirical distribution. We were not interested in elegance; so, to evaluate the expected value we resorted to numeric integration, plugging this probability distribution into the integrand.

And so our model really performs the appropriate integrations and differentiations, using numerical techniques based on the empirical distribution to arrive at an option evaluation.

One of the other questions we had was: Does it make a difference in valuation that the distribution is significantly different from lognormal? The fact that the distribution is significantly different from lognormal may not have any bearing on option evaluations. It may be that by the time we mashed through the numeric integration, and determined the value of an option, it will turn out to be not much different from that using the lognormal distribution as a basis. Table C-1 shows a brief description of the discrepancy between the valuations produced by our calculation and the evaluation produced by the Black-Scholes model. It is for you to judge whether there is any material difference between the kinds of calculations that we produced and the kinds of calculations that the Black-Scholes model produced.

Table C-1. Comparison between Valuations by Gastineau and Madansky and by Black and Scholes

Assumptions:

Daily stock price variance (log)	0.632×10^3
Interest rate	10% per annum
Remaining life of option	3 months
Exercise price	$40
Dividends, commission, and taxes	No adjustment

(1) Stock Price	(2) Gastineau- Madansky Option Value	(3) Black-Scholes Option Value*
$28	$ 0.22	$ 0.13
32	0.70	0.60
36	1.76	1.72
40	3.72	3.67
44	6.59	6.38
48	10.12	9.66
52	13.99	13.29

* Fischer Black, "Fact and Fantasy in the Use of Options," *Financial Analysts Journal*, July–August 1975, pp. 36–72.

Some 3 years later, now that we are rich and famous and don't have to work out of my garage anymore, I can report the results of a study of a larger set of 4 years' worth of data, this time much cleaner data. (I will not tell you who provided us with our earlier data, but it was a data source other than CRSP.) About a year ago we studied 4 years' worth of daily stock price data on 389 optionable stocks. The number of optionable stocks increased from our original 40, mostly because the number of stocks that were already trading was over 200 on the various exchanges. We were interested in seeing whether the distribution that we had developed a number of years ago was a reasonably accurate description of what would happen with a larger universe of stocks and with a change in the time period. And the answer is that there is no significant difference between the cumulative distributions—the one we developed a number of years ago and the one that we developed recently—based on the larger sample.

There is a small practical difference, of course, if one uses this amended distribution in our evaluation integration, as can be seen from Table C-2. But in the worst case, we are

Table C-2. Option Values Based on the Revised Empirical Distribution

Stock Price	Revised Option Value
$28	$ 0.25
32	0.70
36	1.70
40	3.68
44	6.62
48	10.19
52	14.06

talking about some 7-cent difference in the valuation of the option, which I think is in the noise level relative to other factors such as commissions.

What I was more interested in pursuing, though, was the question of how different, on a stock-by-stock basis, was this portmanteau-generalized empirical distribution from a lognormal distribution. We broke up the 4-year period into 16 quarters and compared the empirical distribution and the lognormal distribution to see how well they fit with each of the 16 quarters' distributions for each of the 389 stocks.

We used two statistical tests: one that you should all be familiar with, the chi-squared test, and another called the *Kolmogorov-Smirnov test*, for testing goodness of fit of distributions. The reason that we used both tests is that the chi-squared test has the propensity of saying that things are significant if the tails are off. It weighs the tails much more heavily than perhaps it ought to. The Kolmogorov-Smirnov test treats the tails in a little gentler fashion. It does not reject hypotheses very rapidly if the tails are off. And so, as a fair test of comparison between the two distributions, we performed both the Kolmogorov-Smirnov test and the chi-squared test on each of these 389 stocks in 16 time periods.

Table C-3 gives the results. Using the chi-squared test, out of 389 comparisons, if we looked at 5-day lags, for example, we found only one case where the normal distribution surpassed the empirical distribution. The import of Table C-3 is that, in the preponderance of cases, the empirical distribution is at least as close to the distribution of the changes in stock

Table C-3. Comparison between Normal and Empirical Distributions

Lag	No. of Stocks for Which Normal Distribution Surpassed Empirical Distribution		No. of Stocks for Which Normal Distribution Was at Parity with Empirical Distribution	
	Based on χ^2 Test	Based on K-S Test	Based on χ^2 Test	Based on K-S Test
5	1	18	6	53
21	6	43	30	80
63	7	60	24	76
126	5	47	36	53

prices as is the best-fitted lognormal distribution based on the variance estimated from the data for that particular time period.

There is a technical problem associated with what distribution one fits to the log of the return (or to the log of the changes in stock prices). The only distribution for which the variance as a function of time is equal to t times the variance, among all so-called "stable distributions," is the normal distribution. And so we were concerned about whether, in fact, the reason for the discrepancy between the lognormal distribution and the data distribution had to do with the fact that the formula

$$\sigma^2(t) = \sigma^2 t$$

is breaking down. We looked at a number of cases to shed light on this question, and I am anecdotally reporting on three which I have selected to illustrate some points. Two that I have selected are Johns Manville and General Foods.

If one were to plot the returns for Johns Manville and plot the returns for General Foods, Johns Manville is about as close as one can get to lognormality. (Bell Telephone is good, too, but I picked Johns Manville because everybody picks on the telephone company.) General Foods represents one of the most extremely deviant from lognormal data sets in my set of 389 stocks.

And so I took these two extreme cases and looked at the

variance divided by the one-period variance in order to see what the behavior is as a function of time. In theory, if the distribution were lognormal, then the column $\sigma^2(t)/\sigma^2(1)$ in Table C-4 should equal t, the lag that is being carried along. And you can see that for a 5-day lag, it is very good; for a 21-day lag, it is also very good; for a 63-day lag, it starts to get worse; at 126, it is still worse; and at 189, it is still worse.

Table C-4. Comparison between Johns Manville and General Foods

Lag t	JM $\sigma^2(t)$	$\sigma^2(t)/\sigma^2(1)$	GF $\sigma^2(t)$	$\sigma^2(t)/\sigma^2(1)$
1	0.00050205	1.00	0.00036986	1.00
5	0.002579	5.14	0.0018688	5.05
21	0.010542	21.00	0.0077321	20.91
63	0.0267757	53.30	0.017432	47.14
126	0.047315	94.25	0.036179	97.83
189	0.064289	128.07	0.040446	109.37

The reason I selected these two is that the patterns look about the same for both. So just looking at a plot of $\sigma^2(t)/\sigma^2(1)$ for the two stocks, I cannot tell whether the data distribution is going to be lognormal or is not going to be lognormal. I conclude that the deviation from lognormality may be, but is not necessarily, a function of whether the variance is linear in time. That is the import of the Johns Manville–General Foods comparison.

The other kind of phenomenon that I wanted to point out is illustrated by Table C-5. In terms of deviations from lognormality, Ralston Purina is about as deviant from lognormality as General Foods, and yet the pattern of $\sigma^2(t)/\sigma^2(1)$ is quite markedly different from that of General Foods and, in fact, is devastatingly bad. Look at what happens as the lag gets larger and larger. In effect, the variance as a function of lag is not linear in t; it suddenly stops growing, and the ratio actually drops for lag 189. But on a judgment call, I would say it is pretty flat after about 63 days.

Well, these are the results of our work in checking and comparing the use of empirical and lognormal distributions

Table C-5. Ralston-Purina

Lag t	$\sigma^2(t)$	$\sigma^2(t)/\sigma^2(1)$
1	0.0002827	1.00
5	0.0015669	5.54
21	0.0057551	20.36
63	0.013107	46.36
126	0.016292	57.63
189	0.015257	53.97

in options evaluation. I do want to make another comment, though, on the relation of this work to puts. It becomes very clear in puts, especially in the formulation given by Myron Scholes, that one can plug in any distribution and do the dynamic programming or backward analysis to obtain the put evaluation. I decided to try to approximate the lognormal distribution with the 22-point approximation and calculate the put value, assuming not the lognormal distribution, but rather the 22-point approximation to the lognormal distribution. It turns out that I get results that are markedly different from the Parkinson* calculations when using 0.5σ intervals. If we were to take the 0.5σ-interval approximation to the lognormal distribution and use it in our call program, we would get numbers that are about a penny off of what the Black-Scholes formula would produce. My suspicion is that for puts a much finer grid on an empirical distribution than 0.5σ intervals is needed in order to enable one to build an empirical put evaluation model.

* Michael Parkinson, "Option Pricing: The American Put," *Journal of Business,* January 1977, pp. 21–36.

APPENDIX D
ANNOTATED BIBLIOGRAPHY

The Annotated Bibliography is divided into three sections. The first section reviews the major publications available from the option exchanges, particularly the Chicago Board Options Exchange and the American Stock Exchange, and from The Options Clearing Corporation. These publications probably contain the best elementary discussions of options available. Any user of options should read this material carefully, particularly those items marked with an asterisk, which are worthy of particular attention.

Not all the books and articles reviewed in the second part of the Bibliography are recommended. Heavily promoted books are included because they tend to be readily available, not because they are worthwhile reading. Major academic articles are listed and reviewed. The bibliographies in these academic papers will help a researcher find additional information.

The third section of the Bibliography summarizes the information available from option advisory services. While this summary does not evaluate these publications, Chapter 7 contains some comments on the merits of the option evaluation techniques used by several services. Most advisory services will provide free sample copies or low-cost introductory subscriptions to help an investor appraise the publication.

1. Exchange Publications

Some of the best basic discussions of option topics have been published by The Options Clearing Corporation and the option exchanges.

Items on this list marked with an asterisk are particularly good and should be studied carefully by anyone interested in the topic which the pamphlet covers. Copies of most of these publications are given to brokerage firm customers without charge. Research studies sponsored by the CBOE are reviewed in the Books and Articles section of the Bibliography.

Options Clearing Corporation
Prospectus: Exchange Traded Put and Call Options

Chicago Board Options Exchange
Understanding Options
Are Call Options for You?
Are Put Options for You?
Option Spreading
Call Option Writing Strategies
Tax Considerations in Using CBOE Options (Revised October 1976)
Buying Puts, Straddles and Combinations
The Robbins-Stobaugh Study: A Summary
The Nathan Report: A Summary
Market Statistics (annual)
Constitution and Rules (not ordinarily distributed free)
CBOE Reference Manual (not ordinarily distributed free)
Margin Manual (not ordinarily distributed free)

American Stock Exchange
The Versatile Option
Spreading Strategies
Tax Planning for Listed Options
Introducing Puts
Guide to Listed Options (not ordinarily distributed free)
Options for Institutions (three booklets)
Protecting Your Investments with Options
Increasing Your Income with Options
Buying Options for Profit Opportunities
Amex Stats (monthly)

Philadelphia Stock Exchange
The Anatomy of an Option Order
Guide to All Listed Options
*Argus Options Service Quarterly Fundamentals (not ordinarily distributed free)

In addition to the material listed, the Securities and Exchange Commission requires that each option exchange publish a review of quarterly high and low prices covering a 5-year period for each underlying stock.

2. Books and Articles

This listing is an attempt to catalog most of the important books and articles on options and related subjects which might be of interest to the reader who wishes to explore a particular topic in depth. With a few exceptions, articles originally published in academic journals are not listed separately if they are reprinted in one of the volumes of readings, such as those edited by Cootner and Lorie. Some papers and books which the author found to be of minimal value are omitted. Aside from important journal articles which have not been reprinted in a form readily available to the average investor, the reader can obtain most of this material through a bookseller or local library. If a reader is interested in undertaking a comprehensive survey of option literature, most material not listed here is mentioned in one or more of the articles and books which are listed.

Alverson, Lyle: *How to Write Puts and Calls*, New York, Exposition Press, 1968.

> While he covers some of the same material as the Asens' book (see below), Alverson's book is much less comprehensive.

Ansbacher, Max G.: *The New Options Market*, New York, Walker & Company, 1975.

> A basic book describing most major option strategies, tax treatment of option transactions, and margin requirements. Ansbacher's style is quite readable, although he sometimes achieves clarity by

oversimplifying. After examining his unequivocal arguments against the purchase of call options, one is left with the feeling that he does not fully understand the mechanism of stock price change and the determinants of option value.

Asen, Robert, and R. Scott Asen: *How to Make Money Selling Stock Options*, West Nyack, N.Y., Parker Publishing Company, 1970.

This book is written almost exclusively from the viewpoint of the option writer. While the text tends to drag at times, the explanations of complex topics are clear and comprehensive. Margin requirements are more complex today than when this book was written, but the Asens' explanation of the application of margin rules to basic conventional option transactions is unusually clear.

Auster, Rolf: *Option Writing and Hedging Strategies*, Hicksville, N.Y., Exposition Press, 1975.

This is a difficult book to evaluate. Where it is good it is very good, and where it is bad it is very bad. Auster is an accounting professor, and, as one might suspect from that background, he has the mechanics of options down cold. Auster's greatest weakness is an almost total lack of appreciation for the mechanism of stock price change and the techniques of option evaluation. Though he cites a number of articles on option evaluation in his bibliography, the comments he makes on premium levels and stock price–option price relationships suggest that his knowledge of this literature is superficial.

Black, Fischer: "Fact and Fantasy in the Use of Options," *Financial Analysts Journal*, July–August 1975, pp. 36–72.

An excellent analysis of the risk characteristics of various option and stock positions. In this article Black goes a long way toward shattering much of the conventional wisdom concerning the risks of option trading. Must reading for the serious investor.

Black, Fischer: "The Pricing of Commodity Contracts," *Journal of Financial Economics*, January–March 1976, pp. 167–179.

When commodity options begin trading on exchanges in the United States, this article will be the frame of reference for sophisticated users of commodity options, just as the original Black-Scholes papers have served users of listed stock options.

Black, Fischer, and John C. Cox: "Valuing Corporate Securities: Some Effects of Bond Indenture Provisions," *The Journal of Finance*, May 1976, pp. 351–367.

An excellent example of the application of option theory to some of the problems of corporate financial policy.

Black, Fischer, and Myron Scholes: "The Valuation of Option Contracts and a Test of Market Efficiency," *The Journal of Finance*, May 1972, pp. 399–417.

In this article Black and Scholes test their model against actual conventional option transactions. During the period studied, they concluded that options on highly volatile stocks tended to be underpriced, while options on less volatile stocks tended to be overpriced. They found that transaction costs in the conventional option market largely eliminate any chance for consistently superior profitability.

Black, Fischer, and Myron Scholes: "The Pricing of Options and Corporate Liabilities," *The Journal of Political Economy*, May–June 1973, pp. 637–654.

The basic article in which Black and Scholes derive their option valuation model. The article has some useful comments on alternative models as well.

Bokron, Nicholas R.: *How to Use Put and Call Options*, Springfield, Mass., John Magee, Inc., 1975.

Glowing dust-jacket testimonials to the contrary notwithstanding, this is neither the best nor the most understandable of the basic books on options. Apart from the fact that the author's terminology is frequently at variance with that used by most option investors, the examples and diagrams are difficult to follow.

Boness, A. James: "Elements of a Theory of Stock-Option Value," *The Journal of Political Economy*, April 1964, pp. 163–175.

A clear explanation of a general probability model. Somewhat technical.

Bookbinder, Albert I. A.: *Security Options Strategy*, Elmont, N.Y., Programmed Press, 1976.

This is not the worst book reviewed here, but it is by far the most disappointing. Anyone with Bookbinder's credentials should have produced something better. He devotes an inordinate amount of space to a review of studies of the profitability of buying and writing call options. Bookbinder's understanding of the significance of many of these studies, particularly the work of Fischer Black and Myron Scholes, is quite limited. He embarks on his own "analysis" of the returns to various option market participants. Because he does not seem to understand the difference between the volatility of an individual stock and the volatility of broad market averages, his results are meaningless. The balance of the book simply restates material found in exchange booklets or other basic option publications.

Branch, Ben, and Joseph Finnerty: "Option Listing and Stock Price Performance," Amherst, University of Massachusetts School of Business Administration, Working Paper.

This paper examines the effect of an option listing on the price of a company's stock. The conclusion is what most observers would expect: Newly listed option stocks significantly outperform the market after their listing is announced.

Brealey, Richard A.: *An Introduction to Risk and Return from Common Stocks*, Cambridge, Mass., The M.I.T. Press, 1969.

Brealey, Richard A.: *Security Prices in a Competitive Market*, Cambridge, Mass., The M.I.T. Press, 1971.

These two books provide an excellent nontechnical introduction to the literature of portfolio theory and stock price behavior. The second book has an excellent review of various studies of option writing and buying results. Brealey concludes that transaction costs in the conventional option market are so high that in the long run only the put and call broker will make a profit. The bibliographies are excellent.

Brennan, Michael J., and Eduardo S. Schwartz: "Convertible Bonds: Valuation and Optimal Strategies for Call and Conversion," Vancouver, University of British Columbia, Working Paper no. 336, July 1976.

The basic technique for extending option theory to the analysis of other convertible securities is discussed here and in the Ingersoll papers listed below.

Brennan, Michael J., and Eduardo S. Schwartz: "The Valuation of American Put Options," *The Journal of Finance,* May 1977, pp. 449–462.

Most readers will find this to be a clearer discussion of the put evaluation problem than the Parkinson paper.

Brickel, Robert W.: *Planned Profit through Hedging,* privately published by the author, 1974.

This booklet suffers from the author's lack of understanding of the economics of short selling and from the use of hypothetical transactions that would rarely be possible.

Buskirk, Richard H., and Benjamin R. Howe: *Preplanning a Profitable Call Writing Program,* Larchmont, N.Y., Investors Intelligence, 1970.

This book, devoted exclusively to option writing, falls between the Alverson and Asen books in both complexity and overall quality.

Bussman, Richard L.: *The Statistical Game Theory of Speculation,* Deerfield Beach, Fla., R. L. Bussman Press, 1975.

This rather unusual book will satisfy few readers. Academic critics will find fault with Bussman's eclectic mathematics. The typical investor will be lost by page 3. Grammarians and opponents of creative spelling will be aghast. Nonetheless the text is more informative than that of most books for the nonprofessional market.

Cary, Elgin: *Profitable Spreading Strategies Using Listed Call Options,* New York, Austin Advisory Services, 1976.

If an investor relies on Cary's tables of probable spread price relationships to any large extent, this book could be misleading.

Charell, Ralph: *A Great New Way to Make Money: 51 Consecutive Profits in 5 Months,* New York, Stein and Day Incorporated, 1976.

Charell is a self-styled consumer advocate. Readers who examine his "performance record" in detail will soon reach the conclusion that they need someone to protect them from Charell. While the book provides adequate descriptions of a number of basic option strategies, the "51 consecutive profits in 5 months" claimed by the author are questionable. They seem to have been obtained by the simple expedient of taking small profits whenever possible and letting losses run. At the end of the 5-month period, Charell had a series of 51 small realized gains and an apparent accumulation of unrealized losses.

Chen, Andrew H. Y.: "A Model of Warrant Pricing in a Dynamic Market," *The Journal of Finance*, December 1970, pp. 1041–1059.

One of the better probability-based option and warrant evaluation models. Slightly easier reading than most, but still fairly technical.

Clasing, Henry K.: *The Dow Jones–Irwin Guide to Put and Call Options*, Homewood, Ill., Dow Jones–Irwin, Inc., 1975, revised edition 1978.

This book does a fair job of explaining the basic characteristics of the listed option contract. Unfortunately, Clasing's descriptions and risk-reward characterizations of various stock and option strategies suggest that he has only a limited understanding of option evaluation and listed puts. The revised edition does not correct these weaknesses.

Cloonan, James B.: *Stock Options: The Application of Decision Theory to Basic and Advanced Strategies*, Chicago, Quantitative Decision Systems, Inc., 1973.

A hodgepodge of explanatory material on basic option terminology and strategies and the author's ideas for what is, in essence, filter-rule trading of stocks and options. Cloonan proposes that the investor cover and uncover an option writing position as the stock price moves up and down. Any trader who feels that such an approach will give superior results should read Chapter 16 of Cootner's book. (See reference below.)

Cootner, Paul, ed.: *The Random Character of Stock Market Prices*, Cambridge, Mass., The M.I.T. Press, 1964.

An excellent collection of academic journal articles and doctoral thesis extracts on the subject of the probability distribution of stock prices. Any serious student of options will find this book invaluable. An interesting feature of this book is that so much of the work on stock price fluctuations has been done in connection with the development of option pricing models. Unfortunately, most of the material is highly technical, and an ability to deal with complex mathematical formulations is essential.

Cox, John C., and Steven A. Ross: "The Valuation of Options for Alternative Stochastic Processes," *Journal of Financial Economics*, January–March 1976, pp. 145–166.

Cox and Ross cope with the shortcomings of the Black-Scholes evaluation formula by building a shift in the distribution into the model. The approach is roughly similar to Merton's.

Cunnion, John D.: *How to Get Maximum Leverage from Puts and Calls*, Larchmont N.Y., Business Reports, Inc., 1966.

One of the better basic books on conventional options.

Dadekian, Zaven A.: *The Strategy of Puts and Calls*, New York, Charles Scribner's Sons, 1968.

This introductory book on option writing is much less comprehensive than the Asens' book in its treatment of taxes, margin, and other technical topics. Dadekian does, however, stress the importance of stock price volatility as a factor in option pricing. His calculations of return on investment are seriously misleading, but the decision process he advocates is more rational than that suggested by most basic option books. Unfortunately, his techniques are not very helpful in analyzing listed options.

Davis, Gary A., and M. Alan Jacobson: *Stock Option Strategies*, Cross Plains, Wis., Badger Press, 1976.

Though this book seems to be intended as an intermediate-level discussion of stock option strategies, it contains nothing in the way of substantive information or insights beyond the material provided by elementary books and pamphlets. This lack of substance and a rather "cutesy" writing style (e.g., two hypothetical bearish investors are given the names Fred Grisly and Karl Kodiak) suggest that the authors may have received their Ph.D.'s in areas quite unrelated to options, perhaps zoology.

Dimson, Elroy: "Instant Option Valuation," *Financial Analysts Journal*, May–June 1977, pp. 62–69.

Dimson, Elroy: "Option Valuation Nomograms," *Financial Analysts Journal*, November–December 1977, pp. 71–74.

These two articles describe the use of nomograms, a graphic version of the Black-Scholes option evaluation model. Nomograms can be useful to an investor who (1) wants to evaluate only a few options,

(2) has sound estimates of the stock's standard deviation (volatility), and (3) is able to make quick mental dividend adjustments. Most investors will find computer printouts easier to use.

Fama, Eugene F.: "Efficient Capital Markets: A Review of Theory and Empirical Work," *The Journal of Finance*, May 1970, pp. 383–423.

An outstanding review of the literature on the efficient markets model and the random walk hypothesis.

Fama, Eugene F., and Marshall E. Blume: "Filter Rules and Stock-Market Trading," *The Journal of Business*, January 1966, pp. 226–241.

An excellent discussion of filter rules and similar mechanical trading techniques. In spite of articles like this one, mechanical rules continue to attract attention. Anyone who is ever tempted by seemingly good results from a mechanical technique should study this paper carefully.

Fama, Eugene F., and Merton H. Miller: *The Theory of Finance*, New York, Holt, Rinehart and Winston, Inc., 1972.

A standard textbook that covers not only portfolio and capital market theory but a number of topics of particular interest to advanced students of options. The bibliographic references at the end of each chapter will be particularly helpful to the reader wishing to pursue a specific topic in depth.

Filer, Herbert: *Understanding Put and Call Options*, New York, Popular Library, 1966.

This is the book that many brokerage firms have used to explain conventional put and call options to registered representatives and customers. Filer does an excellent job of explaining the conventional option market clearly and accurately. In addition to definitions of the basic terms in the option vocabulary, Filer provides brief illustrations of various strategies that can be employed using options.

Galai, Dan: "Tests of Market Efficiency of the Chicago Board Options Exchange," *The Journal of Business*, April 1977, pp. 167–197.

An interesting examination of the magnitude of pricing anomalies on the Chicago Board Options Exchange. Unfortunately, the technique is oversimplified, and the results are open to question.

Galai, Dan: "Characterization of Options," *Journal of Banking and Finance*, December 1977, pp. 373–385.

This is an excellent summary of the ways option theory can be used to analyze the economic value of a variety of assets and income streams.

Galai, Dan, and Ronald W. Masulis: "The Option Pricing Model and the Risk Factor of Stock," *Journal of Financial Economics*, January–March 1976, pp. 53–81.

A good example of the application of option theory to corporate finance decisions. In this case the authors study the effect of increasing and decreasing the leverage of the firm through the use of debt.

Gaylord, Sherwood: *Sensible Speculating with Put and Call Options*, New York, Simon and Schuster, 1976.

As a topical paperback published 2 months after listed option trading began, this book might have been helpful to some investors. It provides no useful information not available from free pamphlets published by the options exchanges.

Geske, Robert: "The Valuation of Compound Options," unpublished working paper, University of California at Berkeley, December 1976.

This article forges even stronger links between the theory of option evaluation and modern capital market theory than were forged by the initial Black-Scholes papers. Geske's compound option formula considers a call as an option on shares of common stock, which are, in turn, options on the assets of the firm. The compound option concept is advanced as one of several possible explanations for the fact that stock prices are not lognormally distributed.

Giguère, Guynemer: "Warrants: A Mathematical Method of Evaluation," *The Analysts Journal*, November 1958, pp. 17–25.

One of the earliest attempts to develop a simple formula to relate the value of an option or warrant to the stock price.

Granger, Clive W. J., and Oskar Morgenstern: *Predictability of Stock Market Prices*, Lexington, Mass., D. C. Heath and Company, 1970.

Probably the most comprehensive single book on the predictability of stock price behavior. Granger and Morgenstern review the major studies of stock price behavior and test the random walk hypothesis and various trading rules. Unfortunately, most of the book is highly technical.

Gross, Leroy: *The Stockbroker's Guide to Put and Call Option Strategies*, New York, New York Institute of Finance, 1974.

As the title implies, Gross focuses on ways the registered representative can keep clients happy. While his explanation of the mechanics of option trading on the CBOE is excellent, much of the trading advice Gross offers is of doubtful value.

Henin, Claude G., and Peter J. Ryan: *Options*, Lexington, Mass., D. C. Heath and Company, 1977.

Although this book provides useful insights into a few of the more obscure characteristics of options, most readers will find it extremely frustrating. Less sophisticated readers will be distressed by the authors' extensive use of mathematical notation. More sophisticated readers will be appalled by unjustified departures from the mainstream of option valuation theory, by unnecessary oversimplification in constructing an option model, and by the intrusion of technical analysis of stock price movements.

Herzfeld, Thomas J.: "Closed End Funds," *Bull & Bear*, August 1977, pp. 8–9.

In this short article Herzfeld suggests using options to hedge the stock market risk associated with owning a closed-end fund. When an option hedging strategy is combined with an effort to determine when the fund shares themselves are selling at an inappropriately large discount, the results can be excellent. Using ordinary closed-end funds as the long position seems more attractive than the Noddings approach (see below), which focuses on dual-purpose funds.

Hutchinson, James D.: *Fiduciary Implications of Investments in Exchange Traded Stock Options*, Chicago, Chicago Board Options Exchange, 1977.

A reprint of a speech by the former administrator of pension and welfare programs at the U.S. Department of Labor, this pamphlet summarizes the legal status of listed options in certain institutional portfolios. While Hutchinson may err in the direction of conservatism, he does an excellent job of pointing out possible hazards in the use of options by fiduciaries.

Ingersoll, Jonathan E., Jr.: "A Theoretical and Empirical Investigation of the Dual Purpose Funds," *Journal of Financial Economics*, January–March 1976, pp. 83–123.

Readers interested in option strategies using dual fund capital shares should compare Ingersoll's analysis with the latest book by Noddings listed below. Ingersoll's work suggests that dual fund capital shares are systematically overpriced by the market, not underpriced, as Noddings argues. Ingersoll also has some interesting comments on the nonlognormality of securities price distributions.

Ingersoll, Jonathan E., Jr.: "A Contingent Claim Valuation of Convertible Securities," *Journal of Financial Economics*, May 1977.

In this article Ingrersoll constructs a generalized model for the evaluation of convertible bonds and preferred stocks. While corporate financial officers will be interested in the implications of this paper for the optimal capital structure of the firm, investors will be interested primarily in the increased sophistication that option theory has brought to the evaluation of convertible securities. Ingersoll's efforts are a marked contrast to earlier work on convertible securities.

Ingersoll, Jonathan E., Jr.: "An Examination of Corporate Call Policies on Convertible Securities," *The Journal of Finance*, May 1977, pp. 463–478.

Ingersoll's work suggests that most corporations wait too long to exercise the call privilege on their convertible securities, that the original terms of a convertible security could be more favorable to the corporation if a higher call price was used, and that the appropriate evaluation of most convertible securities is an extraordinarily complicated process.

Kassouf, Sheen T.: *A Theory and an Econometric Model for Common Stock Purchase Warrants*, New York, Analytical Publishers Co., 1965.

A reprint of Kassouf's doctoral dissertation, this short book provides detailed background information on the construction of the Kassouf model for anyone wishing to apply the Kassouf approach to options.

Kassouf, Sheen T.: "An Econometric Model for Option Price with Implications for Investors' Expectations and Audacity," *Econometrica*, October 1969, pp. 685–694.

A good summary of Kassouf's doctoral thesis.

Kassouf, Sheen T.: *Evaluation of Convertible Securities*, New York, Analytical Publishers Co., 1969.

A slightly more technical version of the material available in Thorp and Kassouf's *Beat the Market*.

Kassouf, Sheen T.: "Option Pricing: Theory and Practice," Columbia University Graduate School of Business, The Institute for Quantitative Research and Finance, Spring 1977 seminar.

Probably the best summary of Kassouf's arguments for the inherent superiority of covered call option writing. The validity of these arguments is challenged in Chapter 10.

Keynes, Milton: *Put Options*, Englewood Cliffs, N.J., Cliffs Financial Publishing Inc., 1976.

Probably the first book devoted primarily to put options. Though Keynes spends a great deal of time discussing the factors affecting the value of a put option, he really does not understand the relationship between put and call premiums. He does not deal with the importance of dividend payments in determining the value of a put.

Klemkosky, Robert C.: "The Impact of Option Expirations on Stock Prices," *Journal of Financial and Quantitative Analysis*, September 1978.

This is the first serious study of stock price behavior during the week before and the week after options expire. Klemkosky concludes that expiration of an option series appears to cause a 1 percent average residual stock price decline in the week prior to expiration followed by a partially offsetting 0.4 percent advance the following week. This paper should set an example for future systematic studies of the effect of option trading on the underlying stock.

Latané, Henry A., and Richard J. Rendleman, Jr.: "Standard Deviations of Stock Price Ratios Implied in Option Prices," *The Journal of Finance*, May 1976, pp. 369–381.

This article features an excellent discussion of the concept of implied volatility. Unfortunately, the empirical work was done with a Black-Scholes model that had not been adjusted for dividends. The absence of a dividend adjustment is enough to invalidate the conclusions.

Lefèvre, Edwin: *Reminiscences of a Stock Operator*, New York, Pocket Books, Inc., 1968.

This fictionalized biography of Jesse Livermore provides an excellent account of the activities of the "bucket shops," which provided investors with optionlike contracts prior to the passage of strict securities legislation.

Levasseur, Michael G.: "An Option Model Approach to Firm Liquidity Management," *Journal of Banking and Finance*, June 1977, pp. 13–28.

Levasseur applies option theory to the determination of the firm's optimum cash (liquidity) balances. This article illustrates the application of option theory to a corporate finance problem.

Lloyd, Humphrey E. D.: *Spread Trading in Listed Options*, Beverly, Mass., privately printed, 1975.

Unless an investor has capital gains to defer to a subsequent tax year and/or an unusually skillful broker, spread transactions should probably be avoided. Because of the sizable commissions that spreads generate, various brokerage firms have focused intensively on spread recommendations and the "analysis" of spread positions. Most of the published material on spreads is of limited value to the reader or investor who is interested in a careful explanation and appraisal of the principal types of spreads. Lloyd's book is probably the best work available on the subject. One word of caution: Some of the positions he suggests or uses as examples are impossible or extremely difficult to establish in simultaneous transactions. While it is less original than Lloyd implies, the ultimate spread (a combination put and call spread with the short option position qualifying as a straddle for tax purposes) had a great deal to recommend it before the tax treatment of straddles was changed.

Lloyd, Humphrey E. D.: *The Moving Balance System: A New Technique for Stock and Option Trading*, Brightwaters, N.Y., Windsor Books, 1976.

Lloyd makes some interesting comments about the psychological problems faced by many investors.

Lorie, James, and Richard Brealey, eds.: *Modern Developments in Investment Management*, New York, Praeger Publishers, 1972.

While relatively few of the articles reprinted in this volume pertain directly to options, much of this material will help readers integrate their understanding of options with other aspects of investment and capital market theory. This volume is the only place the author has seen Shelton's original articles reprinted.

Mackay, Charles: *Extraordinary Popular Delusions and the Madness of Crowds*, New York, The Noonday Press, Inc., 1969.

This reprint of Mackay's classic provides an excellent description of the Dutch tulipomania.

McMillan, L. G.: *How to Make Money with Stock Options*, Hicksville, N.Y., Exposition Press, 1975.

The best features of this book are the author's discussion of CBOE trading and floor procedures and his suggestions for order entry. While much of the basic explanatory material is good, there are numerous factual errors. Many of the errors are due to changes in the rules for margining and exercising listed options. McMillan relies too heavily on some inaccurate rules of thumb in his evaluation of specific option contracts.

Madansky, Albert: "Some Comparisons of the Use of Empirical and Lognormal Distributions in Option Evaluation," *Proceedings of the Seminar on the Analysis of Security Prices*, University of Chicago, May 1977, pp. 155–168.

Reproduced in this volume as Appendix C.

Malkiel, Burton G., and Richard E. Quandt: *Strategies and Rational Decisions in the Securities Options Market*, Cambridge, Mass., The M.I.T. Press, 1969.

Malkiel and Quandt's introductory chapter discusses the historical background of options and the organization of the modern option market (pre-CBOE). In addition, this chapter provides a theoretical framework for the rational evaluation of options. While this theoretical framework is far from comprehensive and is not in a form useful to the investor, it should help the reader appreciate the inadequacies of "back of an envelope" option evaluation techniques. Chapter 2 outlines and graphically illustrates the wide variety of strategies available to the option writer or buyer and provides a quick summary of the contemporary tax treatment of each of these strategies. The remainder of the book is more technical and deals primarily with utility theory and the application of utility theory to option transactions.

Mayo, Herbert B.: *Using the Leverage in Warrants and Calls to Build a Successful Investment Program*, Larchmont, N.Y., Investor's Intelligence, 1974.

While the approach is different, readers will find little material in this book that was not covered in Thorp and Kassouf's *Beat the Market* and Prendergast's *Uncommon Profits through Stock Purchase Warrants*. The section on listed call options is very brief; it stresses the similarity between options and warrants.

Merton, Robert C.: "Theory of Rational Option Pricing," *The Bell Journal of Economics and Management Science*, Spring 1973, pp. 141–183.

A comprehensive review of option valuation formulations based on the stock price probability approach. The discussion is rather technical, but many nonmathematically oriented readers will find it possible to follow much of Merton's argument. Merton's bibliography is quite extensive.

Merton, Robert C.: "The Impact on Option Pricing of Specification Error in the Underlying Stock Price Returns," *The Journal of Finance*, May 1976, pp. 333–350.

This article describes Merton's efforts to quantify the error introduced into the option evaluation process by assuming stock price lognormality. Merton's results differ materially from those described in Chapter 7, probably in part as a result of a different specification of the volatility variable.

Merton, Robert C.: "Option Pricing when Underlying Stock Returns Are Discontinuous," *Journal of Financial Economics,* January–March 1976, pp. 125–144.

Merton extends the original Black-Scholes formula to a more general case in which underlying stock returns are generated by a mixture of continuous and jump processes. Although the efforts of Merton, Geske, Cox and Ross, and others have helped overcome the empirical weaknesses of the Black-Scholes formula, these expanded models are too complicated for use by even the most sophisticated option trader.

Merton, Robert C.: "An Analytic Derivation of the Cost of Deposit Insurance and Loan Guarantees," *Journal of Banking and Finance,* June 1977, pp. 3–11.

This short article is typical of the work being done to apply option theory to a variety of financial problems.

Merton, Robert C., Myron S. Scholes, and Mathew L. Gladstein: "A Simulation of the Returns and Risk of Alternative Option Portfolio Investment Strategies," *The Journal of Business,* April 1978, pp. 183–242.

Its flaws notwithstanding (see pages 289–306 above), this is by far the most ambitious study of the risk and return characteristics of various option strategies. Apart from the analysis of return patterns, the article contains useful insights into the impact of options on a portfolio. Virtually all the key points can be understood by a reader who lacks mathematical sophistication.

Miller, Jarrott T.: *Options Trading,* Chicago, Henry Regnery Company, 1975.

There is little material in this book that the reader cannot get from CBOE or brokerage house publications. Miller's trading advice and option selection approach are questionable. His stories about the use and misuse of options by Jay Gould, Jesse Livermore, Russell Sage, and their contemporaries are the best feature of the book.

Miller, Jarrott T.: *The Long and the Short of Hedging,* Chicago, Henry Regnery Company, 1973.

The virtue of this book is that it contains a fairly comprehensive discussion of the margin rules as they apply to certain arbitrage-type operations. Unfortunately, the discussion of margin rules does not extend to options.

Murphy, Robert W., et al.: *Evolving Concepts of Prudence*, Charlottesville, Va., Financial Analysts Research Foundation, 1976.

This collection of seminar papers presents some differing viewpoints on the concept of prudence under ERISA. Additional discussions of prudence can be found in the articles by Hutchinson, Pozen, and Reiser listed here, in the June 1976 issue of the *Columbia Law Review*, and in many recent issues of the *Financial Analysts Journal*.

Noddings, Thomas C.: *The Dow Jones–Irwin Guide to Convertible Securities*, Homewood, Ill., Dow Jones–Irwin, Inc., 1973.

Though it covers much of the same material as the Thorp-Kassouf and Prendergast books, this work has little that is unique to recommend it. Some of the material on evaluation of convertible securities is misleading.

Noddings, Thomas C.: *How the Experts Beat the Market*, Homewood, Ill., Dow Jones–Irwin, Inc., 1976.

A marked improvement over Noddings's earlier efforts. While it provides insights that the nonprofessional investor may find useful, Noddings's analysis is often annoyingly incomplete and naïve. To cite a simple example, he strongly advocates the sale of assorted call options against a long position in the capital shares of a dual fund. The virtues of this position, christened the "Superhedge," are extolled at length. However, it is not clear that Noddings understands the true risk characteristics and return potential associated with this strategy. He appraises the income and capital shares separately rather than recognizing that a more appropriate technique would be to calculate the overall discount on both types of shares and then treat the income shares like the debit balance in a margin account. He notes the similarity of dual fund capital shares to options and warrants but does not pursue the point. In spite of these and similar errors and omissions, the book has enough good points to justify a quick but cautious reading. Investors interested in dual funds should read the Ingersoll article reviewed above.

Noddings, Thomas C., and Earl Zazove: *CBOE Call Options: Your Daily Guide to Portfolio Strategy*, Homewood, Ill., Dow Jones–Irwin, 1975.

Because this is a "how to do it" book, the question at issue is how well the Noddings-Zazove approach "does it." In contrast to most such books, this one focuses on option evaluation. Unfortunately, the graphic evaluation system these authors present is oversimplified and is based on what they assert is normal value rather than fair value. On the basis of an analysis of the curves they provide, it appears that they markedly overvalue out-of-the-money calls and undervalue in-the-money calls. Though actual market prices show some tendency to reflect this same pattern, the distortions in the Noddings-Zazove graphs are probably due to misuse of the unadjusted Kassouf equation, not to any empirical study of actual prices. Other important failings of the Noddings-Zazove approach are that the authors ignore the effect of interest rates completely, that they do not adequately adjust for dividends, and that they use an inappropriate measure of stock price volatility. The edition reviewed had outdated margin data and incorrect and incomplete commission information. The book's loose-leaf format allows for updates and corrections, but the price ($75 including quarterly updates for one year) seems high, even with this service.

Parkinson, Michael: "Option Pricing: The American Put," *The Journal of Business*, January 1977, pp. 21–36.

The definitive article on the evaluation of the type of puts listed on options exchanges. Parkinson's technique for determining the effect on put option values of early exercise is as basic as the neutral hedge technique described by Black and Scholes. Unfortunately, Parkinson's article is more difficult to read than the Black-Scholes papers, and it suffers from some unfortunate typographical errors in the equations. These obstacles do not detract from the importance of Parkinson's work, but they make it hard for the average reader to understand.

Pauley, Milton: *The Do's and Don'ts of Puts and Calls*, Fairfield, N.J., Reference Book Publishers, 1976.

This book, by one of the leading writers of options on over-the-counter stocks, provides an insight into some practical aspects of option trading when the underlying stock is highly volatile and lightly traded. The short sections on puts and listed options are of limited value.

Pihlblad, Leslie H.: *On Options,* New York, Pershing & Co., 1975.

This small pamphlet, written by the chairman of the board of The Options Clearing Corporation, is by far the best basic explanation of listed options yet published. Available from Pershing & Co., 120 Broadway, New York, N.Y. 10005. Price $5.

Platnick, Kenneth B.: *The Option Game: Puts and Calls and How to Play Them,* New York, CommuniConcepts, Inc., 1975.

Despite a propensity to use gambling terminology in many places where it is both unnecessary and inappropriate, Platnick does a fair job of explaining some of the very basic option strategies. The principal weakness of the book is that it uses a series of hard-to-follow numerical examples to illustrate strategies. There is virtually nothing of substance in this book that a reader could not obtain easily and more understandably from the pamphlets published by the exchanges.

Pounds, Henry M.: "Covered Call Option Writing: Strategies and Results," *The Journal of Portfolio Management,* Winter 1978, pp. 31–42.

Using techniques roughly analogous to those in the Merton-Scholes-Gladstein study, Pounds examines various covered call writing strategies in more detail and for a different time period than the Merton-Scholes-Gladstein paper. The article makes some interesting comments about the effect of commission costs, the consequences of selling underpriced options, and the merits of "rolling up" and "rolling down."

Pozen, Robert C.: "The Purchase of Protective Puts by Financial Institutions," *Financial Analysts Journal,* July–August 1978, pp. 47–60.

This article is a classic in both option and legal literature. A concise explanation of the risk-reward characteristics of buying protective puts and selling covered calls is followed by a carefully reasoned legal analysis of the protective put under the common law and ERISA versions of the prudent man rule. Must reading for fiduciary and institutional investors.

Practicing Law Institute: *Option Trading,* Corporate Law and Practice, Course Handbook Series, no. 146, New York, 1974.

Contains reprints of many important regulatory documents. The general reader will find the study prepared for the Chicago Board of Trade by Robert R. Nathan Associates of greatest interest. This study examined the public policy aspects of option trading in preparation for the Board of Trade's application to start the CBOE.

Prendergast, S. L.: *Uncommon Profits through Stock Purchase Warrants,* Homewood, Ill., Dow Jones–Irwin, Inc., 1973.

Prendergast is a cofounder of a leading warrant and option advisory service, and his understanding of the techniques of warrant and option hedging is excellent. The reader who has read and thoroughly mastered *Beat the Market* should proceed to the Prendergast book. The material covered is slightly more difficult, and the strategies discussed are occasionally more complex. The basic evaluation technique, however, is identical. Prendergast (and presumably his advisory service, C&P Research, Inc.) uses the Kassouf model for the evaluation of warrants.

Press, S. James: "A Compound Events Model for Security Prices," *The Journal of Business,* July 1967, pp. 317–335.

One of the better discussions of the probability distribution of stock market prices. This article plus those cited in Press's bibliography will tell the reader much about stock price probability distributions.

Prestbo, John A.: *The Dow Jones Stock Options Handbook,* Princeton, N.J., Dow Jones Books, 1977.

This is the first of what is apparently intended to be an annual series of publications on the option market. The 1977 edition contains (1) a brief summary of 1976 developments in the option market, (2) a short glossary, (3) three articles on options reprinted from *The Wall Street Journal* and *Barron's,* and (4) skeletal earnings data and price charts on all stocks for which listed options were available at the end of 1976. At least half of the book is taken up by (5) an extended summary of monthly volume and price changes in every listed option contract. The pertinence of *monthly* option price changes is unclear.

Reinach, Anthony: *The Nature of Puts and Calls*, New York, Book-mailer, 1961.

One of the better books focusing on the over-the-counter option market. Unfortunately, even the conventional option business has changed since 1961.

Reiser, Robert E.: "Puts and Portfolio Strategy," *Trust & Estates*, February 1977.

Although this article focuses primarily on the prudence of using puts as part of a portfolio strategy, it contains a number of useful comments on broader topics of legally permissible option invest-ment strategies.

Robbins, Sidney M., and Robert B. Stobaugh: *The Impact of Exchange Traded Options on the Market for New Issues of Common Stock of Small Companies*, Chicago, Chicago Board Options Exchange, 1977.

As the title indicates, this monograph explores the effect of the options market on financing for small companies. Any such effect is probably small and almost certainly not precisely measurable. The authors of this study have not put the issue to rest.

Robert R. Nathan Associates: *Review of Initial Trading Experience at the Chicago Board Options Exchange*, December 1974.

The first comprehensive study of listed option trading activity. Unfortunately, several key questions were left unanswered. For example, the report concludes that option trading may slightly reduce the overall volatility of the underlying stock. Although they may accept this conclusion as generally valid, many observers believe that stocks with listed options are *more* volatile during the week or two preceding and following an expiration date. This hypothesis is so widely accepted that testing it would seem to be almost mandatory. A careful examination of the impact of option trading on the short interest in the underlying stock would also have been desirable. The report has an excellent appendix written by Myron Scholes.

Rodolakis, Antony, and Nicholas Tetrick: *Buying Options: Wall Street on a Shoestring*, Reston, Va., Reston Publishing Company, 1976.

Although a good book for option buyers could help offset the mass of material directed solely at option writers, Rodolakis and Tetrick do not quite meet this need. Part One of their book lightly covers the basic material that an option buyer has to know, but it is largely an elementary discourse on chart reading and divers other stock market subjects. Part Two and several appendixes are devoted primarily to option evaluation. Because the evaluation approach is neither highly sophisticated nor easy for the average investor to use, it will probably be ignored by most readers. The virtue of the book is that it may introduce the concept of option evaluation to some beginning investors.

Rogalski, Richard J.: "Variances in Option Prices in Theory and Practice," *The Journal of Portfolio Management,* Winter 1978, pp. 43–51.

This article makes some interesting points about the nonlognormality of stock price distributions and the various techniques used to estimate variances in option pricing models.

Rosen, Lawrence R.: *How to Trade Put and Call Options,* Homewood, Ill., Dow Jones–Irwin, Inc., 1974.

The material in this book would have made an excellent 40-page pamphlet for free distribution by a brokerage house. Unfortunately, the basic "pamphlet" is fattened with a variety of extraneous forms and newspaper clippings, apparently in an attempt to justify the $9.95 price tag. Save your money.

Rosenberg, Barr. "The Behavior of Random Variables with Nonstationary Variance and the Distribution of Security Prices," Berkeley, Institute of Business and Economic Research, Research Program in Finance, Working Paper No. 11.

Though highly technical, this paper presents some of the best research available on the deviation of stock price distributions from lognormality.

Ross, Stephen: "Options and Efficiency," *Quarterly Journal of Economics,* February 1976, pp. 75–89.

A comprehensive analysis of the role of the options market in promoting stock market efficiency. Ross justifies option trading from the viewpoint of economic theory. He demonstrates that put options and options on broad market averages are as important as call options in promoting market efficiency.

Rubinstein, Mark: "The Valuation of Uncertain Income Streams and the Pricing of Options," *The Bell Journal of Economics,* Autumn 1976, pp. 407–425.

Rubinstein applies option theory to the valuation of income streams under uncertainty. His work has implications for capital budgeting decisions as well as for the valuation of securities.

Rubinstein, Mark (assisted by John C. Cox): *Option Markets,* Englewood Cliffs, N.J., Prentice-Hall, Inc., forthcoming.

Readers of *The Stock Options Manual* who want to explore the mysteries of option evaluation in greater depth will find Rubinstein's book an excellent transition between the material presented in Chapters 7, 9, and 10 and that provided in the academic journal articles listed in this Bibliography. In addition to an extensive discussion of option evaluation, Rubinstein's book contains important chapters on order entry and floor trading procedures, on techniques for incorporating dividend adjustments into option evaluation models, and on the economic justification of options. Extensive use of symbolic notation may be a problem for readers who are not comfortable with mathematical relationships.

Samuelson, Paul A.: "Mathematics of Speculative Price," *SIAM Review,* January 1973, pp. 1–42.

An excellent, though rather technical, summary of the literature on option value and stock price fluctuations. The bibliography is unusually comprehensive.

Samuelson, Paul, and R. C. Merton: "A Complete Model of Warrant Pricing That Maximizes Utility," *Industrial Management Review,* Winter 1969, pp. 17–46.

One of the most comprehensive recent adaptations of the classic probability model. Unfortunately, the work of Black and Scholes makes some of the features of this utility model unnecessary. The article is highly technical.

Sarnoff, Paul: *Puts and Calls: The Complete Guide,* New York, Hawthorn Books, Inc., 1968.

Sarnoff does a good job of explaining how the conventional put and call market operates. Specific examples illustrate his points and make the text quite readable. Unfortunately, Sarnoff's flair for examples does not extend to his discussion of margin requirements, which is not particularly readable or complete. Sarnoff's discussion of taxes is misleading and should be omitted entirely. Apart from Chapter 4, Section D, and the article by Stoll cited below, Sarnoff's chapter on conversion techniques is one of the few generally available discussions of conversion.

Sarnoff, Paul, ed.: *An Empirical Examination of the Options Business*, Hempstead, N.Y., Hofstra University School of Business, 1977.

This imposing volume (nearly 500 pages in an 8½ by 11 format) should make the Guinness list as the largest option book yet published. The book is a collection of theses prepared by the editor's students in 1974, shortly after the beginning of listed option trading. As might be expected, the quality of these essays is extremely uneven. The paper on special price expiration options (down-and-out calls and up-and-out puts) will probably be of greatest interest to the reader already familiar with most aspects of option activity.

Scholes, Myron: "Taxes and the Pricing of Options," *The Journal of Finance*, May 1976, pp. 319–322.

Although the change in the tax treatment of option transactions in late 1976 makes some of the material in this article obsolete, the basic argument is still sound. Scholes amplifies the point originally made by Fischer Black in his "Fact and Fantasy" article: Other things being equal, a low-tax-bracket investor will find the purchase of options relatively advantageous, and a high-tax-bracket investor will find the sale of options relatively advantageous. This article should be read by all investors making extensive use of options.

Scholes, Myron: "Some Comments on the Use of Puts," *Proceedings of the Seminar on the Analysis of Security Prices*, University of Chicago, May 1977, pp. 135–154.

An excellent summary of some of the problems encountered in developing a practical model for the evaluation of put options.

Sharpe, William F.: "Risk, Market Sensitivity and Diversification," *Financial Analysts Journal*, January–February 1972, pp. 74–79.

A brief, clear explanation of the impossibility of diversifying away market risk without options.

Sharpe, William F.: *Investments,* Englewood Cliffs, N.J., Prentice Hall, Inc., 1978.

This basic investment text departs from tradition in attempting to explain modern portfolio theory without higher mathematics. It is probably the first text to integrate options and portfolio theory.

Shelton, John P.: "The Relation of the Price of a Warrant to the Price of Its Associated Stock," *Financial Analysts Journal,* May–June 1967, pp. 143–151, and July–August 1967, pp. 88–99.

The original articles describing the Shelton model. Not highly technical.

Siegel, Robert M.: *How You Can Make More Money with Stock Options,* Miami Beach, Fla., Carillon Publishers, 1976.

You can "make more money with stock options" by spending the price of this book in some other way.

Smith, Clifford W.: "Option Pricing," *Journal of Financial Economics,* January–March 1976, pp. 3–51.

An excellent review of the major developments in the history of option theory from 1900, when Bachelier's first paper was published, to the present. A nonmathematically oriented reader will find the text to be unusually clear for an academic journal article. An extensive bibliography is a key feature of this paper.

Stoll, Hans R.: "The Relationship between Put and Call Option Prices," *The Journal of Finance,* December 1969, pp. 801–824.

A slightly technical and dated discussion of the economics of conversion.

Thayer, Peter W.: "Options Achieve Respectability with Trust Departments," *Trust & Estates,* September 1976.

On the basis of a survey of 200 of the largest banks in the United States, Thayer concludes that the banks which have spent the most time examining options have decided that options can be a useful tool in portfolio management.

Thomas, Conrad W.: *How to Sell Short and Perform Other Wondrous Feats,* Homewood, Ill., Dow Jones–Irwin, Inc., 1976.

This book, like two previous works by the same author, promises far more than it delivers. Thomas's surefire approach to portfolio management is to buy low and sell high. Some unnecessary algebra and some unusual graphs are used to make this simple proposition seem complicated. Some of Thomas's criticisms of the random walk hypothesis and the capital asset pricing model are sound but not original. Most of his criticisms, however, stem from misinterpretations of modern portfolio theory. The most serious failings of the book are that it discusses short selling only peripherally and that the author does not communicate even a basic understanding of either the mechanics or the economics of short selling.

Thorp, Edward O.: "A Public Index for Listed Options," *Proceedings of the Seminar on the Analysis of Security Prices*, University of Chicago, May 1977, pp. 169–205.

The principal difference between Thorp's primary index and the index described in Chapter 9 is that Thorp's index relates option premium levels to a moving, short-term measurement of stock price volatility, while the index proposed here relates premium levels to a fixed, long-term stock price volatility base. Thorp hopes his index will give a rough indication of option overpricing or underpricing *relative* to recent stock price volatility levels. The index described in Chapter 9 is a measure of *absolute* option premium levels.

Thorp, Edward O., and Sheen T. Kassouf: *Beat the Market: A Scientific Stock Market System*, New York, Random House, Inc., 1967.

Chapters 4 and 6 of *Beat the Market* provide one of the best discussions of the basic principles of hedging to be found anywhere. Chapter 8 discusses reverse hedging with warrants. The warrant hedge and the reverse warrant hedge are analogous to the option hedge and the reverse option hedge. Chapter 9 discusses the things that can go wrong in hedging. Chapter 10 extends the basic principles of warrant valuation to the evaluation of other convertible securities, principally convertible bonds. There are brief discussions of convertible preferred stocks and call options. Chapter 13 is one of the most interesting chapters in the book. It discusses the difficulty of persuading investors to engage in hedging activities. The excellent publicity generated by the CBOE and the weak markets of the past several years probably make hedging easier to sell to a skeptical public than it has ever been in the past. While there are several option and warrant evaluation techniques that give more useful results than the Kassouf econometric model, this book is a classic and should be read by any serious student of options.

Tso, Lin: *How to Make Money in Listed Options*, New York, Frederick Fell Publishers, 1976.

One of numerous books aimed at the average investor's desire to find an easy way to master options. Though the organization is weak in spots, most readers will have little difficulty following Lin Tso's discussion. The book does not cover some key option topics at all and is rather superficial in its treatment of other topics. The Pihlblad book is far superior.

U.S. Securities and Exchange Commission: *Report on Put and Call Options*, August 1961.

This document is relatively scarce and somewhat out of date, but even today it is the only comprehensive empirical study of the conventional option market. Copies may be obtained by writing directly to the SEC.

Value Line Convertible Survey: *More Profit and Less Risk: Convertible Securities and Warrants*, New York, Arnold Bernhard & Co., 1970.

This slightly dated handbook (it refers to real estate investment trusts as "prestigious" and as "prime quality financial intermediaries") is distributed to all *Value Line Options and Convertibles* subscribers. While it is easy to criticize Value Line's tendency to oversimplify the analysis of convertible securities, this book will help the reader appreciate how diverse convertible securities have become.

Wellemeyer, Marilyn, ed.: "The Values in Options," *Fortune*, November 1973, pp. 89–96.

An excellent description of the Black-Scholes model and some of the things investors are doing with it.

Wyser-Pratte, Guy P.: *Risk Arbitrage*, New York, Institute of Finance of New York University, 1971.

Because this book predates the CBOE, options are mentioned only in passing. Nonetheless, Wyser-Pratte's work is required reading for any investor involved in a merger situation.

Zieg, Kermit C., Jr.: *The Profitability of Stock Options*, Larchmont, N.Y., Investor's Intelligence, 1970.

This book describes what is probably the most extensive study ever made of the profitability of conventional stock option transactions. Zieg concludes that option buyers, particularly straddle buyers, appear to have an edge over writers. Like all other examinations of option profitability, this one is highly dependent on the time period it covers. In the terminology used in the chapters on option evaluation in the present text, options were undervalued relative to the magnitude of stock price fluctuations during the period Zieg studied.

3. Option Advisory Services

Table D-1 lists the major option advisory services and describes their offerings. With the exception of the heavily promoted *Options Alert* service from Merrill Lynch, brokerage firm publications are excluded from this tabulation. The inclusion or exclusion of a service should not be construed as endorsement or disapproval.

Key to Table D-1

Prob	Probability type, usually a variant of Black and Scholes
Econ	Econometric type, usually a variant of Kassouf
Hist	Historical volatility, weighted or unweighted
Calc	Calculated volatility, including historic and implied volatilities
Judg	Judgmental volatility estimate
RE	Return if exercised
RU	Return if stock price unchanged
EAR	Expected annualized return

ORC	Other return calculations
D	Dividend information
Ltd	Limited but more than, or different from, earnings and dividend data
EX	Extensive data on underlying stocks
Tech	Technical ratings of stocks
Fund	Fundamental ratings of stock

Table D-1. Information Provided by Option Advisory Services

Name and Address	Evaluation of Premiums								Stock Information			
	Values Provided		Hedge Ratio	Type Model	Volatility Estimates or Data	Return Data	All Option Stocks Covered	Statistical	Recommendations	Technical or Fundamental	Data on Nonoption Securities	Market Opinions
	Calls	Puts										
Advanced Investment Strategies Thomas C. Nodding & Associates, Inc. 135 S. LaSalle St. Chicago, Ill. 60603	No	No	No	None	None	None	Selected strategies	Ltd	Convertibles	Tech	Convertibles, dual funds	No
Fischer Black 50 Memorial Dr. Cambridge, Mass. 02139	Yes	Yes	Yes	Prob	Calc	None	Yes	D	No		No	No
CMI's Option Trader CMI Business Services, Inc. 1133 N. North Camano Dr. Camano Island, Wash. 98292	No	No	No	None	Hist	ORC	56	No	Yes	Tech	No	Yes
Chartcraft Weekly Option Service Investor's Intelligence, Inc. 2 East Ave. Larchmont, N.Y. 10538	No	No	No	None	None	RE, RU	Yes	P&F charts	Yes	Tech	No	Yes
Dunn and Hargitt's Option Guide 22 N. Second St. Lafayette, Ind. 47902	No	No	No	None	Hist	No	209 stocks	Ltd	Yes	Tech Fund	Some	Yes
EVM Stock Option Letter EVM Analysts, Inc. 1001 Gayley Ave. Suite 208, Westwood Village Los Angeles, Calif. 90024	Yes	Yes	Yes	Econ	Calc	RE, RU	Yes	Ltd	Yes	Tech	No	Yes
The Holt Trading Advisory T. J. Holt & Company, Inc. 277 Park Ave. New York, N.Y. 10017	Yes, graphs	Planned	No	Econ	Hist	No	156 stocks	Ex	Yes	Tech. Fund	No	Limited
The Option Trader 119 W. 57th St. New York, N.Y. 10019	No	No	No	None		ORC	No	Ltd	Yes	Fund, Tech	No	Yes

Table D-1. Information Provided by Option Advisory Services (*Continued*)

| Name and Address | Evaluation of Premiums | | | | | | Stock Information | | | | |
| | Values Provided | | Hedge Ratio | Type Model | Volatility Estimates or Data | Return Data | All Option Stocks Covered | Statistical | Recommen- dations | Technical or Fundamental | Data on Nonoption Securities | Market Opinions |
	Calls	Puts										
Option Weekly 4838 Randolph Dr. Annandale, Va. 22003	Some	Some	No	Econ	Hist	ORC	102	No	No	No	No	No
Options Alert Merrill Lynch Pierce Fenner & Smith, Inc. P.O. Box 967 Farmingdale, N.Y. 11737	Yes	Yes		Prob	Calc	RE, RU	Yes	Ex	Yes	Tech, Fund	No	Yes
The Put and Call Tactician Barry Vaniel & Co., Inc. 312 E. Brook Hollow Rd. Phoenix, Ariz. 85022	Yes	Yes	No	Prob	Judg	EAR, ORC	Selected strategies	Ltd	Yes	Tech	No	No
Stock Option Guide Daily Graphs P.O. Box 24933 Los Angeles, Calif. 90024	Yes	Yes		Prob	Calc		Yes	Ex	No		No	No
Systems and Forecasts P.O. Box 1227 Old Village Station Great Neck, N.Y. 11023	Occa- sional	Occa- sional	Occa- sional	Prob	Hist	No	No	Ltd	Yes	Tech. Fund	Yes	Yes
Trade Levels Option Report Trade Levels Inc. Suite 400 Mutual Savings Building 301 E. Colorado Blvd. Pasadena, Calif. 91101	No	No	No	None	Calc, beta	RE, RU	Yes	No	Yes	Tech	No	Yes
Value Line Options and Convertibles Arnold Bernhard & Co., Inc. 5 E. 44th St. New York, N.Y. 10017	Yes	Yes	Yes	Econ	Hist	None	Yes	D	Yes	Fund	Convertibles, warrants	No

APPENDIX E
GLOSSARY

Adjusted striking price or adjusted exercise price: When a dividend is paid on the stock subject to a conventional option or any capital change occurs on the stock subject to either a listed or conventional option, the striking price is adjusted to reflect the change. If necessary, the number of shares subject to option is also changed. For example, if a stock is split three for two and the original striking price of an option was $60, the adjusted striking price is $40 and the option becomes an option on 150 shares of the split stock.

Aggregate exercise price: The exercise price of an option contract multiplied by the number of units of the underlying security covered by the option contract.

American option: A put or call that can be exercised at any time prior to expiration. All listed options, including those on European exchanges, are American-type options. *See* EUROPEAN OPTION.

Arbitrage: Technically, arbitrage is purchasing a commodity or security in one market for immediate sale in another market. Popular usage has expanded the meaning of the term to include any activity which attempts to buy a relatively underpriced item and sell a relatively overpriced item, expecting to profit when the prices resume a more appropriate relationship. In trading options and other convertible securities, arbitrage techniques can be applied whenever a strategy involves buying one and selling the other of two related securities.

At the money: The striking price of an option equals the market price of the underlying stock.

Average price of an option: *See* NORMAL PRICE OF AN OPTION.

Beta factor: A measurement of stock price volatility *relative* to a broad market index. Because it measures relative rather than absolute volatility, the beta factor can be seriously misleading if used in option evaluation.

Box spread: A combination of a horizontal, or calendar, call spread and a horizontal put spread. Both spreads have the same expiration date on their respective long and short positions. This position can also be visualized as a combination of (1) a long straddle and (2) a short straddle which expires before the long straddle and has the same striking price. An alternative form of box spread might combine vertical put and call spreads with identical expiration dates. Box spreads are used almost exclusively to transfer gains from one tax year to the next.

Break out: The process of undoing a conversion or a reversal, reestablishing the option buyer's original position.

Butterfly spread: Although some traders use different definitions, a common butterfly spread combines a vertical bull and a vertical bear spread with the same expiration date on all options and the same striking price on all options written. This position is sometimes known as a *sandwich spread.*

Buy-in: When a call is exercised against an option writing account that does not hold sufficient shares of the called stock, the broker will "buy in" the necessary shares for delivery to the option holder. Also, in short selling, if no stock can be borrowed to continue a short position, the broker will "buy in" the shares for delivery, forcing the short seller to cover. This type of buy-in occurs in stocks with large short interests and/or small floats.

Calendar spread: The option purchased expires after the option sold. The number of contracts purchased equals the number sold, and both options have the same striking price.

Call option: An option to buy, ordinarily issued for a period of less than 1 year. *See* OPTION, TERMS OF OPTION CONTRACT.

Call spread: A spread consisting of a long position and a short position in calls on the same underlying stock.

Capital change: A stock split, stock dividend, merger, or spin-off that affects the number of shares of stock owned by an investor without necessarily affecting their value.

CBOE call: *See* CHICAGO BOARD OPTIONS EXCHANGE, LISTED OPTION, CALL OPTION.

Chicago Board Options Exchange: A registered securities exchange sponsored by the Chicago Board of Trade, set up to trade options which differ from conventional options in a number of respects. (1) The contract terms are standardized. (2) The traditional link between the buyer and the writer is severed because The Options Clearing Corporation is the primary obligor on every option. (3) There is a secondary market for CBOE options. (4) The striking price is not adjusted as a result of payment of ordinary cash dividends on the optioned stock.

Class of options: All listed option contracts of the same type covering the same underlying security, e.g., all listed Texas Instruments call options.

Closing purchase transaction: A transaction in which an option writer terminates his obligation by purchasing an option having the same terms as an option previously written.

Closing sale transaction: A transaction in which the holder of an option liquidates his position by selling an option having the same terms as an option previously purchased.

Collateral: An obligation or security attached to another obligation or security to secure its performance. For example, an option writer may deposit, with his bank or broker, common stock in the company on which an option is written as collateral to guarantee his performance on the option. He may also deposit securities convertible into the underlying stock or unrelated securities with an appropriate collateral value.

Combination option: An option consisting of at least one put and one call. The component options may be exercised or resold separately, but they are originally sold as a unit. *See* SPRADDLE, STRADDLE, STRIP, STRAP, SPREAD.

Commodity Futures Trading Commission (CFTC): The regulatory agency charged with regulation of commodity futures and commodity option markets.

Commodity option: An option to buy (call) or sell (put) a specific commodity or commodity futures contract at a given price within a specified time. Commodity options have been more widely used in the United Kingdom than in the United States. The Commodity Futures Trading Commission has been formulating rules under which expanded trading in commodity options will be permitted in the United States.

Conventional option: An option contract negotiated and/or traded off a securities exchange. While the contract is negotiable, it does not usually change hands after the original transaction. The terms of conventional option contracts are not standardized.

Conversion: The process by which a put can be changed to a call, and a call to a put. To convert a put to a call, the conversion house buys the put and 100 shares of stock and issues a call. To convert a call to a put, the conversion house buys the call, sells the stock short, and issues a put. *See* REVERSAL, BREAK OUT.

Covered writer: A call option writer who owns the underlying stock which is subject to option. An investor setting up an option hedge or writing multiple options may be covered with respect to part of the option position and uncovered with respect to the rest. *See* OPTION HEDGE, UNCOVERED WRITER.

Day trade: A day trade occurs when a stock or option position is bought and sold during the same trading session.

Delta factor: *See* NEUTRAL HEDGE RATIO.

Diagonal bear spread: Regardless of whether puts or calls are used, this position involves the purchase of a relatively long-term option contract and the sale of a shorter-term contract with a lower striking price. Ordinarily, the number of contracts purchased equals the number of contracts sold.

Diagonal bull spread: Regardless of whether puts or calls are used, the option contract purchased expires later and has a lower striking price than the option sold. Ordinarily, the number of contracts purchased equals the number of contracts sold. Like other spreads, these diagonal spreads are best analysed by using stock equivalents.

Double option: An option to buy (call) or sell (put) but not both. Exercise of the call causes the put to expire, and exercise of the put causes the call to expire. Double options are used primarily in commodity option trading.

Down-and-out call: A conventional-type call option that expires if the market price of the underlying stock drops below a predetermined expiration price. These options are written by a number of major brokerage firms and sold only to clients able to accept substantial risk.

Econometric model: As applied to options and other convertible securities, a series of mathematical relationships, usually derived by multiple regression analysis or a similar technique. The model is designed to predict the average or normal price of an option or other convertible security when the stock price and other revelant variables are inserted in the formulas that make up the model.

Elasticity: *See* NEUTRAL HEDGE RATIO.

Endorsement: In conventional option transactions a New York Stock Exchange member firm endorses the option contract on behalf of the writer to guarantee his performance on the option. The Options Clearing Corporation performs an analogous function for listed options.

European option: A put or call that can be exercised only on the expiration date. Options listed on European options exchanges are American options in the sense that they can be exercised prior to the expiration date. *See* AMERICAN OPTION.

Exercise of an option: Purchase or sale of the underlying stock at the striking price by the holder of a put or call.

Exercise price: *See* STRIKING PRICE.

Expiration date: The date after which an option is void. The option buyer should check carefully into the time of day by which he must notify his broker to exercise or sell an option. *See* EXTENSION.

Extension: An agreement between the buyer and the writer of a conventional option to lengthen the life of the option beyond the original expiration date. Extensions are not common because both parties have to agree to the extension and to the price to be paid for it. There is no mechanism for extension of listed options.

Fair value of an option: The option value derived by a probability-type option valuation model. The fair value of an option is the price at which both the buyer and the writer of the option should expect to break even, neglecting the effect of commissions, after an adjustment for risk. Fair value is an estimate of where an option *should* sell in an efficient market, not where it will sell.

Fungibility: The standardization and interchangeability of listed option contracts permits either party to an opening transaction to close out a position through a closing purchase or sale of an identical contract.

Hedge: To reduce the risk of loss from an investment position by making approximately offsetting transactions that will largely eliminate one or more types of risks. The term is often used loosely, and hedging in the broader sense typically involves partially offsetting a long position in one security with a short or short equivalent position in a related security. *See* OPTION WRITING, OPTION HEDGE, REVERSE OPTION HEDGE, SPREAD.

Hedge ratio: *See* NEUTRAL HEDGE RATIO.

Historical volatility: The variance or standard deviation of the change in the underlying stock price for a designated period of time.

Horizontal spread: *See* CALENDAR SPREAD.

Implied volatility: The value of the stock price volatility variable that would equate option price and fair value. Alternatively, the value of the volatility variable that buyers and sellers appear to accept when the market price of an option is determined.

In the money: A term referring to an option which has intrinsic value because the current market price of the stock exceeds the striking price of a call or is below the striking price of a put. For example, a call exercisable at $100 is said to be three points in the money when the stock is selling at $103. *See* AT THE MONEY, OUT OF THE MONEY.

Intrinsic value of an option: The market price of the stock plus or minus the striking price of an option. The intrinsic value cannot be less than zero.

Leg-in: A phrase used by traders to describe a procedure in which one of two offsetting positions is taken in the hope that a subsequent change in the price of the other position will permit execution of the entire trade on favorable terms. When this procedure does not work, the trader "gets legged."

Listed option: An option traded on a national securities exchange.

Long option position: The position of the holder or buyer of an option contract.

Margin: The required equity that an investor must deposit to collateralize an investment position.

Mark to the market: In the event that a writer has written options on more shares of a given security than he owns, he will be required to put up more margin if the stock moves against him. The broker will ask for more margin to mark his account to the market.

Match market: A match market occurs when a buyer and a writer for a given option enter the market at about the same time and a put and call broker can bring them together on mutually satisfactory terms. Since the dealer's task is simplified by this common interest and he does not have to look around for one side of the trade, the spread between the price paid by the buyer and the price paid to the writer should be smaller than usual.

Naked option writing: An option writing position collateralized by cash or by securities unrelated to those on which the stock option is written. *See* OPTION HEDGE.

Net margin requirement: The margin required after any option premium received by the investor is deducted.

Neutral hedge: A combination of long and short positions in related securities that is designed to be equally profitable whether the underlying stock goes up slightly or down slightly in price.

Neutral hedge ratio: The fraction of a point by which the price of an option contract is expected to change in response to a one-point change in the price of the underlying stock. For example, if its neutral hedge ratio is given as 0.5, an option contract should change in price by about 50 cents for each $1 change in the price of the underlying stock. Also called *delta factor, sensitivity,* and *elasticity.*

Normal price of an option: The option price predicted by an econometric model or similar technique used to estimate typical stock price–option price relationships. The normal price is an estimate based on the assumption that relationships that existed in a prior period are still meaningful. Normal price is a prediction of what an option price will be, not necessarily what it should be. *See* FAIR VALUE OF AN OPTION.

Open interest: The number of listed option contracts outstanding at a particular time. Open interest figures are available on each listed contract.

Opening purchase transaction: A transaction in which an investor becomes the holder or buyer of an option.

Opening sale transaction: A transaction in which an investor becomes the writer or seller of an option.

Option: A stipulated privilege of buying or selling a stated property, security, or commodity at a given price (striking price) within a specified time (in the United States, at any time prior to or on the expiration date). A securities option of the type discussed in this book is a negotiable contract in which the writer, for a certain sum of money, called the *option premium,* gives the buyer the right to demand within a specified time the purchase or sale by the writer of a specified number of shares of stock at a fixed price, called the *striking price.* Unless otherwise stated, options are written for units of 100 shares. They are ordinarily issued for periods of less than 1 year. *See* CALL OPTION, PUT OPTION, COMBINATION OPTION, COMMODITY OPTION, TERMS OF OPTION CONTRACT.

Option buyer: The individual or, less frequently, institutional investor who buys options to increase his leverage, hedge the risks in his portfolio, or attain other investment objectives.

Option contract: In conventional options, the actual contract is in bearer form and sets forth the provisions of the contract. It is endorsed or guaranteed by the New York Stock Exchange member firm which holds the option writer's account. Unless the buyer specifically requests a certificate evidencing his ownership of the option, the terms of a listed option are as stated in the prospectus. The buyer's evidence of ownership is his confirmation slip from the executing broker.

Option hedge: A hedged position in which the writer sells more than one call option against each round lot of the optioned stock he owns. The net effect of this position is to maximize the writer's pretax profit when the stock sells at the striking price on the expiration date. The rate of return declines if the shares sell either above or below the striking price. The writer loses money only if the stock rises or falls drastically before the expiration date. Some writers use the terms "option hedge" and "reverse option hedge" with opposite meanings to those used in this book. *See* REVERSE OPTION HEDGE, NAKED OPTION WRITING.

Option portfolio: Any portfolio that includes long option positions or collateralizes option writing positions.

Option writer: The individual or institutional investor who sells options collateralized by a portfolio of common stock and other securities.

Optioned stock: The underlying common stock which is the subject of an option contract.

Options Clearing Corporation: The guarantor of listed option contracts. It is owned proportionately by each of the exchanges trading listed option contracts in the United States. Similar organizations act as guarantors in most option markets outside the United States.

Options exchange: One of the securities exchanges authorized to trade listed options.

Out of the money: A term referring to an option that has no intrinsic value because the current stock price is below the striking price of a call or above the striking price of a put. For example, a put at $100 when the stock is selling at $105 is said to be five points out of the money. *See* AT THE MONEY, IN THE MONEY.

Parity: The circumstance in which option's premium over intrinsic value is zero.

Premium: Technically, the amount of money an option buyer pays for a conventional put or call or the quoted price of a listed option. Unfortunately, many analysts use the word to designate the amount by which the price of an option exceeds its intrinsic value. For example, if an option to buy XYZ Corporation at $100 is selling at $9 and the stock is selling at $103, the premium is said to be $6. To avoid confusion, the term "option price" or "premium" is used to designate the market price of an option, and the term "premium over intrinsic value" is used to designate the amount by which the stock price must rise before the expiration date for the option buyer to break even, neglecting commissions.

Put and Call Brokers and Dealers Association: For many years this was the principal self-regulatory organization for the conventional option market. Today it exists largely on paper.

Put option: An option to sell, ordinarily issued for a period of less than 1 year. *See* OPTION, TERMS OF OPTION CONTRACT.

Put spread: A spread consisting of a long position and a short position in puts on the same underlying stock.

Pyramiding: Though the term is sometimes used loosely, it generally refers to the practice of using the excess margin or "buying power" generated by a successful speculative operation to increase the commitment to that operation. In options, an example might be the naked writer who writes more options as the change in the price of the stock frees up some of his margin. Pyramiding is common in commodity futures trading where margin requirements are usually lower than in options.

Rate of return on net margin required: A method of expressing option writing profitability adopted for convenience and clarity. See Appendix B for a detailed explanation.

Ratio spread: *See* VARIABLE SPREAD.

Ratio write: *See* OPTION HEDGE.

Ready market: An active option market. Dealers' spreads will be relatively narrow, and the prices quoted by various dealers will be practically identical.

Reconversion or reversal: The process of changing a call into a put. Occasionally used to describe the exchange of a put for a call if the put was originally created by conversion of a call.

Reverse option hedge: A hedged position in which the investor owns more than one call option for each round lot of the optioned stock he is short. This position becomes profitable as the market price of the stock moves away from the striking price of the options *in either direction. See* OPTIONS HEDGE.

Rolling over: Substituting an option with a different expiration date and/or a different striking price for a previously established option position. Rolling over usually involves substituting an option with a more distant expiration date for the existing option position. The process is called *rolling up* when an option with a higher striking price is substituted and *rolling down* when an option with a lower striking price is substituted for the previous option position.

Sandwich spread: *See* BUTTERFLY SPREAD.

Securities and Exchange Commission (SEC): The regulatory agency charged with regulation of securities and securities options markets in the United States.

Sensitivity: *See* NEUTRAL HEDGE RATIO.

Series of options: All listed option contracts of the same class having the same exercise price and expiration date, e.g., all Texas Instruments July $100 calls.

Short-against-the-box: A short sale of securities when an equal amount is owned in the account but will not be delivered against the sale until a later date. A short-against-the-box is used to defer taxes on profits.

Short option position: The position of the writer or seller of an option contract.

Short sale: The sale of a security not previously owned by the seller in the expectation that it will be possible to repurchase that security at a lower price some time in the future. The term is ordinarily applied to the sale of stocks or other conventional securities, but an equivalent short sale position can be attained through the sale of an uncovered call option or the purchase of a put.

Special expiration price option: *See* DOWN-AND-OUT CALL, UP-AND-OUT PUT.

Special options: Conventional options available for sale out of an option dealer's inventory. Some of these are advertised in the newspapers by put and call dealers to stimulate inquiries. These "specials" include some very good buys, but the fact that an option is advertised does not necessarily mean it is a bargain. Unfortunately, many of the most attractive special options will be unavailable on the advertised terms when a buyer calls, either because another caller got through first or because the dealer has changed the price.

Spraddle: A combination option similar to a straddle in which the put side and the call side have the same expiration date but different striking prices. The put striking price is below the call striking price, and thus there is a range of prices on the expiration date at which the spraddle will expire worthless.

Spread: (1) For listed options: The purchase of one option and the sale of another option on the same stock. The investor setting up the spread hopes to profit from a change in the difference between the prices of the two options. (2) In the conventional option market: A straddle in which the put side and the call side are written at different striking prices. Typically, the put striking price is below, and the call striking price is above, the market price of the stock at the time the spread is established. In the listed option market this position is usually called a *spraddle*. (3) The put and call dealer's margin between the option premium paid by the buyer and the premium paid to the writer is also called a *spread*. *See* CALL SPREAD, PUT SPREAD, CALENDAR SPREAD, BUTTERFLY SPREAD, etc.

Stock equivalent: As the price of the underlying stock changes, a simple or complex option position will change in value as if it were a position in the shares of the underlying stock. The option position has risk characteristics similar to those of the number of shares it imitates. The share equivalent of an option position is approximately equal to the neutral hedge ratio times 100. *See* NEUTRAL HEDGE RATIO.

Straddle: A combination option consisting of one put and one call. Either option is exercisable or salable separately and the striking prices are usually identical.

Strap: A combination option consisting of two calls and one put.

Striking price: The price at which an option is exercisable. While the striking price is set at the time the option contract originates, it is subject to adjustment under certain circumstances. The striking price of a conventional or over-the-counter option is reduced by the value of any cash dividend, right, or warrant issued to holders of the optioned stock, and both the striking price and the number of shares under option are adjusted for stock dividend or splits. Listed options are adjusted for other distributions, but not for ordinary cash dividends.

Strip: A combination option consisting of two puts and one call.

Terms of option contract: The terms of an option contract are defined by the conventions of the market in which it is traded and the terms of the specific contract. A securities option is defined by (1) exercise or striking price; (2) expiration date; (3) security on which the option is written; (4) dividend adjustment, if any; (5) adjustment for splits and other capital changes; and (6) quantity of the underlying security that makes up the unit of trading.

Transaction costs: Transaction costs associated with a trade include the purchase or sale commission charged by the brokerage firm executing the trade and the spread between the bid and the asked price. Even relatively sophisticated traders have been known to overlook the bid-asked spread when estimating their transaction costs.

Type of option: The classification of an option as a put, a call, or a combination option.

Uncovered writer: A writer who does not own the underlying stock which is the subject of an option. *See* COVERED WRITER, NAKED OPTION WRITING.

Underlying stock: *See* OPTIONED STOCK.

Unmarginable calendar spread: This spread gets its name from the fact that in order to obtain favorable margin requirements on spread transactions, the option purchased must expire on or after the expiration date of the option sold. In this case the option purchased expires before the option sold, and both have the same striking price. This type of spread is used to control the timing of gains and losses and to obtain arbitrage profits from price disparities.

Unmargined spread: A spread in which, for one or more of the following reasons, the short option is margined as a "naked" option rather than as part of a spread: (1) The long option expires before the short option. (2) The price relationships in certain vertical or diagonal spreads may be such that the margin requirements for a naked option are more favorable than those for spread margin treatment. (3) One or both of the options are unlisted.

Up-and-out put: A conventional-type put option that expires if the market price of the underlying stock rises above a predetermined expiration price. These options are written by a number of major brokerage firms and sold only to clients able to accept substantial risk.

Variable spread: Offsetting long and short positions are taken in two options of the same type and class but with different striking prices and/or expiration dates. The number of contracts short will be different from the number of contracts long.

Vertical bear spread: Regardless of whether puts or calls are used, the option purchased will have a higher striking price than the option sold. The number of contracts purchased will equal the number sold, and both options will expire on the same date.

Vertical bull spread: Regardless of whether puts or calls are used, the option purchased has a lower striking price than the option sold. The number of contracts purchased will equal the number sold, and both options will expire on the same date.

Volume or size buyer: A buyer who wants to buy a large number of options on a single stock.

Volume or size writer: A writer who is willing to sell a large number of options on a single stock.

Warrant: An option to purchase securities at a given price and time, or at a series of prices and times outlined in the warrant agreement. A warrant differs from a call option in that it is ordinarily issued for a period in excess of 1 year and is usually issued by the corporation whose securities it represents the right to purchase. Warrants are issued alone or in connection with the sale of other securities, as part of a merger or recapitalization agreement and, occasionally, to facilitate divestiture of the securities of another corporation. Ordinarily, exercise of a warrant increases the number of shares of stock outstanding, whereas a call is an option on shares already outstanding.

Whipsaw: A sharp price movement quickly followed by a sharp reversal.

Work-out market: A market in which any quote an option dealer may furnish is subject to his ability to find the other side of the trade. Frequently, these markets are thin and the option dealer is not willing to commit his own capital to the option except at a prohibitive markup. Prices quoted by different dealers may vary greatly in a work-out market.

Index